Joyful
Literacy Interventions
Early Learning Classroom Essentials

Janet Nadine Mort PhD

Printed by CreateSpace, An Amazon.com Company
ISBN-10: 1502513617
ISBN-13: 978-1502513618

Dedication

I dedicate this book to vulnerable children everywhere and the educators who work tirelessly to help them succeed. Significant among these educators are two international heroes who have invested their careers inspiring us to "do the right thing" on behalf of vulnerable children who can't help themselves.

Canadian scholar, the late Dr. Clyde Hertzman
Officer of the Order of Canada

and

American scholar, Dr. Richard Allington
Researcher and Outspoken Advocate for the Rights of Vulnerable Children

A Remarkable Mom and Dad – Margaret and Henry Swain
They believed in literacy and in me: I thrived as a result. I was one of the "lucky" ones.

My partner of 45 Years – Michael Mort
Wise, gentle and kind: I was lucky in love too.

These five people, and others, have been my mentors and helped me to understand the urgency of working for those who are vulnerable in all walks of life. They taught me how to find the courage to make our voices heard amidst life's chaos.

Who needs our advocacy more than our most vulnerable children?

Join the chorus. Make our voices heard.

Vulnerable children can and will thrive.

Contents

Acknowledgements

I felt a sense of urgency about writing this book. Thousands of vulnerable children enter kindergarten every year and leave the primary grades still vulnerable. The new research is compelling. We have learned much in the past three years by implementing the new theories in pilot projects. This book documents our progress and is a compilation of the wisdom, energy and insights of many:

- Renowned researchers and authors whose selected wisdom is quoted and acknowledged;
- *Vancouver Island University* (VIU) who sponsored the Summits: *When Vulnerable Children Thrive Dreams Come True*;
- Speakers at the Summits who helped raise awareness and propose action plans for vulnerable readers;
- My school district colleagues and their teaching staff who had the courage to take risks and prove we could raise literacy levels through case study documentation:
  - School District 84 Gold River,
  - School District 28 Quesnel, and
  - School District 59 Peace River South;
- Students in my *Early Intervention* university courses (502 and 503) who experimented and implemented new approaches, reported on results and gave me permission to share their experiences in *Teacher's Stories;* and
- Close friends who supported me throughout the documentation and writing process.

I am grateful to my wonderful Early Intervention VIU students and their contributions to the book: Rose Boulton, Shauna Buffie, Sarah Cochrane, Wendy de Groot, Vicky Dodge, Teresa Fayant, Michelle Fitterer, Ruth Irving, Nicole Kauwell, Alison Kimmerly, Heather Marshall, Margie Radigan, Jennifer Schmidt, Kohle Silverton and Kathleen Lougheed-Mercier. I also extend a special thank you to contributors Ann George and Shauna Lothrop.

There are so many of you I cannot begin to list the names, but I will be sure to thank you in other ways. Thanks to Yuni Wong, graphic designer, for the book cover design and ongoing support for the Summits.

Extra special thanks to three lifelong friends and cheerleaders who have always shared my passion for vulnerable children and who agreed to play pivotal roles in the book and Summits:

- Neil Hughes – Summit Manager and Cover Photographer
- Gay Pringle – Internal Graphic Design and Summit Registrar
- Linda Smith – Prime Editor (Sally Jennings – back-up editor)

Thanks to each and every one of you for this truly collaborative effort.

Janet N. Mort PhD

About this Book: Joyful Literacy Interventions

Using Stepping Stones to reach the Grade 2 Milestone

My Intentions

This was a very intentional book. I knew that over 90% of all children should be successful (not just 70%) by the end of grade 2. I wanted to do what I could to change the trajectory of the lives of the vulnerable children. With this in mind, I believed that you would want the following information:

- Compelling recent research about what will have greatest literacy impact by grade 2;
- Recommended sources for further exploration;
- Motivating stories and photos of teachers, schools and school systems that are achieving success;
- Strategies for engaging families;
- A checklist describing the ideal classroom; and
- Practical ideas for implementation.

There are no programs and no sequential *steps* for teaching literacy. The joyful part of teaching children is the holistic excitement of discovery through a variety of mutually reinforcing experiences. Letters become words, sounds become shapes, drawings become stories, books become inspiration, writing becomes reading, upside down becomes right side up and reversals turn around. No two children develop literacy skills in the same way or in the same order. In "the old days" that's what we counted on—and it didn't work. We used the shotgun approach—shoot programs into the classrooms and cross our fingers.

We now know the specific essential skills children must learn in order to be competent readers by the end of grade 2. Although these skills will have the greatest impact on future literacy success, there is no universally recommended order for teaching them. To the untrained eye, the ideal classroom might look like a chaotic theater of experiences that may or may not be linked. Yet the capable teacher connects them in a joyful choreography of interdependence.

The Metaphor

How do I describe this process in an orderly way when there is no apparent order? There is no series of steps. I decided to use the metaphor of *Stepping Stones*. Each chapter begins with an image of *Stepping Stones* in water. Consider crossing a pond with natural stone formations. We make our way across, but those following us or leading us do not necessarily take the same route; however, we have the same objective—to make it safely and successfully to the other side.

Think about it this way.

- As we consider our path across the pond, we look for different signs. Which stones look slippery? Shoes become a consideration.

- Which stones are surrounded by water lilies? I might want to stop there to enjoy their fragrance or the creatures submerged beneath.

- Could I explore downstream using a route different from yours and still end up on the other side? Perhaps, but if not, I could always backtrack and try a different route.

- Although I feel confident today and ready to take risks, you want to stay in the shallow areas. It's okay to want to feel safe.

- One pair of stepping-stones requires a big jump; if I stay and practice, I'll bet I can conquer it.

- My friend has never crossed a pond before and is afraid. My parents and I have been here before—I think I'll teach him how.

The Connection between the Stepping Stones Metaphor and Literacy

And so it is with literacy development. Literacy skills and concepts are the *Stepping Stones*. Literacy success by the end of grade 2 is the *Milestone*. We know we must offer multiple routes to the other side of the pond—giving children choices that support their comfort levels: offering them challenges; providing alternatives; creating safe places where they can linger and practice new skills; designing a privacy screen that allows them dignity; making sure that their individual path is just right for them—no competition or comparisons with others necessary. Self-esteem is high on our priority list.

We must offer all essential literacy skills and concepts from the get-go. Some children will be ready, and some will not. We have to encourage them to try different paths to the other side. We have to "catch them before they fall." We have to celebrate every effort no matter how small or how little progress is made. We have to model and encourage their peers to model what it could look like when vulnerable children find the courage to try. Trying is all we ask and want.

As educators, we must use assessment, teaching, and tracking progress—just like scientists—to ensure we are doing the right thing. There is no room for guesswork when it comes to children's lives. We have to be patient and provide multiple "doses" for those who need practice—and we have to make it FUN!!!

Stepping Stones to Milestones

The nine Stepping Stones identified in Figure 1 are the Chapter organizers. The research and skills described within these Chapters will have the greatest impact on children's future literacy success. There are other important *Stepping Stones*—highly desirable ones such music, art, drama, physical exercise and dance. In the early years many of these experiences can be integrated into literacy in meaningful ways. The *Milestone*, however, is literacy by grade 2, achieved in a happy and playful environment. We have to keep our "eye on the prize" as my dear friend Clara often reminds me.

The Structure of this Book

Figure 1. Nine *Stepping Stones* to the Grade 2 Milestone

This graphic is a summary of the *Stepping Stone* Chapters 1 through 9. The central circle emphasizes that the chapters are constructed on a central research base, and it also identifies the components considered as essential skills and concepts. The numerical order does not imply a sequence. Within each chapter you will find suggestions for integration of skills and concepts and cross-referencing among them. Indeed, it was difficult to separate the topics but for multiple reasons—especially to provide order for the reader—it was necessary. Each chapter features a reflection about the importance of the chapter topic; a research summary and authors' opinions as well as recommended books; practical teachers' stories describe ideas and experiences about putting the research into action in classrooms and school districts. The summary challenges us to take action.

On a Personal Note

I wrote this book for vulnerable children, as well as those who work with them, in the hope that we can accelerate a systemic response to their needs through a grassroots movement. Time is running out. Educators could make the difference—to our economy, our social system and its growing pains—but more importantly, to the 30% of our population who are vulnerable and need us to speak and act on their behalf. There is no time to waste. I wrote the book under tight time pressures, limited resources and took a calculated risk in doing so. Now it's over to you.

Any part you can play in moving vulnerable children through the *Stepping Stones* to the other side of the pond will be a *Milestone* for each vulnerable child at the end of grade 2. I cheer you on! Let me know if there is anything I can do to help you along the way.

Urgent Advice for Administrators

Kindergartens are in crisis. They are often unsupported by administrators who may not understand the emerging predicament in our countries. More and more children, for economic and social reasons, are entering kindergarten vulnerable; most have not previously been in public institutions and their conditions go undiagnosed. These children absorb all a classroom teacher's available energy and time when systemic supports have not been put in place and are not available early in the year. If you are an administrator, please take a leadership role in addressing this issue. If you are a kindergarten teacher, please appeal to your administrator with this information. Other primary teachers may need the same support in very vulnerable neighborhoods.

At the beginning of the kindergarten classroom year I recommend that all extra human resources such as counsellors, speech language pathologists and learning resource staff be assigned to these classes on an urgent basis. Obvious behaviors and challenges must be assessed as quickly as possible and be afforded immediate, appropriate support.

I also recommend that the kindergarten teachers receive additional adult support in the classroom for several hours a day; this would allow them to conduct the alphabetic principle, phonological awareness, sight words and print concept assessments as described in Chapter Two of this book.

Without such support, the kindergarten teacher will be left, for safety reasons, to struggle with managing behavior as her top priority. She will have no time to assess literacy skills and related small group instruction; this will result in leaving challenged children to remain un-assessed, perhaps until their grade one year, simply delaying
progress for all.

All the best, Janet N. Mort PhD
jnmort@shaw.ca

Connecting letters and shapes to make a train around the room.

CHAPTER ONE

Stepping Stone

Create a Dynamic Learning Environment

"Learning environments are largely invisible yet permeate everything that happens in the classroom. Perhaps because of their invisibility, we tend not to talk about them very much in faculty meetings, staff development sessions, or professional conversations. These missed opportunities diminish teachers' awareness of this critical aspect of schooling and their intentionality in developing environments that actively invite learning." - Sousa & Tomlinson, 2011

 ## Janet's Introduction

Radiating the 'WOW' Factor

Classrooms are for children. Sometimes we forget that and in our commitment to our profession we create an environment that best suits our need to teach rather than a child's need to learn. Desks in orderly rows were such a convenient way to organize restless, busy, active bodies when I first started teaching many years ago. It didn't take me long to begin to question the tradition that had been my own school experience as a child in schools. My classroom transformation and the WOW factor happened in such an accidental way!

In my second year of teaching I had a class of significantly different ability levels. No matter how carefully I grouped them and worked with them in round-robin style, I found myself focusing on the struggling readers while the more capable children finished everything I assigned them before I was ready to take them the next step instructionally. One day I had a bright idea. I put a few desks at the back of the room with extra, interesting activities as a special reward for their hard work. Children who had completed their assigned work could move to the back of the room to play quietly until I was ready for them again.

You guessed it and you've probably experienced it too. I discovered the advanced group worked even faster to get to the fun activities; my struggling readers wondered, longingly, if they'd ever get a chance to play as well. It wasn't long before I set aside a half hour each day when the whole class had optional, playful choices where they could practice skills at their own reading level independently. Of course, success breeds success! Within that school year I began to organize my entire classroom as a learning-centered classroom with practice centers. Once the classroom was settled in productive individualized work, I was free to pull children into small groups for targeted instruction. It was the most inventive and exciting time in my teaching career; it was the beginning of my discovery about the importance of the WOW factor. Children are our best advisors.

Building a magical space to play and work.

When I became a principal, this learning became part of my leadership plan. As a staff, we decided that our school should be child-designed. Every class was invited to submit a proposal for a theme or school-wide décor. The 20 themes were listed on a ballot; teams from each class—even kindergarten—visited other classes to campaign for their nomination (great oral language practice and lots of fun). Once the voting was complete and the winning theme announced, the whole K to 7 school was assigned space for their art creations—the ceilings, sections of the hallway, the principal's office and even the washrooms. I remember so many magical themes: space, circus, clowns, fairy tales, spring, flowers, jungles, dinosaurs and bugs. Our school was a cornucopia of color, movement and pride. Why was it so important? Why did it work?

Simple! It's because it appealed to their natural instincts. If we ask a child to make a choice for a weekend experience or a thrilling holiday there is little hesitation. In their real-life world they choose: laughter, movement, color, action, success, friendly competition, relationships, variety, imagination, joy and self-satisfaction. They choose Disneyland, the water slides, the bug zoo, the golf putting games, the merry-go-round and jumping on the trampoline.

Children spend at least five hours a day in our classrooms. Other than prisons, schools are one of the only places people are required by law to reside. The difference is children have done nothing wrong! We owe it to them to design spaces that appeal to their interests and sensitivities. The more we emulate the experiences they would choose, the greater the possibility we can inspire, motivate, challenge and successfully teach our vulnerable learners. "WOW" can become the operative classroom word!

Janet

Linking block building, reading, imagination and comfort.

The Model: Early Intervention Essentials

When we first began the Summit series on Early Intervention we established two goals: (1) to raise awareness about the early intervention needs of vulnerable children and (2) to raise awareness about the complexity of the issues facing teachers who teach them. An unintentional outcome was our discovery that teachers, and often school districts, were addressing vulnerable children's needs in piecemeal ways. Some were focusing on the social emotional needs; others focused on data collection and analysis; some focused on classroom offerings and innovative resources; others featured playful environments and exciting inquiry projects. Very few had coherent connected strategies in place and few were aware of recent research on the topic.

It became apparent that there was a need to understand the importance of each element of a potential model and begin to consider them in an integrated and holistic way based on the latest best research. By the third Summit we had designed this research-based model (Figure 1) to help us collectively understand how the needs of vulnerable children—and in fact all children—must be considered in an all-inclusive and interconnected way.

Janet

When Vulnerable Readers Thrive
Dreams Come True   JANET N. MORT PhD

© Mort (2014)

Figure 1: The Model: Early Intervention Essentials

Model Highlights:

- Vulnerable children need *A Supportive Environment*; one where they feel safe, welcome and successful. This is the teacher's prime responsibility.

- Within this supportive environment there are specific *Early Intervention Essentials* that vulnerable children will need to achieve their full potential. This book defines the early intervention essentials in a nine-step method that will result in success by grade 3 for vulnerable children. No step is optional.

- The learning environment must be *Play- and Inquiry-based*. Young children learn best through play. When inquiry opportunities are built into the play environment children have the opportunity for rich oral language experiences, developing imaginative and creative problem-solving capacities, and cooperative and collaborative relationships.

- Some vulnerable children enter school with *Social and Emotional* challenges. School and district resources need to be available and applied at the school-entry level to mitigate the impact these challenges have on learning. In many cases the school system provides the first opportunity for professionals to engage with and support children and families. Some of the challenges can be successfully addressed in the classroom at a tier two level; however, teachers need to seek extra support for children at the tier three level as soon as possible to address their needs through specialized services and to maximize classroom opportunities for all children.

- At the same time teachers need to create classroom systems and processes that encourage *Self-Regulation*.

- Recent scientific studies have identified the *Foundational Literacy Skills and Experiences* children have to master in order to be fluent readers and writers in their future school experiences and ultimately achieve success in life.

Working on reading, working on writing.

Janet's Comment

Implementing this integrated model effectively will provide us with the opportunity to close the experiential gaps for the children who enter school "unlucky in literacy." Research is our guide. All of our decisions must be research-driven so we can create optimal opportunities for our must vulnerable but capable children.

Janet

Research and Recommended Books

Research Part 1:
The Environment Sets the Stage!

Most literature on the classroom-learning environment has focused on classroom organization, room arrangements, instructional materials, scheduling, grouping and variety in activities for children. These are important and necessary organizers technically, but recent scientific understandings about brain development deepen our understanding about what we need to offer. What is missing in this technical list is recent knowledge about how the brain responds to the environment and consequently the child's social and emotional response to what is happening in his immediate surroundings. Critical considerations in teachers' planning processes must be what triggers negative reactions and what promotes positive reactions. I have carefully chosen the best books and research I could find to guide you.

Blocks and building are always favorite choices during free play. We hear wonderful conversations about planning and cooperation.

About Brain Research

Janet's Comment

I was delighted to discover Sousa and Tomlinson's book *Differentiation and the Brain: How Neuroscience Supports the Learner-Friendly Classroom* (2011). I highly recommend it for your personal library. The following selected quotes explain why the holistic Model in Figure 1 is so important.

Janet

Differentiation and the Brain: How Neuroscience Supports the Learner-Friendly Classroom

(Sousa & Tomlinson, 2011)

"The model of brain-friendly differentiation (around which this book is developed) counsels teachers that virtually all students enter their classrooms seeking affirmation, contribution, purpose, challenge and power." - National Research Council, 2009

Emotions Associated with the Learning Environment (Classroom Climate)

Positive environments leads to endorphins in the blood stream, which:

- Generate feelings of euphoria;
- Raise pain thresholds;
- Stimulate the frontal lobe so that the situation and the learning objective are remembered.

Negative environments lead to cortisol in the blood stream, which:

- Raises anxiety level;
- Shuts down processing of low-priority information, for example, the lesson objectives;
- Focuses the frontal lobe on the cause of the stress so that the situation is remembered, but not the learning objective.

Figure 2.2. The Impact of the Learning Environment on Body Chemistry

Teachers who believe that all students come to school desiring to learn will figure out different ways to reach and teach them when they are uninterested or frustrated. This positive mindset has a profound impact on the ways that teachers respond in the classroom, especially to those students who are struggling. When students lose faith in their ability to learn, they often turn to counterproductive ways of coping, such as misbehaving or withdrawing. This situation is less likely to occur in a differentiated classroom, where students of varying ability have a better chance of success and where teachers' negative assumptions are far less apt to prevail (p. 22).

Classroom Environments and Differentiation

Learning environments are largely invisible yet permeate everything that happens in the classroom. Perhaps because of their invisibility, we tend not to talk about them very much in faculty meetings, staff development sessions, or professional conversations. These missed opportunities diminish teachers' awareness of this critical aspect of schooling and their intentionality in developing environments that actively invite learning (p. 30).

This was so great because it wasn't until after I took a picture of the finished product that the girls told me they had drawn up plans and used ideas from each one to build the "chopper."

Classroom environments are no less critical to outcomes for young learners who typically lack power and autonomy in school settings. In many ways, in fact, classroom environments are harbingers of cognitive and academic outcomes. Just as their environment affects adults, students are encouraged or discouraged, energized or deflated, invited or alienated by classroom environments. Positive learning environments prepare students for the difficult task of learning. They open students up to the possibilities of what lies ahead. In that way, learning environments have profound implications for learners, affectively and cognitively (pp. 30-31).

Learning Environments, Student Affect and Differentiation

In the classroom, maintaining safety and security includes having structures, such as class rules and routines that lend predictably to the day. It extends to the assurance that students do not make fun of one another, belittle one another or bully one another. Many students at all grade levels come to school each day feeling vulnerable to peers, to society and even to their families. If the learning environment is crafted to address issues of safety and security, the classroom becomes an oasis of order in an otherwise unreliable world. If the learning environment feels unsafe and insecure, an intangible but very real barrier stands between the students and academic growth. Every student—not just the ones that we might identify as vulnerable—needs an abiding sense that the classroom has protective "rules of the road" and that those rules will be universally followed. Such assurance and knowledge provide a stability that allows attention to move to the next higher level of need.

With adequate attention to safety and security, students seek belonging, affection and love. Shaped by a fluid or growth mindset, the teacher's positive regard for each child sends initial signals that the

My class was grouped by varying ages and abilities to retell the story *Baboon's Nest*. It was a terrific story and they loved re-telling it with actions.

classroom has a place for everyone and that everyone is worthy of respect. A teacher who is attuned to students' needs helps the students work collaboratively, celebrate one another's successes, support one another's needs and create positive memories as the year progresses. In this way, the classroom becomes a community (p. 31).

Learning Environments, Student Cognition and Differentiation

Brain-imaging studies are providing increasing evidence that stimulating learning environments may be responsible for more rapid and robust neuron development in children and adolescents. Although genetics certainly play a role in brain growth, many neuroscientists suspect that environmental influences probably play an even greater role. Maintaining a rich learning environment, of course, should be the goal of all schools, but the research implies that school experiences for children and adolescents may have a significant impact on an individual's brain development and eventual level of intelligence. That bears repeating. What happens in classrooms may actually raise or lower a student's IQ (p. 33).

Following directions to build a marble run, or choosing from a variety of activities and materials.

The National Research Council (1999)

Among the qualities that make learning environments conducive to developing student cognition, we know that three are particularly important:

1. Our best knowledge and understanding of the nature of the learning process points to "learner-centered" classroom environments. That is, teachers teach better when they systematically study their students to increase their understanding of both the age group as a whole and the individuals within that

age group. This understanding enables them to focus the content on student needs.

2. Our best knowledge of how people learn leads to the conclusion that learning environments must be "flexible" in order to maximize students' cognitive development. That is, teachers must be prepared to use time, space, materials, groupings, strategies and other classroom elements in multiple ways to address students' multiple developmental trajectories. To assume that all students in a particular class will benefit from trying to learn the same thing in the same way, over the same time period and with the same support systems, rejects what we know about student variance.

3. Our best knowledge of how people learn indicates that in environments that serve as catalysts, students' cognitive work is "rich and stimulating." That is, the learning environment provides materials, models and human interactions that tap into and feed students' natural interests, learning preferences, curiosity and desire for successful autonomy. Because students have different interests, inclinations, strengths, weaknesses and approaches to learning, instructional resources will necessarily have to be both varied and matched to student needs. Remember that the brain is a strong pattern-seeker. It is continually looking for ways to weave new learning and past learning into conceptual patterns that make sense and have meaning. Rich and stimulating environments are the places where such connections, pattern development and retention of learning can best occur.

Classroom environments with the three qualities just listed are mindfully designed to promote student responsibility, self-awareness as a learner and learning for the satisfaction of learning. They are not about creating cute bulletin boards or protective cocoons, but rather about building a context that capitalizes on the human inclination to learn in order to achieve one's potential and to contribute to the time and place in which one lives (pp. 33-34).

As we weave together the skills and strengths of each student in the classroom, we build and strengthen the learning strands of the group and create a tapestry of mindful learners.

Janet's Comment

About Debbie Diller

Through our work in the Summits we have had the privilege of getting to know not only Debbie Diller's work in her six books, but also her charming and energetic personality and her deep commitment to children. In the 70's my entire school was organized through work stations and our staff were considered to be on the leading edge of innovation with active learning. Northridge School was my inspiration for my autobiographical book *Teaching with the Winning Touch* (Good Apple, 1981). When I discovered Debbie Diller's work on Learning Stations and the learning environment, I felt like I had found my professional soul mate. I highly recommend all of her books for your library; I assigned them as required texts in my university courses and my students were delighted with the change and the rich results when her ideas were implemented in their classrooms.

Janet

Literacy Workstations: Making Centers Work

(Diller, 2003)

Engaging the Brain

The term "workstations" helps to remind teachers that these are not an extra. They are not something students turn to when their work is finished. Workstations are for all children. The tasks that students do at their workstations take the place of worksheets. The emphasis is on hand-drawn learning that engages students.

Eric Jensen (1998) writes about getting the brain's attention in his book, *Teaching with the Brain in Mind*. He suggests that to increase students' intrinsic motivation and keep their attention, teachers should provide choices, make learning relevant and personal and make it engaging (emotional, energetic, physical). These are exactly the factors that make literacy workstations successful in classrooms.

Jensen writes that a change in location is one of the easiest ways to get the brain's attention. At literacy workstations, students move to various places in the classroom to participate in learning with partners. He also suggests that teachers provide a rich balance of novelty and ritual. In contrast to seatwork, literacy workstations provide novelty as children participate in a variety of tasks around the classroom. Teachers can do much to set up success for students by considering what students pay attention to and what engages them (p. 2).

Spaces and Places:
Designing Classrooms for Literacy

(Diller, 2008)

Why Look at Classroom Space?

You walk through the door and are transported to a place where children and literacy can blossom. The space isn't big, but every inch is being utilized thoughtfully... This room is a place where the teacher works to meet the needs of *all* students in a variety of instructional settings, including whole group, small group, one-on-one, partner work at stations and cooperative groups. It is a place where children are valued.

Most of us dream of this kind of classroom, where we walk in and find all the materials we need for our whole group, teaching right where they belong . . . where everything we need is organized and ready to roll in the small group space. Our desks are not dumping grounds, but instead are workspaces, with room to write our plans or organize our anecdotal notes. We can spend our time with children rather than losing valuable minutes looking for stuff.

Teachers often struggle with space. Our classrooms may be small or antiquated; we have lots of materials and supplies and there is never enough room for (or time to organize) everything. Add twenty-plus children to the mix and it can feel downright challenging.

Maximizing space to organize students' reading boxes.

In this book, you will find before and after pictures that show how we changed spaces like this, plus step-by-step instructions on how to do it. Restructuring classroom spaces often leads to improved instruction. It provides the structure necessary for instruction to be more successful and allows kids to add their stamp and make the room better (pp. 1-2).

Journey to Literacy: No Worksheets Required

(Flemington, Hewins & Villiers, 2009)

The Impact of Brian Cambourne: The Whole Story

He taught us that children require opportunity, demonstration, choice, instruction, practice, timely feedback and a chance to make and learn from mistakes. We understood the importance of the learners taking responsibility for their own learning, but more significantly seeing the need for the learning. Engagement is the culmination of Cambourne's conditions of learning. He says that children become engaged in their learning when all the conditions are present. The following are Cambourne's seven conditions:

1. *Responsibility:* Encourage children to take responsibility and ownership for their own learning by making choices and decisions about their work and learning.

2. *Immersion:* Immerse children in a print-rich environment, full of meaningful literacy materials and experiences.

3. *Expectation:* Expect that all children can and will succeed.

4. *Demonstration:* Provide demonstrations to help ensure that children have many opportunities to experience a variety of instructional techniques such as modeling, observing and direct instruction, as well as referring to books and other materials for information.

5. *Use and Practice:* Provide regular opportunities for students to use their developing skills. Doing so makes improvements and consolidation possible.

6. *Approximation:* Since children have different abilities and skills, all their efforts are respected and encouraged. Children are invited to take risks, to "have a go," to move towards increasingly accurate conventions and skills. They are not all expected to do the same thing at the same time. Differences are expected and do not stand out for critical evaluation or compassion.

7. *Feedback/Positive responses:* Offer encouragement so that developing learners will continue to take risks and make further attempts with the learning. This encouragement might include oral comments, written messages, or constructive suggestions that will provide immediate incentive for children to keep striving.

Literacy in all the Centers

As we reflected on Cambourne's work, we saw how his principles of learning could apply to *all* learning and that they would be valuable in creating kindergarten classrooms with a strong literacy focus. We were excited by the fact that we could easily integrate Cambourne's learning conditions into our play-based kindergarten programs. Into every center in the classroom, we infused a wide range of literacy experiences, drawing upon books, photographs, authentic artifacts and recording materials. We began to link our "read aloud" times, shared reading times, shared writing times, and "borrow a book" program to the work at the centers.

Quesnel School District 28
early literacy activities

Thanks to our understanding of Cambourne's perspective and the need to make literacy learning relevant, the kindergarten environment had become rich in literacy learning (pp. 8-9).

The Limitations of Worksheets

By infusing literacy activities into every facet of our program, we were able to demonstrate to parents, other teachers and administrators that we had no need to resort to worksheets to help children develop their literacy skills.

We recommend a viable alternative to worksheets: either blank sheets or templates. Worksheets, either commercially produced or teacher-made, paper and pencil assignments, often include many extraneous instructions, illustrations and titles. They typically require the learner to connect ideas, complete a blank, circle a correct answer, copy the text, or match images and letters. In contrast, teachers can make use of blank pieces of paper or templates (which are bridges and blank sheets and worksheets).

A template has an organized format designed by the teacher and provides the children with the opportunity to add their ideas and knowledge to the organizer…

Thus, we saw worksheets as having limited use for diagnosing future teaching points and developing individual literacy skills—these fit into a more teacher-directed kindergarten program. By contrast, templates are blank sheets providing more opportunity for differentiated response and instruction. They fit well into a play-based, learning center-based kindergarten program (pp. 9-11).

Designs for Living and Learning: Transforming Early Childhood Environments

(Curtis & Carter, 2003)

Expanding Our Vision of What is Possible

If we embrace the idea of the environment as a significant educator in our early childhood programs, we must expand our thinking beyond the notion of room arrangements. We must ask ourselves what values we want to communicate through learning environments, and how we want children to experience their time in our programs. From the physical to the social and emotional environment, how are we demonstrating that we respect and treasure childhood and the identity of particular children and their families? Are we showing pride in our work and an ongoing commitment to developing ourselves and our profession?

Children deserve to be surrounded with beauty, softness and comfort, as well as order and attention to health and safety. Childhood is a time of wonder and magic, where dreams and imagination get fuelled and issues of power are explored. In their early years, children need multiple ways to build a solid identity and connections with those around them—their family, peers, role models, culture and community and the natural world. Children bring a powerful drive to learn and understand what is around them. They learn best when offered interesting materials, ample time and the opportunity to investigate, transform and invent, without the interruptions of a teacher's schedule.

The children spontaneously created a polar bear habitat on an ice flow. This engaging, imaginative activity provided an assessment opportunity as the students exhibited their understanding of a habitat. Their play represented that they knew they needed food, shelter, water and an area to survive.

Children come to us with experiences and skills that need to be acknowledged and drawn upon as we coach them into new learning. They have vivid imaginations and theories about the world, which need to be taken seriously and explored more fully. Children have active bodies and a desire for adventure; they have the right to show us how powerful and competent they are. They have a wide range of strong feelings; they deserve to express their feelings and be respected. Their emotional intelligence is as important to cultivate as intelligence related to academic pursuits... Emotional intelligence is essential to academic learning.

We titled this book *Designs for Living and Learning* because we believe it is a mistake to make artificial distinctions between how young children live, play, relate and learn. Their bodies, minds, emotions and spirits come to us as a package all wrapped up in an ever-accumulating set of experiences, relationships and connections that shape learning. Teachers must act with intention to make our beliefs about the value of children, childhood, family, community, and the learning and teaching process visible in the environments we create in children's programs (pp. 6-7).

Research Part 2: The Significance of Play

Let the Children Play:
Nature's Answer to Early Learning

Prepared by the Early Childhood Learning Knowledge Centre
Retrieved from: Canadian Council of Learning November 8, 2006
http://www.ccl-cca.ca/pdfs/LessonsInLearning/Nov-08-06-Let-the-Children-Play.pdf

1. Play is essential for optimal development.

Play enhances every aspect of a child's development and learning, forming the foundation of intellectual, social, physical and emotional skills necessary for success

A vibrant, dynamic learning environment encourages play and learning.

in school and in life. Play "paves the way for learning," fostering creativity and flexibility in thinking. There is no right or wrong way in play, only many possibilities. Pretend play promotes communication, conversational skills, taking turns, and using perspective; it encourages social problem solving such as persuading, negotiating, compromising, and cooperating. Play allows children to make sense of their experiences while discovering the intimacy and joy of friendship. When self-directed, it leads to feelings of competence and self-confidence.

2. The nature of children's play is changing and we need to create opportunities for play.

Not only are children's opportunities for play changing, but also their access to play environments. It is becoming increasingly rare for children to have long, uninterrupted blocks of time to play indoors and outdoors by themselves or with their friends. As more Canadians move into cities, their children are less likely to have access to outdoor play spaces in natural environments. Technology, traffic, and urban land-use patterns have impacted the natural play territory of childhood. At the same time, growing numbers of children are spending substantial time in settings that focus on structured educational and recreational activities, leaving little time for participation in open-ended, self-initiated free play.

Children need access to environments that support rich, spontaneous play; their learning occurs while playing with hands-on, concrete materials that encourage exploration, discovery, manipulation and active engagement. The quantity, quality, and selection of play materials influence the resulting interactions. By providing long, uninterrupted periods of spontaneous play and a variety of materials, we can let children entertain themselves for their own purposes. We can encourage them to manipulate the environment, engage with others on their own terms while we take an interest in their play, ask questions, offer suggestions and join in eagerly when invited.

3. Educators need to create optimal conditions for children to learn from play.

Both processes of play and learning stimulate one another in early childhood; there are dimensions of learning-in-play as well as dimensions of play-in-learning. Children do need time to play without adult interruption although some active adult involvement can be beneficial, resulting in longer, more complex episodes of play. Educators can support children's learning by becoming co-players, guiding and role modeling; this is especially important when the play becomes frustrating for the child or when it is about to be abandoned for lack of knowledge or skill.

Maryjane made an "M" and Lukus found an "L" outside on our letter hunt.

Outdoor free play.

Educators can provide valuable information to parents about the benefits of unstructured free play in early childhood and should convey to them the importance of play and engaging with their children in play. Educators can provide adequate conditions and time for play, providing a balance of child-initiated free and directed play. They must also create tools to assess the quality and learning in play in context.

Chopsticks and Counting Chips: Do Play and Foundational Skills Need to Compete for the Teacher's Attention in an Early Childhood Classroom?

NAEYC (National Association for the Education of Young Children)
https://www.naeyc.org/files/yc/file/200305/Chopsticks_Bodrova.pdf

1. Studies show links between socio-dramatic play and many foundational skills and complex cognitive activities.

Play not only helps children develop skills and concepts necessary to master literacy and math but builds a foundation for more general competencies necessary for successful learning in school and beyond (including cognitive skills and emotional self-regulation).

The ks are resting after the letter hunt.

2. There are four principal ways that, through play, influence child development.

1) Play affects motivation (and ability to delay gratification).

2) Play facilitates cognitive decentering (which helps to develop reflective thinking and metacognition).

3) Play advances the development of mental representations (using their imagination or replicas to substitute for real objects).

4) Play fosters the development of deliberate behaviors: physical and mental voluntary actions. Learning to follow the rules of play extends to mental processes such as memory and attention. For a variety of reasons, many kindergarten-aged children today have not had enough opportunities for rich, imaginative play situations; as a result, with these developmental foundations missing, the child may experience difficulty adapting socially to school with teachers and peers or in content learning.

"Play expands intelligence, stimulates the imagination, encourages creative problem solving, and helps develop confidence, self-esteem, and a positive attitude towards learning." – Dr. Fraser Mustard, 1999 Early Years Study

3. Socio-dramatic play is the kind of play that helps children develop all four foundations.

Teachers can scaffold mature play. Help children create an imaginary situation by providing non-specific, multipurpose props. Help children act out various roles. In each new setting, explore the many different roles people play and how these roles may be related.

Help children plan their play by encouraging children to discuss the following possibilities:

- the various characters and their roles,
- the theme of the play,
- the story line and what might happen.

Planning helps children maintain and extend their roles.

"Play needs time and space. It needs mental and material stimulation to be offered in abundance. Creating a rich play environment means creating good learning environments for children." - M. Kalliala, *Play Culture in a Changing World*

Teachers' Stories

Janet's Comment

I provided my university students with *The Ideal Classroom* Checklist (Chapter 8, p. 217). After discussing the possibilities and reviewing the relevant research I asked them to consider how they might apply it in their classroom to achieve the WOW factor for young children. I was impressed with their suggestions. They represent a vision of the Outcome Statements outlined in the Critical Criteria.

Janet

Recycling for Functional Structures and Learning

(Margie Radigan)

Materials: glue gun, clean, empty, sealed milk jugs

For three consecutive years my students and I collected and assembled an igloo structure by gluing together milk jugs row by row. Having the students participate collaboratively in the igloo construction was an engaging learning experience as they discovered that recycled materials could be used to create creative functional structures. The end product provided a space where students could relax or work quietly. As the igloo grew in size so did the excitement of the students.

The students were fascinated to see how naturally the structure began to arch inwards as it became taller (without caving in), and by the time the sides met at the ceiling the igloo was tall enough for the students to stand up inside. They brought pillows and quilts from home to create a comfortable quiet learning space. The purpose of the igloo was to support the *Physical Science Learning Outcome: Describe how the basic needs of plants and animals are met in their environment.* However, it was transformed throughout the year to create and support other learning outcomes. Each year the igloo was uniquely different in structure and transformed into a variety of different centers. It served as a friendship fort, a quiet reading center, the inside of a developing chick embryo when learning about the lifecycle of a chicken, a cave during a dinosaur unit and a bat unit (simply by draping a large piece of solid dark fabric over the structure) and a mini-music center where the students brought a basket of instruments and explored making music.

Creating a Play Theater

(Margie Radigan)

Materials: old white sheet, long wooden dowel, large amp light source [camping light or a portable light used for working on a car], a variety of materials and objects to create puppets and props

In a corner of the classroom hang a sheet draped over a dowel that is suspended from the ceiling to act as the theater screen. Secure a light source on the wall at the backside of the sheet. Ensure that there is room for a few students to be able to set up their shadow play safely. Provide an assortment of interesting objects to use as props, for example: bicycle pump, various kitchen utensils or paper plates attached to Popsicle sticks. Students thrive when they have the opportunity to learn through exploration as it unleashes their imaginations. This example would tie in nicely with the socio-dramatic dress-up.

Quesnel School District 28: Performing with puppets.

Thinking About Building Multi-dimensional Spaces in the Classroom

(Rose Boulton)

- A trellis decorated with plants and found objects from nature or a hanging sheet painted by the children could be used to create dividers and separate spaces.

- A two-story tree house or fort that allows places to work alone or collaboratively with a ladder of 3 to 5 steps to reach the upper level and be high enough underneath for children to sit comfortably. This structure could be modified to represent a tree house by adding branches and birds, a fortress with the addition of a border around the top and drawbridge, a playhouse or spaceship. The structure also lends itself to a quiet reading corner with comfy pillows, a puppet theater, and a great place to display art and photos.

- A rubber, inflatable dinghy such as a Zodiac. This center would invite the children to role-play as fishermen, pirates, explorers, coast guard or whale watching tour guides. It could also be used as a language or math center where children fish over the sides for matching letters or numbers on cards with magnets. "Go fish!" To continue exploration of natural objects the middle section of the dinghy could be filled with beach sand and students could dig for beach glass (which has had all rough edges smoothed away), shells and driftwood, then sort, classify, graph, and draw their findings.

Enjoying a dirt and mud sensory table.

- Shadow puppetry can be explored with lighting behind a hanging barrier.

- A cozy corner made up with bean bag chairs, throw cushions, a reading lamp and a water fountain would make an ideal resting or reading space that helps children transition from home to school.

- A child-sized picnic table with a patio umbrella or gazebo, to minimize the institutional nature of the classroom, could facilitate communicating and sharing.

- Active learning could be encouraged through centers such as a miniature portable greenhouse (2 x 3 x 4 feet), a bicycle mounted on a repair stand with simple tools, a mannequin with samples of fabric, and a sawhorse with a saddle and blanket.

- There are numerous ways to make the classroom feel more like a home such as bringing in an electric fireplace for a reading corner, plants, a rug, standing mirror, welcome mat, a loveseat, lamps, etc.

- Some ideas we have discussed implementing include making curtains on a sliding cord to conceal storage shelves, particularly closed centers, and to change our display of the children's baby photos to family photos. I am currently hunting for an old dresser with a mirror and a coat rack to dress up our dress-up center!

- Other items could include marionettes, chimes, Christmas lights, vines, flags, a birdcage, disco ball, kites, and a toy net to hold stuffed animals or puppets.

Dynamic design and structures

(Shauna Buffie)

Currently in my classroom some structures that are creating the WOW factor for my students are a couple of small sized IKEA tents covered in white thrift store sheets. These "igloos" are decorated with clear small Christmas lights and large pieces of cotton batting to look like snow. You may see a sign taped up: *"Penguins onle: No polr bars!"* Only the stuffed penguins that have overtaken our classroom are allowed in, because they all know that penguins and polar bears do not live together. This structure readily promotes imaginary play, oral language and literacy.

My classroom has a very high ceiling design. Strung across the classroom in an X shape from the corners is string with clothes pegs. Often students' work and letters of the alphabet we have been focusing on hang there. Currently there are also sparkly stars and snowflakes hanging down as well as some silks in one area. There is one wall of windows that have some very big, glittery snowflakes found at the dollar store hanging in them from fishing line.

Celebrations are important – Thanksgiving turkeys!

Approaching this assignment and reading the research has given me wonderful ideas for making my classroom more dynamic. Being more mindful of cultural backgrounds and making stronger family/school connections is inspiring and refreshing. I can now take ideas I have used in the past and provide a richer, more meaningful experience for the students. Centers and materials need to be changed regularly to keep students interested and inspired. I am fortunate that our community resources are so diverse and affordable.

The greatest challenge I think all teachers face (especially kindergarten teachers) in this regard is storage. Collecting materials, structures and devices requires more space. Storage is already at a premium at our school and in my home! Perhaps our class can brainstorm solutions to this problem as well. [Note: The class **did** subsequently brainstorm and came up with the idea of getting parents to pour a concrete pad on school property (with district permission and supervision, of course) and construct or buy an outdoor shed to provide storage for teachers. Why not?]

Connecting with Reggio Emilia and Light Tables

(Wendy de Groot)

I love the idea of working with a light table. I have not used one before and had not really thought about it until this past summer when I had the opportunity to visit the 100 Languages of Children display in New Westminster. Wow! Events like this start an idea percolating in the back of my mind; this assignment triggered that idea once again.

Here is my idea for making a simple, inexpensive light table, one that made the most sense to me and would be the most versatile: presenting the "Plastic Tote" light table.

I took a plastic tote (scrapbook) and lined the bottom and sides with foil paper and the top with white paper to soften the glow. I then inserted a 15-foot rope light and notched out an area for the plug coil to come out the back. Next, I took a second tote and attached it to the "light tote" with packing tape. This provided a surface that could "hold items" and allow us to experiment with various materials, both solid and liquid.

Creative light table.

Objects to use on it:

- Colored plastic cups,
- Clear beads,
- Plastic cellophane,
- Clear stones,
- Colored Epsom salts,
- Leaves,
- Gel packs, and
- X-rays and magnifying glasses.

The ideas are endless!

Skills to develop while working with light tables:

- Color mixing,
- Pattern searching in nature,
- Tracing,
- Experimenting with texture,
- Fine motor skills,
- Focusing and concentration,
- Imaginative play,
- Sensory exploration,
- Cognitive and language development, and
- Hand-eye coordination.

I would use the light table as a center by itself. The themes and materials would change throughout the year as our focus of study changes.

Using a Jewelry Case for a Light Table

(Jen Schmidt)

- Jewelers: old display cases, boxes, costume jewelry;
- Glass Shop: mirrors, beveled glass, colored glass, Plexiglas samples;
- Lighting Store: bulbs or rope light, old fixtures, chandelier crystals, switch plates, lamp shades, chains;
- Beach: sea glass, shells; and
- Dollar Store: salt, Kool-Aid powder, Freezies, water beads.

Children respond with enthusiasm to visible invitations to learning and exploration.

An old freestanding jewelry display case would make a good base for a light table. The case can be constructed out of wood or plastic with a glass or Plexiglas top to view the jewels. Paint the inside with metallic paint to reflect the light and add rope lights. The display case could have existing drawers that could be used to store the materials. The treasures listed above would create a wonderful discovery center for children. They could use salt, colored with Kool-Aid crystals, for drawing or printing with fingers, or use tools like wooden spoons and stir

Penguin water bead sensory bin.

sticks. Water beads are great for math activities such as counting, adding and subtracting, or "more" and "less" concepts. Freezies, sea glass, and glass samples provide opportunities to experiment with color.

IDEA: Creating a Drama Trunk

(Vicky Dodge)

A drama trunk allows students to interact with common and less common objects in a new way. When children are dressing up or playing in a dramatic play area, they try various roles to help process and understand their world. Children respond with enthusiasm when there is a visible source of imagination like a drama trunk in their classroom. Children are developing their social skills and ability to play with others, while using their imaginations and being creative. The variety of items that can be used is endless. Here are a few ideas:

- *Bubble wrap:* storytelling, exploring sound and textures;

- *Crowns and tiaras:* for improvisation, storytelling;

- *Magnifying glass and an old makeup brush:* dusting for fingerprints;

- *Masks:* a mask will help a child get into character more easily. A child may pick up a mask and suddenly act as a super hero, an animal, a princess or someone else that comes to mind depending on how the mask is decorated;

- *A jar of bubbles:* creating a new atmosphere. Bubbles can be used in warm-up and concentration exercises, blowing several and everyone following one with just their eyes or their bodies until the bubble pops;

- *Wigs and assorted hats:* a beret, a beanie with a spinner on top, a big floppy lady's hat, and a fedora, a chef's hat, mop heads (yacht and strip mops). The urge to dress up and become someone else is a human trait, and putting on a hat is the simplest way to signal a change of character;

- *Fake and dried flowers:* recreating the seasons. Students may pretend they are gardeners, or that they own a flower shop;

- *Patterned fabric:* can be used as a tablecloth, a surrendering flag, any kind of garments, fort-building material;

- *Kitchen linens:* oven mitts, apron, tea towels. These will help children recreate scenes that they have observed in their own homes while watching family members in the kitchen;

- *Rubber gloves:* may be used in play as cleaning items. Children may like the sounds when they rub the gloves on objects or snap the rubber;

- *A roll of aluminum foil:* for improvisation. Foil can be moulded into pieces of jewellery, armour, or turn someone into a robot;

- *Mirror:* for practicing facial expressions, monologues, concentration exercises, and helping to retell fairy tale stories (Snow White and the Seven Dwarfs), or a signaling device to attract rescuers;

- *Several pairs of sunglasses and eyeglasses:* may help a child get into character more easily. A child may pick up a pair of adult glasses and suddenly act as an older person, nutty professor, cool guy or someone else that comes to mind;

- *Slinky:* could be inspiration for a movement, used as an instrument, worn as a bangle, or be a unique hand prop for a character;

- *Flashlight:* for instant special effects, such as a spotlight and also a good starting point for an improvisation;

- *Puppets:* useful if the puppets' mouths are moveable to more easily imitate facial expressions;

- *Balloons:* improvisation, inspiration for movement, used to understand friction or static electricity, sound to let the air out or for popping;

- *Stuffed animals:* used in improvisation of taking care of an animal, recreating classroom discussions earlier in class, creating a new story or playing vet;

- *Clothing and costumes:* for improvisation, storytelling;. They may include scarves, socks, ballerina's tutu, scrubs, and rescue worker uniforms, old Halloween costumes;

Dress-up play time; a variety of items and endless ideas.

- *Plastic bowls, old pots and pans, helmets:* used as drums for budding rock stars; and

- *Pool noodles:* for fairy tale retelling, super heroes, weighs, fairies, building structures like boats and buildings.

Finding an Old Beat-up Trunk for Drama Excitement

(Margie Radigan)

I recently obtained an old beat-up, blue metal travel-trunk and transferred my socio-dramatic props into it; I continue to add creative items to promote the students' imaginations. At present, my dress-up trunk holds an assortment of outfits: my old bridesmaid dresses, a silk dress from Japan, various skirts and blouses, a hospital lab coat, doctor scrubs, a medical bag, a chef apron and hat, clown, mouse and cat outfits, two boas (one lime green, the other hot pink), a hula skirt, various styles of sunglasses, crowns, magic wands, plastic masks (peacock and clown), purses, bags and men's jackets.

In addition, I would add the following props: a fishing rod and tackle box, rubber boots, a dog leash, a butterfly net, a cape, pirate items (treasure, hat, eye patch, map-making materials, gold coins, jewels, a spy glass, costume jewelry), a picnic basket and blanket, a pair of slippers, a road map of our city, some car keys, an old camera, a small IKEA tent, airplane tickets, fairy wings, butterfly or bumblebee wings, and a package of blank face masks, to be decorated in connection with stories read earlier; students could simply use their imaginations to guide their mask decorating.

My Family's Old Canoe

(Margie Radigan)

I would also like to bring in my family's old canoe, mounted securely on two wooden stands. The students' imaginations could soar with the endless possibilities of all the places to travel. The canoe would allow them to imagine portaging rivers in wilderness regions or magically flying through the night sky to fantasy worlds or places.

Celebrating Culture

(Michelle Fitterer)

Picture your classroom ceiling as an opportunity to celebrate culture, while also exciting your students as they walk through the door. Flags from various countries around the world, can be pinned and draped from the ceiling to add color and

comfort to the classroom. Be sure to steer clear of sprinkler heads and lights when planning the layout of your flags. Some choices to consider may be: pinning 2 out of 4 ends of the flag, using mini or full-sized flags, adding a new flag each month to celebrate different cultures or hanging them all at once.

Having students and their families complete a family tree could help you decide which flags to hang. As well, a great time to try this would be during the summer or winter Olympics. Hanging flags could be linked to a math center where students could identify patterns, count numbers of stripes or symbols, or contrast and compare flags by their colours and designs. An alternative to hanging flags would be to hang different colored origami, lanterns, or fabric inspired from different countries. I believe that this would invoke a sense of wonder for students, as well as foster an environment where different family cultures are respected and valued.

Tower building and flag raising.

Flags are an excellent way to display the values and history of the multicultural families within one's classroom. Even though our schools have become multicultural, it is not uncommon that the national flag is the only flag represented in a classroom. I feel that students and their families may feel proud to walk into a classroom where multiple flags are displayed.

Changing the Mood with Light

(Michelle Fitterer)

Your class has just finished eating lunch and are about to move on to their next activity reading and looking at stories on the carpet. Now picture the same activity with the lights dimmed, soft lamps lit in each corner of the classroom, flameless candles burning on the windowsills, and students curled up on a cozy bathmat of their own. Some of these home-like objects may be similar to those found in your students' homes. Children need some time to themselves where they can daydream and relax in a quiet space. Lamps and candles are a welcome change from the ordinary fluorescent light sources in the classroom.

A teacher at my school recently placed a few lamps in her classroom and it is amazing how they have contributed to a calmer working atmosphere. You can feel the homelike nature of her classroom by simply walking by her door. Clearly, making small changes to the classroom environment can lessen the stressful transition from home to school in kindergarten.

Bringing the Real World Inside

(Michelle Fitterer)

Children take pleasure in structures outside of the classroom such as hockey and soccer nets, rubber tire swings or platforms to play on. We can draw on these interests when designing a learning environment. A hockey net could serve as a medium to hang artwork or nametags, a sporty nook to play or read books in or simply as a creative divider on the floor. Rubber tires and platforms, after being cleaned and adorned with colourful pillows, would provide students with multilevel spaces for climbing, playing, or reading. Using structures that are not normally found in the classroom as dividers on the floor can serve several purposes, including physically separating activity areas and creating a floor divider that remains transparent for the teacher.

Building my own reading platform.

Encouraging Curiosity About Nature: Making a Loom

(Michelle Fitterer)

Children love picking up natural materials from the ground at recess and are sometimes asked to leave them outdoors when they enter the classroom. We can embrace their interest in the natural environment by creating a nature-themed center with baskets of shells, rocks, pinecones and leaves. Students could bring a natural object from home and place it in a "touchy-feely" box for other students to guess what it is. Hanging nearby would be plastic magnifying glasses to awaken the young scientist in our students.

There are so many uses of natural materials that it is difficult to choose just one center that this could apply to. Science, sensory, fine-motor, inquiry, numeracy and art centers could all include outdoor objects. A burlap loom, that can be purchased online, is another interesting artifact where natural materials can be interwoven. Similar to a chalkboard on wheels, the burlap loom can function as a divider in the classroom, an ongoing art project and a center that develops each child's fine-motor skills. Pieces of yarn, lace or ribbon as well as leaves, vines and branches can be woven through the loom to create different patterns and designs. Once the loom has been filled it can be displayed and celebrated.

The loom experience.

We have the opportunity to reconnect children with nature by bringing natural materials into the classroom and weaving them through everyday activities. With the advance and availability of technology in our society, it is even more important to give students the chance to explore natural materials within the classroom.

A Classroom Focal Point

(Wendy de Groot)

Currently I have a fake palm tree (approximately 9 feet tall) located in the middle of my classroom. I purchased it from the vegetable department of our local food store. I happened to ask the manager what they do with the display items like the palm tree when they are done with them. He came up with a dollar amount that I could not refuse! It is attached to the ceiling of my classroom by fishing wire and sits in a large pot of dirt so it is secure.

It is a focal point to my classroom, particularly at the beginning of the year when the walls are quite bare and shelves minimally stocked. Typically this is used for my literacy focus: we cover it with alphabet letters and student names. I use it throughout the year, as we add the "Letter of the Week."

We often examine the tree together and review what we know. We create various *Chika Chika Boom Boom* activities to create classroom literacy themes. It can also be used as a Numeracy Center with the title *Chika Chika 1, 2, 3.* Students can climb the tree [figuratively speaking] with numbers they recognize (Velcro patches make this work). Learning our phone numbers and addresses might also be incorporated on the tree; we add them as we learn them ... lots of motivation around our tree.

It is our very own *Chika Chika Boom Boom* Tree!

Using the Ceiling for Displays

(Wendy de Groot)

I love the use of the ceiling to display children's work, identifying the space being used in the classroom, representing the area of study or theme, and giving the space a sense of wonder. Each year at the beginning of the year I take a picture of the children with their parent or caregiver: that picture is hung from the ceiling all year. I tell the children that if they ever feel like they miss their Mommy or Daddy, all they have to do is "look up" to where their picture is and that is sure to remind them that Mommy/Daddy are close by and they will see them at the end of the day. I hang a separate peg beside each picture to display varied artwork throughout the year, which reflects the area of study.

- I have hung Chinese kites and lanterns when we learned about Chinese New Year; each year I hang a butterfly net where we "grow" artistic butterflies. I also have a tank display so that we can watch the real cocooning process.

- I have used doorway streamers at Halloween to indicate "a wonderful, spooky world." The children love it and as I only have it up for a short period of time, it does not become a problem. I even had it up when I had a student with extreme "sensory issues" and he was fine with it.

- Fabric looped over dowels to give the sense of billowing clouds in the sky. That makes a marvelous quiet reading area. A few pillows with a small area rug underneath and a wicker basket of books add to the enjoyment!

Butterfly net and "rocket ships" use important ceiling space.

- The best thing I have ever used that hangs from the doorways and windows is children's hula skirts! We have a wasp problem at our school. As a result, the wasps often make their way into the classrooms. We have no screens and the only option to avoid this is to keep doors and windows closed. Recently I tried hanging the 'hula skirts' made of raffia. I cut them so they are about 6 inches in length and put them up over my doorways and windows. We look kind of festive but more importantly the bees don't like the movement of the grass skirts and they stay away. Brilliant!!

Janet's Summary

Play: The Best Stage for Thriving Vulnerable Readers

These ideas are vital to creating vibrant learning environments that appeal to the many types of children we meet and their diverse needs. The institutional nature of schools is not inviting and does not appeal to the social and emotional needs of young children. Helping them feel relaxed, and giving them a sense of comfort from home, reduces their natural anxiety about leaving home for an extended period of time and replaces it with curiosity. I want my classroom to be so full of changing themes that even the most anxious wee ones quickly forget their worries and get caught up in the learning adventure!

The Learning Environment is purposefully the first chapter in this book. It sets the stage for all that follows. The classroom is now designed to be a place of excitement, joy and wonder. It is a stage set for a child's notion of theater. It is also a stage set for literacy. As children are ready they will naturally begin to experiment with offerings in the environment once they become comfortable and feel safe.

Our love for each of them, our excitement and our joy in their every achievement, will become the never-ending exploration through play that incorporates essential literacy skills they need in life.

You set the stage for literacy! Let the reading and writing begin!

"Brain-imaging studies are providing increasing evidence that stimulating learning environments may be responsible for more rapid and robust neuron development in children and adolescents. Although genetics certainly play a role in brain growth, many neuroscientists suspect that environmental influences probably play an even greater role. Maintaining a rich learning environment, of course, should be the goal of all schools, but the research implies that school experiences for children and adolescents affect an individual's brain development and eventual level of intelligence. That bears repeating: What happens in classrooms may actually raise or lower a student's IQ" (p. 33). - Sousa & Tomlinson

Janet

Students brought items from home to celebrate our IOO's display. Some brought 100 and a few brought ten.

Vulnerable Children Need Explicit Instruction and Tracking

 ## Janet's Introduction

Play is Not Enough

Play is NOT enough. The following two quotes from highly credible organizations in the USA and Canada assert:

"Although the *learning* in play is powerful, *it is often incidental.* The child is not necessarily motivated by a need or even a desire to learn principles; *learning is a by-product of play*, individually *unpredictable* and not its purpose." - National Learning Panel, 2009

"The pedagogical value of play *does not* lie in its use as a way to teach children *a specific set of skills* through structured activities called play." - Canadian Council on Learning, 2009

These are succinct answers to the question that drove me back to university at age 59 after 40 years in the education system. *Why, after witnessing 40 years of innovation and effort by many gifted teachers practicing the latest theories and methods, do I still witness that over 30% of children still do not succeed in school?*

Remember that over 30% of the children entering preschools and kindergartens have limited literacy experiences. We provide playful choices for them but even if centers are enriched with literacy activities, vulnerable children are likely to choose the experiences they are most comfortable with—sand, blocks and toys. They are unlikely to choose the alphabet center when they don't even understand what letter symbols mean especially when peers around them do.

Word work – alphabet sort.

≤≥v∞√ ⌘≅ ⏏: This is what a word or sentence might look like to a child who has had no preschool literacy experience.

Other children who have already learned to print their own names at home will excitedly engage in letter work at the alphabet center experimenting with matching and making new words. So, the "lucky children" (those who entered school with rich literacy experiences) get richer and the "unlucky children" (those who have limited literacy experiences) get poorer—unless they have a teacher who assesses, teaches and tracks sequential literacy skills until mastery is achieved.

Why Did We Fail to Understand the Limitations of Play in Early Learning?

In the last decade there has been considerable attention paid to the role of play in early learning. The importance of play to young children is indisputable but the interpretation placed on it by people who are implementing programs in preschools and schools has not always been beneficial. While the importance of play in preschools typically drives the preschool program, in the kindergarten and primary classrooms play is the theater stage for the increasingly important essential literacy skills.

Unfortunately, some leaders and classroom practitioners have misinterpreted the importance of play in early learning as being the basic function of the kindergarten classroom. There is a reason for this. Many jurisdictions introduced full-day kindergarten in the mid 2000 decade. Unfortunately this pre-dated the NELP (*National Early Literacy Panel*) 2008 scientific report on the latest 500 research studies that focus on the impact of essential skills on early learning. Therefore, in some classrooms, only play activities are offered leaving children with little skill instruction and no explicit instruction related to basic literacy skills. Experienced and effective kindergarten teachers understand that the play-based classroom must incorporate skill development so they plan and act accordingly. However, many teachers graduating from university report that they have had no instruction in the basics of literacy skills. They do not know which skills are required for reading achievement, nor do they know how to assess children to determine deficits. While many children may absorb essential skills through play activities, we know that the same is not true for vulnerable children who need repeated explicit teaching.

Similarly, teachers who have been practicing for many years, and have experienced limited professional development in the literacy and the early learning field, will be using out-dated practices in their classrooms: Most of the best research on the science of literacy and brain development has only been published since 2008.

The result is that the 30% of children who enter kindergarten vulnerable in cognitive areas and requiring explicit instruction are arriving in the grade 1 classroom just as vulnerable as they were when they entered kindergarten. This puts excessive pressure on grade 1 teachers who are expected to be effective literacy instructors and close the experiential gap before the end of grade 1—an almost impossible task. Many kindergarten teachers report that their school districts do not provide learning assistance support or other forms of special education for kindergarten classes because senior administrators believe that a play-based environment does not require special education support. This is flawed thinking and is inconsistent with the prevailing literature.

The following are examples from highly respected academic work, in both the United States and Canada that speak to the issue:

- *The National Strategy for Early Literacy* identifies (as one of the barriers to literacy improvement) "the inability of many Canadian schools to identify and deal effectively with children who already lag behind their peers when they first enter school." The same report identifies as a barrier "the need to improve teacher preparation in the area of reading development and reading instruction... Currently, many children who are well prepared to learn when they enter school, nevertheless fail to acquire strong literacy skills alongside their peers due to the uneven quality of literacy related instruction" (*National Strategy for Early Literacy*, 2009).

- The same report continues: "It is clear that most literacy challenges can be prevented through an appropriate mix of (a) effective instruction, (b) early learning experience, (c) systematic assessments to identify any children who experience difficulty at an early age, and (d) appropriate intervention" (*National Strategy for Early Literacy*, 2009).

- A large US database known as the *Early Childhood Longitudinal Study* program reported "major positive gains for children who participated when these children received between 30 to 60% of additional instructional time in reading and math in a child-centered, play-oriented kindergarten program. Higher child outcomes in both reading and math were well documented in these studies." Results from the *Early Childhood Longitudinal Study – Kindergarten Cohort*, (ECLS-K) in 1999 showed that "31% of entering kindergarteners were not proficient in recognizing or naming letters."

- "Effective teaching in early childhood education, as in the elementary grades, requires a skilful combination of explicit instruction, sensitive and warm interactions, responsive feedback, and verbal engagement/stimulation intentionally directed to ensure children's learning in a classroom environment that is not overly structured or regimented." This quote comes from *School Readiness and the Transition to Kindergarten in an Era of Accountability* (Pianta, Cox, & Snow, 2007, p. 8).

How did educators get confused about the role of play in early learning? The answer is simple: we haven't been systematically designing our classrooms to conform to the most recent research (post-2008) that should be informing our practice. We haven't been providing our teachers with the professional experiences that would inform them and enable them to implement best practice. Shame on us!

Worst of all, most governments and school systems have not made *vulnerable children* a priority. The time is now: research provides the roadmap. If we interpret the research into an action plan and implement it faithfully, we could change the future for thousands of vulnerable children in our care. **Time is of the essence.** Every year we delay, thousands remain unlucky—not just for literacy, but now for life.

Students use the Alphabet Strip to help them match uppercase and lowercase letters and put them in order. As they play they talk about the letters they know, and siblings and friends who have names that start with these letters.

Janet

Research and Recommended Books

Research: Assessing, Teaching and Tracking Skills Daily

Janet's Comment

In order to prepare a broad list of skills developmentally appropriate from pre-k through grade 3, I researched many sources including those quoted in this book. Within each skill set are subsets that provide a workable basis for early learning teachers. The task of assessment is listed first in the title for good reason: The first task facing the kindergarten teacher is to find out which children have learned the beginning skills (alphabet and phonological awareness) prior to school entry and which children need explicit instruction immediately to close the experiential gap. Ideally, all children will leave kindergarten with similar foundational skills, although it may take vulnerable children up to the end of grade 2 to reach full mastery. These children will simply require more instruction and more practice in applying the skills in classroom environments. The graphic positions this part of the instructional process.

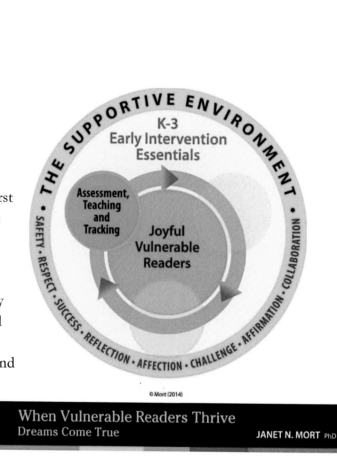

Janet

What are the essential literacy skills?

(Note: This list is intended to be illustrative, not exhaustive. Some children will enter kindergarten with mastery of many skills; others will have little knowledge or experience with these skills. Ideally, all children will leave grade 2 with similar knowledge and experiences.)

Essential Literacy Skills

Letter and Sound Association: Ability to identify:

- Names
- Sounds

Phonological/Phonemic Awareness (Phonemic Awareness is a subset of phonological awareness):
Ability to identify

- Rhymes
- Words/Syllables
- Beginning and ending sounds
- Sound segmenting and blending

Print Concepts: Ability to identify

- Books – including front and back, title, author, illustrator
- Directionality
- Voice to print
- Word and letter concept
- First and last word in sentences
- Punctuation (period, question mark, exclamation mark)

Oral language and Comprehension: Expressive (Speaking) and Receptive (Listening). Ability to

- Demonstrate vocabulary and concept development
- Retell simple narrative and nonfiction text
- Read the illustrations/pictures
- Question and use language for problem solving and inquiring
- Use language to explain, explore, and compare
- Predict
- Enjoy being read to and listening to storytelling, stories being told
- Use language to interact with others, including extending conversations
- Speak in a manner that is readily understood by others, adults, and peers

Word Reading: Ability to identify

- Names, environmental print

Word Work and Phonics: Ability to

- Develop skill in letter/sound correspondence
- Match initial letter sounds and key words/pictures
- Identify high frequency words
- Recognize word families
- Use cueing systems
- Recognize and read punctuation

Word Writing: Ability to

- Name and copy environmental print

Reading: Ability to read

- From memory
- From own writing and shared writings
- From shared readings and environmental print
- From leveled and other simple texts

Writing: Ability to

- Draw and write letter-like forms
- Copy letters
- Write his/her name
- Write words including invented or temporary spelling
- Write sentence(s)
- Leave spaces between words
- Copy and write text such as lists, labels, notes and personal stories
- Illustrate stories

In this list alone there are 41 skills, many of which have skill sub-sets. Research specifies these as the skills that children MUST have to become efficient readers and writers. If you were to test struggling readers in grades 3, 4 and 5 and to assess their degree of knowledge related to these skills, you might find gaps in their learning that impede fluency. We know that a lack of fluency results in a lack of comprehension in later grades. Learning assistant teachers often have to re-teach the "gap" skills in order to create a positive impact on future fluency and comprehension. This is why we need to ensure that these skills are taught methodically and with mastery as early in the primary years, as children are ready to learn them. With vulnerable children, we must provide multiple "doses" of instruction as well as opportunities to practice skills within meaningful contexts.

Building words which are familiar and important.

The Problem

1. So Many Skills

Children must learn over 41 essential skills in their first three years of school. Whether we want to admit it or not, with over 20 children in our classrooms, it is impossible for us to know and remember which children:

- have been taught each skill,
- have mastered each skill,
- need review of a skill,
- need re-instruction of a skill, or
- need support (external to the classroom) for special assessments.

This could amount to over 820 pieces of literacy skill information for one class of 20 children (let alone all the other matters a busy teacher has to remember).

2. Lack of Working Knowledge

The sciences of literacy and the brain have evolved impressively since 2000; some of the best research, articles and books have been published only since 2009. Most practicing teachers don't have time to pursue and analyze the multiple documents that might inform and change their practice. Richard Allington (2014) declared in a recent Summit that teachers need a minimum of 60 hours of professional development per year to be prepared for effective classroom implementation. Few school districts offer this opportunity. Since university bureaucracies are often slow to adopt new curricula; many graduating teachers are not well-informed about essential literacy skills. This is an issue I have confronted in my university classes with beginning **and** experienced teachers. Prior to my last *Kindergarten Intervention* course, I assessed my class—a mixture of nine new graduates and nine experienced teachers—about the degree of essential skill knowledge they possessed. Highlights of my assessment of those 18 qualified primary teachers are as follows:

- Two experienced teachers could name most of the skills;
- Eight teachers, all experienced and with good district professional development programs, could name fewer than 50% of the skills;
- Seven teachers were able to name fewer than 20% of the skills; and
- One teacher was able to name only 8% of the skills.

This was in spite of the fact that the purpose of my course was to plan classroom intervention strategies. How can teachers intervene when they are not even aware of the essential skills? (At this stage I must declare that my class was an exceptional group of dedicated, enthusiastic and self-motivated professionals; these results, therefore, would have to be considered as the high end of the scale. I shudder to contemplate what the results might have been in a group of randomly selected teachers.)

3. Meeting Differentiated Needs in a Typical Classroom

Vulnerable children enter pre-k and kindergarten with very few of the essential skills, while some of their classmates have already started to read. The effective teacher's job at these entry levels is challenging to say the least. Teachers need to be highly skilled and knowledgeable about what the skills are, how to assess them, how to teach them and how to track them. Children must be assessed to determine individual skill knowledge and subsequently grouped and re-grouped daily, according to the mastery-level of each skill. The teacher requires a viable tracking system to monitor individual progress on a weekly basis and one that informs instructional planning for daily and weekly instruction. The classroom must be organized to facilitate all of the above.

4. Managing Emotional and Behavioral Needs

Approximately 10 % of children enter their first school experiences with social and emotional challenges. These can be disruptive, consume teacher time and energy, and distract from others who enter ready and eager to begin learning. This is complicated by the fact that few schools have ways to identify these needs prior to school entry. The system is simply not ready to meet their needs and frequently does not have the appropriate support systems in place such as external expertise and in-class support. Administrators must make this support system their highest priority especially at the start of the school-entry year.

In my book *Teaching with the Winning Touch* (Good Apple, 1981), I described the dynamic learning environment we created throughout our kindergarten to grade 7 school. All classrooms were organized with learning centers, projects, inquiries and choice activities through personal contracts with each child. For its time, the program was a progressive and innovative approach to learning, while desks-in-rows and teacher-led instruction prevailed in other schools.

There was no question that our students were actively engaging in learning, with growing self-esteem and highly-motivated behaviors. The program engendered an atmosphere of love, respect and enthusiasm, with collaboration and respect as the order of the day. We welcomed children from other district schools— vulnerable students thrived in our accepting and inclusive environment.

In retrospect, however, despite higher achievement for all students in the social

Volunteer reading with a student on the library swing.

and emotional domains, I am not certain that academic achievement was adequate for our vulnerable children. Although academically-able students thrived, we were not well-informed about the science of literacy interventions compared to what we know now. Keeping track of who was or was not learning specific skills became a challenging issue. The children were moving from center to center, making tracking of skill mastery and instruction difficult.

The Solution

To address the quandary of uncertainty in tracking skill mastery, I devised the *Circle Charts* as the best possible solution. It has since been field tested in recent pilot sites and revised several times in response to teacher suggestions. The *Circle Charts* and support materials are presently being designed as an "app" for teacher tablets. (Email vulnerablereaders@shaw.ca for an update on product availability.)

Rationale: Why are the Circle Charts SO important?

A synopsis of recent research (NELP, 2008) affirmed that without specific foundational skills in kindergarten and grade 1, most vulnerable children will struggle throughout their school experience due to a lack of specific skills, loss of confidence, and diminished self-concept. Research has now identified skills essential to kindergarten and grade 1 interventions. Further studies declare that 90% of all children can be successful if these skills are mastered in kindergarten, grade 1 and grade 2. Almost consistently in North America less than 70% of children enter school ready to meet literacy expectations and the same number fail to graduate. The problem is that many young children have not had rich literacy experiences between birth and school and we haven't been able to close the experiential gap in their first three years in school.

The *Circle Charts* are a simple tool that can guide initial assessments at kindergarten entry and subsequently track each child's daily progress through the primary years in the essential literacy skills. This ongoing assessment guides daily small-group instruction for vulnerable children in a play-based environment so that many will reach grade 2 or 3 achieving at the same level as their more fortunate peers. The skills identified on the *Circle Chart* are based on the NELP (*National Early Learning Panel*, 2008) report and the work of major literacy experts.

How do the Circle Charts work?

The essential skills are listed across the top of the chart, with children's names listed down the left side. Teachers use informal assessments for skills at the beginning of the school year while observing with the whole group and meeting with small groups or with individuals; the charts are then completed according to the child's response.

- If the child demonstrates mastery, the teacher will fill in the entire circle;

- If in a large-group setting where time is an issue, the teacher can simply make a dot in the center of the circle to be completed later;

- If the child is uncertain about the skill but answers correctly on some examples, the teacher fills in a half-circle indicating a review will be required; and

- If the child shows no understanding, the circle remains empty, indicating the child will need explicit instruction.

Three colors are used on the chart, one for each of the three school terms in the school year. In this way, the teacher can track and report the pace and stages of the child's skill development over the course of the year. Once the chart is completed, the teacher places the chart on a clipboard or in an easily accessible place in the classroom.

A kindergarten *Circle Chart* completed in June: so much success!

Primary teachers would begin the school year with the alphabet, phonological awareness and sight words *Circle Charts*, then move to the next sets of skills as the year progresses. Because the purpose of the process is to inform instruction, it is important that the classroom teacher conduct the assessments. Seventy per cent of children will have already mastered early skills such as the alphabet, allowing assessments to be completed efficiently for most of the children. Teachers report that the *Circle Chart* system works best when the school can provide some human resource support in the classroom to supervise children playing and practicing skills independently, while the teacher conducts initial assessments. This can be accomplished creatively if resources are not readily available as described in the *Teacher Stories* and *Case Studies*.

The *Circle Charts*, while such a simple and easy tool, provide teachers with a profound knowledge of each child and the degree of success with each essential literacy skill; mastery is required by grade 3 if children are to be fluent readers.

Why are the Circle Charts so effective?

There are many reasons. Once each *Chart* is completed teachers can:

- Bring together a small group, all of whom have the same need: the re-teaching or review of a skill; other children can be happily working at literacy practice centers;

- Move from center to center working with individuals identified on the chart as having a need;

- Fill in the circles as children master each skill: complete re-assessments are never needed;

- Introduce the chart to learning assistance teachers, teacher assistants or other adults who can then support the teacher by working with small groups or individuals. In this way vulnerable children can receive multiple "doses" of practice with fun games and supportive adults;

- Share the progress with parents so they can also support the child at home by playing games provided by the teacher; and

- Ask administrators for additional support for children who appear not to be making adequate progress.

Stamping names in Play-Doh.

There are other significant advantages of using the Circle Charts.

- The *Charts* inform daily instruction; teachers can plan their instructional time in order to deliver the greatest benefits with the greatest proficiency. There is no hit-and-miss when using the *Circle Charts*;

- Assessment is ongoing and never has to be repeated, even the following year if *Circle Charts* are passed from grade-to-grade;

- Teachers are accountable and can prove it; administrators are more likely to provide additional human and other resources when teachers can provide evidence that vulnerable children are in need;

- Colleagues, administrators and parents are impressed with teachers' knowledge about each individual child;

- Tier three children (those needing specialized help) quickly become obvious once the initial assessments are completed, especially when after multiple doses: of instruction, the child has made little progress; and

- Teachers feel a sense of accomplishment as they visually review the results of their instructional efforts.

The *Circle Charts* are simple tracking devices that clearly pinpoint skill instruction and progress for over 40 sets of essential literacy skills for the individual student. The goal is skill mastery for tier one and tier two children before the end of grade 2. Tier three children may require external support and perhaps pullout services. *Circle Charts* should be passed from grade-to-grade to avoid unnecessary re-assessments.

How do teachers assess the skills informally?

Assessments are most happily conducted through the use of games, manipulative materials, concrete objects, picture books or other interesting child-oriented attractions. For instance, if teaching the letter *b*, you might empty a bag of ten toys on the table or carpet. Ask the child to say the name of each object, putting the ones starting with *b* back in the bag; point out that *bag* starts with *b* as well. You may ask the child to do any of the following activities:

- Name the letter and say the sound,
- Find the letter in the room or in a book,
- Print the letter on a board, or
- Make the letter using *Lego*.

Using these ideas with a small group will allow teachers to complete the assessment in an expeditious but playful way while completing the *Circle Charts*.

Riley — determined to spell his name. Note the Y!

Teacher Response to Circle Charts in Field Testing

Janet's Comment

How Did Teachers Respond to the Use of the *Circle Chart* in Field Testing?

Over 100 teachers agreed to field-test the *Circle Charts* in their classrooms in either the pilot sites or in my Kindergarten Intervention Classrooms. You will find more responses in the Case Study chapter. The pilot sites used the *Circle Charts* for a full 10 months; the university class used them for three months.

Janet

 ## ASSIGNMENT CIRCLE CHARTS

Teachers were asked to consider their experience with the *Circle Charts* and respond to the following questions:

1. Has the use of the charts changed your teaching practice? If so, how and in what way? If not, why not?

2. Describe how you have used it including frequency, management, sharing of data, or any other description of how it fits into your classroom life.

3. If you were to give suggestions to a friend about how to use it what would be your best advice?

4. Address the time issues involved. How have you managed to complete the assessments and organize small group instruction?

5. How could the charts be improved?

6. Include a copy of your circle chart to date with children's names blocked. Shrink to 8.5 x 11 and explain any analysis of the results so far.

7. To close, tell a story about a child related to the use of the chart.

The following excerpts are representative of the university class students' responses, most of whom were experienced teachers.

Teachers' Stories

The *Circle Charts* Provide Clear Learning Outcomes

(Jennifer Schmidt)

The *Circle Charts* certainly pinpoint the learning outcomes clearly for me as the teacher, as well as for parents and administrators. It is a wonderful tool to show the learning that takes place in a play-based environment! The *Circle Charts* have made me more aware and "tuned in" to what the children know. I am able to plan lessons around the information in the charts; the charts make it so easy to plan for small-group instruction. At a glance I see which children need more "doses" of a particular skill. As a result, I include more small-group instruction in my practice. I can check off some things quickly without having to assess each child on each learning outcome (letter names and sounds—it's even easy to assess in a whole-class setting those who have mastered the skills and it frees up time to focus on those who need more "doses").

I am much more organized and more confident; my teaching is more focused thanks to the *Circle Charts*. My *Circle Charts* are on a clipboard that I carry with me always. I use them multiple times each day. I have the children's first names listed alphabetically because I find that easier than last names to scan and find quickly. During large-group instruction, I am able to fill in the obvious ones quickly. I discreetly complete the charts when we are working in small groups. I prefer them not to be a distraction, so I usually keep the clipboard on my lap and complete them while assessing.

Improvements? Looking to the future, if these were to be sold, it would be great if they were available as a digital document that could be adjusted to suit the class. Technologically savvy teachers would probably appreciate being able to complete the charts digitally on their iPads in the classroom with a quick click to fill in circles. *(Note from Janet: It's in the works!)*

Know Which Students Can Name The Alphabet

(Michelle Fitterer)

How many of **your** students can name all the letters of the alphabet? Which students can produce letter sounds, but may struggle with recalling letter names? Are there any groups of students having difficulty with segmentation, rhyme production, or deletion? If you had asked me those questions four months ago I wouldn't have been able to answer without having to flip frantically through my assessment binder. Now, after completing the *Circle Charts* for both the alphabetic principle and phonological awareness, I can answer those questions both quickly and confidently with one glance at my *Circle Charts*. The use of this assessment tool has helped shape my teaching practice dramatically.

My confidence, as a first-year teacher, has grown since using the *Circle Charts*. Revisiting them daily has helped me understand which stage my students have reached with their learning and how to prepare small-group instruction to improve their skills. Furthermore, the clear format of the *Circle Charts* has made it easier to share this formative assessment with my students, their families, and support staff. As a result, the assessment process in my classroom has become transparent. It is common to see my students and me cheering and high-fiving every time we fill in a circle on the chart. Assessment does not have to be an onerous, time-consuming process. My *Circle Charts*, a colored pencil, and a clipboard are all I need to monitor the progress of my students and plan for further instruction. There is no doubt that I will continue to use this simple and effective assessment tool throughout my teaching career.

In my classroom, everyone knows where our *Circle Charts* are, what the colored-in circles represent, and why we use them.

- They hang behind my desk on a clipboard where I can access them quickly for daily use. It is my goal to review them every day so that I can group students more effectively and choose literacy centers based on areas of need.
- During our *ABC* Tub times I can informally assess my students while they play literacy games in a relaxed atmosphere with their peers.
- As well, I can hold quick conferences with students during free-play centers to discuss their learning on the charts and set goals for the future.
- Sharing the data has been a rewarding process for everyone involved. Students love seeing their line of circles being filled in and they understand what the data means.
- I make an effort to involve families in the learning process and often share the *Circle Charts* with them before or after school. In a matter of moments, a parent and I can share their child's growth and note which alphabet letters or essential literacy skills could be practiced at school and home. In this way, families are receiving more consistent and descriptive feedback on their child's progress rather than receiving three formal report cards in the year.

Now that I have used the charts I realize just how manageable and quick the process is. For example, to assess my students' knowledge of letter names and sounds I used a combination of whole-group, small-group, and one-on-one instruction to gather my data. Once I fell into a rhythm of filling in the circles on the charts I knew I had found an assessment tool that worked for me.

Improvements? Over the past few months I have made subtle changes to the way I fill in the charts to suit my teaching needs. For example, a student had mastered the letter *g* (the circle was completely filled in with yellow pencil crayon), but when I revisited this letter a few weeks later she could no longer remember its name or sound. In response, I decided to place a pencil dot beside the colored-in circle to remind me that she required extra practice with this letter, and when she had regained mastery then I would erase the dot.

Another change I would make for next year is the method I use when filling in half circles. If a student was able to **name** 15 letters of the alphabet I would fill in the left side of the circle; conversely, if a student was able produce the **sounds** for 15 letters I would fill in the right side of the circle. This is an example of how each teacher can make changes to *how* they use a tool, so that it best suits their teaching practice.

The most rewarding part of using the *Circle Charts* as an assessment tool has been sharing the process with my students. Recently, my heart leapt when one of my students pulled a chair up to my desk and said, "Mrs. Cowan, it is my turn next to work on my letters… I have been practicing hard." Just one day earlier, this girl and I had conferred and discovered that she only needed to practice the tricky sounds: q and y. I asked her to think of her favorite words that began with each of those letters, wrote them (queen/yellow) on a sticky note, and then stuck it to her desk for her to practice. I was both surprised and proud that she took the initiative to find me during free center play to show me her learning. She was even more excited when I allowed her to carefully color in the circles herself!

Practicing letters with Play-Doh.

Afterwards, we created a secret handshake to celebrate her success and then she happily quizzed me on my letter names and sounds. Assessment is a quick, fun, and shared process in our classroom, thanks to the *Circle Charts*!

Identify the Students for Specific Instruction

(Shauna Buffie)

The use of *Circle Charts* has changed my teaching practice. They have made it so much easier to see at a glance which children need skill instruction or skill review on a particular upper- or lower-case letter. I know I do more short pullout small-group instruction sessions simply because I can see on a couple of sheets of paper which students need the same direct teaching or review. Before the use of the *Circle Charts* I was using small-group instruction strategies but I was probably not targeting all the right children, because I was pulling them based on my memory not at-a-glance data. My instruction prior to the use of the *Circle Charts* would not have been as individualized or as accurate.

At report card time and parent/teacher/student interview times, it is a useful assessment to share with parents, as it is so easy for them to see what their child has mastered or where they still need some direct instruction or review. As well, using the different colors at different times of the year solidifies when the learning took place and I am able to see and share the progress.

I rely on the *Circle Charts* for organizing small-group instruction because I have several times built into my day where my students are at activities of choice which lends itself to quickly and easily pulling aside a small group to play a literacy game or work on the alphabet through play-based and hands-on learning opportunities.

Shaping letters with dough, and using Wiki Stix to trace over the shapes help children internalize the shape of the letter, while developing their fine motor skills.

Where do My Students Need Support?

(Wendy de Groot)

Using the *Circle Charts* has helped me to clarify where individual students need support. It lets me know exactly what needs to be focused on and it helps me to "at a glance" organize my students into groups for round-table teaching as well as guide me in large-group teaching. In the past I had a ballpark knowledge of who knew what but now I have precise information at my fingertips.

I began using the *Circle Charts* in January as part of a university assignment. I had been using various other data management tools but the *Circle Charts* are much more manageable than the tools I had used previously. You can do the assessments in small chunks of time rather than waiting until you have a larger period of time available; this assists me in getting information quickly.

I used the information for my second-term report cards. For those students that had not yet mastered a significant number of letters/sounds, I set up parent meetings prior to Report Cards going out. I explained and sent home the alphabet binders to give parents who really wanted to support their children at home ideas of how to do so. I then set up a plan to access student support during literacy centers and requested support from our school support staff (through my administrator) to enable myself to work with this small group while my other students were busy doing related activities. Unfortunately I was not given the time because the schedule of support was already set and "it wouldn't be fair" to change it now.

Undeterred, I set up my literacy centers and crossed my fingers that during the teacher-blocked times I would not be interrupted and my students would now be independent enough to move through the schedule with little support. Each week during the first literacy block with my "special guys" I meet with them and we review what we know and choose two letters to focus on for the next couple of days. The letters we started on were letters that were in their name (if those were among the ones not known). I send a note home to their parents to let them know our focus and I have suggestions to help them support their child at home in addition to the alphabet binder. I do this to give them a little reminder that, yes, this is important and we are working on this at school and hope that you will assist the journey by helping at home. Then for the remainder of the week, during centers, odd freed-up times, and other literacy center blocks, I pull these ones aside and we do some quick review using various tools: Play-Doh, Wikki Stix, our bodies, finger tracing, and reviewing rhymes that help us remember.

Making letters with our bodies!

I have made each of my students a small set of cards and put them on a ring. When we choose our letters "to really focus on" we write them on one of the cards on the ring. That is kept close at hand and keeps track of the ones we have been working on recently as well, so it works as a quick review. The *Circle Charts* are also right at my side as we continue to fill in circles for letters/sounds we have mastered and the children are really interested in seeing those circles get shaded in.

To reward success as well as determination, we make a trip down to the office to visit our administrator to share our learning joy! She follows up with a phone call home and I send a "happy gram" in their home folder. I am able to use the *Circle Charts* to show parents and colleagues the progress and summary of progress of my students. It is a quick visual for all to see.

Advice? I would advise getting started right away. It does not take long to get that first phase completed; from then on it is a working document that is never far away. For kindergarten I have only used it for tracking mastery of letter identification and learning letter sounds but I am going to work with my student teacher to help her use it to track skill mastery in the PE unit she is going to teach next month. *(Note from Janet: The Circle Charts can be used as a tracking tool for any set of skills at any grade level – even high school.)*

Avaya is a good example of student success in collaboration with parents. She turned five at the end of October. She is the second child (of three) in a very busy house that has recently experienced a family tragedy. She is very social and not really interested in the academics of school. She just likes to play, draw, and do dress-ups. She has a wonderful sense of humor and has recently started to enjoy playing school with her big sister.

After completing my assessment in January/February and noting the big gaps in her letter/sound mastery, I met her parents and showed them her progress (covering up the names of fellow students) and we discussed how we could support Avaya's learning. They already had learning-fun built into their home routines, although they admitted that perhaps they had been neglecting them recently due to the family situation. When I explained how the alphabet binder works they felt it would fit into their existing schedule nicely. I sent the binder home with them and told them that I would be in touch with them again in early April to check on their progress.

Now [after holidays] we are setting up a concentrated six-week schedule of support for my students. I sat down with Avaya to check her progress on the *Circle Chart* and make our first weekly goal. I was delighted to see that there was significant progress.

She happily chatted with me and told me how she practiced at home and with whom. She was tickled-pink to see her circles get completed. She now knows all of her uppercase letters and sounds, and of the ten lowercase letters that she did not previously know, she only has five more to learn! Wow! While working with her I noticed her making funny contorted faces as she identified the letters. I was about to ask her what she was doing but before I could she told me, "I can do this! I just cross my eyes and bump across the alphabet to figure it out."

Intent on matching the letters and finding the missing letters.

Janet's Summary

The *Circle Charts*, implemented in a play- and inquiry-based environment, are a major key to ensuring success for vulnerable children:

- The diligent use of them facilitates explicit instruction in differentiated small groups;
- They inform daily teacher planning and instruction;
- They track individual progress;
- They facilitate reporting to parents;
- They provide compelling evidence for child advocacy to other professionals as children need specialized support; and
- They provide a sense of self-satisfaction and pride for teachers who witness concrete evidence of their own effectiveness as they document student progress with each skill.

Learning and practicing essential skills together.

Teachers can develop their own circle charts; however, Janet's *Circle Charts* are available as a site license from Early Learning Inc. Please see the Appendix for details about how to purchase a site license for your classroom, school or district.

Janet

Learning to make letters with tiles.

Vulnerable Children Need Explicit Skill Instruction

 ## Janet's Introduction

Teaching essential skills joyfully requires a lot more than a focus on games. Language skills like phonemic awareness are embedded in everyday oral language as well as writing and print experiences. There is a significant link between the use of language and cognitive growth. Self-confidence and emotion are directly connected to a child's openness and willingness to learn. Skills cannot be learned without context and meaningful connections.

That should be enough to capture your attention! This was supposed to be a chapter on teaching essential skills and I have just raised numerous other issues. There's a reason for that. If you read the *Research and Recommended Books* section carefully you may find some remarkable facts that will be important to your classroom practices and planning. In summary:

- Contrary to recent decades of practice, it is now clear that explicit instruction must begin in kindergarten especially for vulnerable children.

- Oral language is the vehicle for phonemic awareness learning; therefore, creating environments that are rich in talk are essential for phonemic awareness.

- "Lucky" children have five times the number of working words in their vocabulary. Does your classroom structure encourage "talk" between the "haves" and "have-not" children?

- Print, as context, is also a vehicle for phonemic awareness learning. Frequent reading and writing experiences enhance phonemic awareness skills.

- At the same time, vulnerable children need explicit instruction in small groups. The classroom organization must make room for both invisibly.

- Peers are "conversational torchbearers." How will you create an environment, rich in peer dialogue, where those who are language challenged can wallow in the experiences of the "lucky ones."

- Emotions allow or block learning. Is your classroom happy, busy, interactive and safe?

- Do you and your children laugh and play with language?

Richard Allington warns us that we must have an early warning system that alerts us to children who are not mastering phonemic awareness (and related skills) by mid grade 1. Dick and I will discuss this one day I'm sure, but I say it's in mid-kindergarten that we have to raise the alarm.

Please read the next section on research. It has been very enlightening for me to prepare this for you and I think you might find some surprises in the research. I did!

Janet

© Mort (2014)

When Vulnerable Readers Thrive
Dreams Come True   JANET N. MORT PhD

Research and Recommended Books

Building Oral Language Skills

(Middendorf, 2009)

Research tells us that phonemic awareness is the primary indicator of readiness for reading instruction, as well as a reliable predictor of future success in reading. Since phonemic awareness is an awareness of (and competency in) oral language, it follows that the more a child practices oral language, the stronger his or her phonemic awareness grows, and the more ready he or she is for phonic connections and ultimately written language (p. 11).

By age three, children from privileged families have heard 30 million more words than children from underprivileged families (p. 12).

Hart and Risley (2003) showed that by age three, children of professional parents had a vocabulary of about 525 words, whereas children in homes considered economically deprived had a vocabulary of 117 words. The researchers found that families who spoke more words to the children were soon increasing the complexity of syntax and sentence structure. Conversation evolved beyond simple, concrete instructions into discussions; and discussions evolved into abstractions, talking about feelings, relating cause and effect, wondering and predicting. This more complex use of language in turn stimulated cognitive growth.

Children at the kindergarten age need to be able to do the following:

- Produce the sounds needed for speech,
- Demonstrate comprehension of spoken language,
- Listen for short periods of time with focused attention,
- Demonstrate phonemic awareness,
- Rhyme, identify initial phonemes, and manipulate sounds,
- Follow two- and three-step directions,
- Verbalize daily experiences and personal needs,
- Incorporate new vocabulary into daily speech,
- Answer simple questions about a read-aloud or story,
- Ask meaningful questions,
- Re-tell events in sequence,
- Hear and respond to patterns in sounds and language,
- Hear and use conventions of speech,

- Engage in conversations with peers and adults,
- Use age-appropriate social language for manners and conflict resolution,
- Demonstrate auditory memory, and
- Use pitch and inflexion to convey meaning.

Many children come to our classrooms already proficient in most of these areas. They are the conversational torchbearers for others, since children learn language from fluent peers as eagerly and as effortlessly as they learn from caring adults who are conscientiously modeling good language (p. 16).

Remember that receptive language develops before expressive. Keep that in mind when a child is struggling to find the right word or stammering to verbalize something to you. Most young children think more quickly than they can find the words to express those thoughts, and our patience is needed as they mentally search for a word or phrase (p. 17).

This student was playing with a rhyming poem we had been practicing. She proudly showed me that she used one of the rhyming cards and found a Word Wall word that rhymed!

Building Oral Language Through Phonemic Awareness Fun

Phonemic awareness as a subscale of phonological awareness is the foundation of literacy. A child with solid phonemic awareness skills learns to read and spell more easily than a child with weak phonemic awareness skills. A child who is phonemically aware can accomplish the following:

- Isolate individual phonemes (sounds) in a word,
- Identify the same sound in different words,
- Segment and count the parts (syllables) of a word,
- Blend individual phonemes together to make a word,
- Eliminate beginning sounds from a word,
- Substitute one beginning sound for another, and
- Create and identify rhyming words.

Oral language that plays with words creates fun for early learners and builds crucial skills. What child doesn't enjoy silly songs and nonsense words? We can easily capitalize on a young child's fascination with language to shape important literacy foundations (p. 27).

Oral Language in Centers

Fact: Children talk during center time. That chatter is cause for celebration rather than concern. According to Erik Jensen (1998), "Talking anchors learning." The more children verbalize about the task at hand, the more neuro-connections they create that will embed what they are learning. Our challenge is in keeping their conversation on task and in encouraging the exchange of higher order thinking while children are interacting in center... Specifically we will examine those centers that are designed to use oral language to reinforce learning:

- Discovery centers,
- Re-telling centers,
- Listening centers, and
- Book centers (p. 50).

What Really Matters for Struggling Readers

(Allington, 2012)

Some students need more expert and intensive instruction for their learning to keep pace with that of other children. Schools must enhance classroom instruction so that the number of struggling readers is minimized and then put into place an organizational strategy that ensures that the children who need intensive, expert instruction receive it (p. 175).

My interpretation of the research suggests that although most children develop adequate phonemic segmentation in the course of routine beginning reading instruction, a small proportion of students fail to acquire the understanding and strategies that underline this skill. These students do not seem to acquire phonemic segmentation from classroom lessons and this lack of development seems strongly related to their difficulties learning to read (p. 175).

Allington (2012) proposes that schools need to ensure three things:

1. Classroom lessons feature activities that foster development of phonemic segmentation,

2. An early warning system that will identify those students having difficulties, and

3. An intervention plan that will target, by the middle of the first grade year, any students who have failed to developed this skill and will provide that student with expert, intensive instruction.

Teaching Struggling Readers: How to Use Brain Based Research to Maximize Learning

(Lyons, 2003)

Marie Clay wrote in the Foreword:

There will always be some children who cannot make it without supplementary, individual instruction. This will be most economically provided in the early stages of learning something. Rather than let them fall behind their peers, we must find ways to accelerate children's learning, so that they catch up and join in with their successful peers. Better classroom education for the majority will never eliminate the need for individual teaching for some learners to acquire basic reading and writing skills… There is a need to make a continuous supply of catch-up education available as a matter of course wherever children are in school. We have done this with speech therapy for decades but have only recently begun to do this for literacy learning, and it is working well. Every child must be given the tools they need to succeed in later education, and sometimes that means giving individual instructions (pp. x, xi).

Carole A. Lyons, author, acknowledges the efforts of early intervention teachers as follows. Your efforts are seldom known, recognized or appreciated, but the children you reach will be forever thankful, for you have prevented them from experiencing a lifetime of frustration and reading barrier. On behalf of all the struggling children you have taught to read and write, and their parents and families, thank you for making a difference in their lives. An extensive body of neurological and psychological research demonstrates that emotions are essential to thinking and are an inseparable part of the learning process. This body of research is especially important for literacy educators to understand because unless students learn to read and write early on, they cannot fully participate in classroom experiences during elementary school years and beyond (p. 3).

I believe that our schools' failure to teach children who are fully capable of learning to read and write is not the children's fault, but rather, due to a reliance on the methods of teaching that ignore the nature of the learning process—specifically, the cognitive and affective dimensions of learning. With our current understanding of the inseparable fusion between cognition (reasoning) and emotion in the development of the mind, all children, with the exception of those with severe neurological difficulties, should be able to become readers and writers. In order to accomplish this goal, however, teachers must learn how to provide the powerful and sustained opportunities that will enable students with varying needs and abilities to learn from the very act of reading and writing itself (p. 5).

Reading and Learning to Read

(Vacca & Vacca et al., 2012)

These studies suggest that the greatest impact on phonemic awareness is achieved when there is interaction with print and explicit attention to phonemic awareness abilities. In other words, interaction with print combined with explicit attention to the sound structure of spoken words is the best vehicle towards growth.

Instruction has its greatest impact on phonemic awareness when teachers balance a high level of interaction with print and explicit instruction in various tasks related to manipulating sounds in words (p. 167).

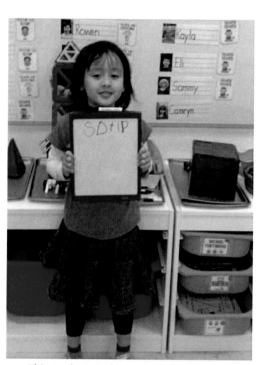

This student is playing with this week's Jolly Phonic letters, names and sounds.

Learning single alphabet letters contributes greatly to learning to read, although it is not sufficient by itself. Often some teachers may be tempted to have children memorize single alphabet letters through the use of flash cards. Schickedanz, (1998), however, recommends avoiding flash cards for teaching young children letter naming and recognition because the practice is devoid of meaningful context. As she puts it, "In meaningful activities, children are able to see and appreciate a connection between what they are learning and some application of it—some reason for its importance or usefulness. If children are exposed to letters and their names through the use of flashcards… the purpose of alphabet letters is not obvious. But if children are exposed to letters and letter names in looking at their own names, classroom signs, or titles of story books, the purpose of letters is obvious" (p. 164).

Definitions:

1. The Alphabetic Principle suggests that letters in the alphabet map to phonemes, hence the word phonics is used to refer to the child's identification of words by their sounds.

2. Phonics – children learn their word can be separated into sounds and that the segmented or separated sound can be represented by letters.

3. Phonemes – are the minimum sound units that can be represented in written language.

4. Phonemic Awareness – this refers to an insight about oral language and the ability to segment and manipulate the sounds of speech and is one of the five essential components of reading.

5. Phonological Awareness – this is the ability to hear, recognize, and play with the sounds in our language. It is the recognition that sounds in English can be broken down into smaller and smaller parts: sentences, words, rhymes and syllables. Phonological awareness is auditory: students can do most phonological awareness activities with their eyes closed. Phonological awareness can be taught and is important for all students (pp. 161-165).

Kindergarten Literacy

(McGill-Franzen, 2006)

Kindergarten Reading Changes Lives:

This study (Hansen & Farrell, 1995) is one of the most comprehensive evaluations of kindergarten ever done. It followed about 4,000 students in 24 districts, in 10 states who had been taught to read in kindergarten. By the time they were contacted and evaluated for this study, more than 12 years had passed between the kindergarten experience and their senior year, yet the researchers found "extraordinary" benefits for the children... Not only did the students who received formal reading instruction in kindergarten exhibit a clear pattern of (a) showing superior current reading skills, (b) having higher grades and better attendance in school, and (c) needing and receiving significantly less remedial instruction in both elementary and secondary school, but they were from families with a significantly lower social class status and parent education, compared to those in the other two comparison groups (p. 93).

Thus, in spite of fewer family resources, students who received kindergarten reading still out-performed higher socio-economic students (SES) who did not (p. 15).

Read, Write, Play, Learn: Literacy Instruction in Today's Kindergarten

(Rog, 2001)

Small Group Instruction: An Extra 30 Minutes Per Day?

It is important to remember that 80% to 85% of students develop this understanding by the middle of first grade simply by living in a world of language (IRA, 1998). As with every other aspect of teaching and learning, we teachers need to assess what our students know so that we can plan the instructions that best meet their needs... For those students in need of an extra dose of phonemic awareness instruction, the *National Reading Panel* recommends small group instruction for about 30 minutes a day for a maximum of 20 hours. In school terms that is only two months, even in kindergarten (p. 19).

Phonological Awareness: Hearing Sounds and Words

The ability to hear, distinguish and replicate the sounds and words (known as *Phonological Awareness*) is the foundation on which reading is built. For young readers to learn to decode and spell words, they must hear these sound structures: syllables, rhymes and phonemes (p. 52).

Guided Reading: In each lesson we blitz a literacy skill, read a new book, and practice sight words and writing.

Literacy Development in the Early Years

(Morrow, 2012)

Phonemic and Phonological Awareness Instruction

Instruction in phonemic and phonological awareness should be playful as teachers read stories, tell stories, play word games and use rhymes and riddles. Instruction in the area should be purposeful and planned; we cannot leave it to chance. In the past, this instruction was spontaneous and incidental. Of course, it could still be spontaneous when the moment arises and should be; however, it must be systematically written into daily plans (p. 158).

An Alphabet Letter a Day?

Children need to learn the alphabet to become independently fluent readers and writers… It has been demonstrated by research to be a predictor of reading success… Systematic teaching of the alphabet is necessary. One of the most common practices is teaching the alphabet from beginning to end with one letter a week… The letter of the week has been criticized if the letter is taught in isolation from meaning and it takes 26 weeks to introduce all the letters. Others have suggested a letter a day or two or three letters a week. This way the alphabet is introduced quickly and you can go back and review each one again. Reutzel carried out a study about teaching kindergarten children the alphabet with a letter of the week approach and another group with the letter of the day. Those in the letter of the day group increased significantly in their letter recognition… The growth was attributed to the constant review of the letters throughout the year, after letters are initially introduced (Reutzel & Cooter, 2009, pp. 162).

Janet's Comment

Teach Essential Skills Joyfully

When I was designing the curriculum for my university early intervention class, I decided to feature the alphabetic principles first for good reason. Without a solid working knowledge of the alphabet, children cannot begin to read. Without a basic understanding of how to teach the alphabet, beginning teachers cannot help vulnerable readers become literate. A preposterous proposition? Not at all!

One September, I had a first-year teacher call me in tears: "I just was assigned a kindergarten class and I'm so scared." I was a bit bewildered as it was my understanding that this was her dream come true. "But I don't know how to teach a letter!" she responded. She was a recent graduate from an elementary university program and she didn't know how to teach an alphabet letter to children? This is when I get angry! I see this situation frequently in my school visits: teachers moving from secondary assignments to grade 1; experienced teachers deprived of updated professional development; teachers who do not read or have time to read the most recent research. I have found children in grade 3 who still don't know some sounds for letters.

Practicing letters with "goop!"

The alphabet is the best place to start with assessments in September in any primary grade. The first task should be to assess every child's knowledge of the alphabet, record the results and start grouping for instruction. Most vulnerable children will require many "doses" of explicit instruction before they reach mastery. You will find the word "doses" used frequently in this book. It's a medical term that our colleague Dr. Clyde Hertzman used to use. He would point out that when we fill prescriptions we are reminded to complete the entire "dose" for maximum medical effectiveness. In literacy skill instruction, some children will learn a skill after one dose. Vulnerable children with limited literacy experience may require 10 doses (instruction and practice) before mastery. We don't give up. We just stay patient and persistent. All children can learn the alphabet!

As a university professor of an early intervention class I wanted to ensure that my students (some of them experienced teachers) were skilled in their alphabet work with children. I assigned them the following task:

VANCOUVER ISLAND UNIVERSITY
EXPLORE. DISCOVER. EXCEL.   THE ASSIGNMENT

ASSESSING AND TEACHING ALPHABET LETTERS

Purpose: The purpose of this exercise is that students experience informal assessments of children individually, in a small group and (if possible) in a full class group of kindergarten children.

Selection of students: Select students that you believe do **not** know the letter(s) you choose to assess (small consonants only). Do not choose tier three students or those who appear to have emotional/social issues. Use the *Circle Chart* distributed in class to record your observations.

Teach and Assess Students: Read the handouts distributed in class and Anne McGill-Franzen's (2009) book (pages assigned for reading) to inform yourself about how to teach and assess letter knowledge. Create a game-like activity to teach and practice the letter. Each of the following three steps should take no more than 10 minutes. Arrange for someone to manage the rest of your class while you are completing Steps 2 and 3:

Step 1: Teach the letter to your whole class. Make note of the children you think knew the letter and sound during the lesson and practice. Put a dot in the center of the circle on the *Circle Chart* to indicate you "think" this child has mastered this letter.

Step 2: Choose five children that appeared not to learn the letter and or sound and in a small group (in the classroom setting) re-teach the letter then assess whether each child can name the letter and make the sound successfully. Practice with your game then re-assess to see if the assessment results change. Mark progress on the *Circle Chart.*

Step 3: Repeat the instructions in Step 2 but this time with only one child who appeared not to learn the letter (someone who was not part of the group of five above).

Document Your Experience:

In approximately two pages (it's up to you) use the following headers to document your experience:

1. The Children (what you observed),

2. The Teaching Game and Practice (what you did),

3. The Difference Between the Large Group, Small Group and Individual Experience, and

4. Your Experience and Learning (as a teacher).

Consider:

- What surprised you?
- What disappointed you?
- What went well/or didn't go well?
- Anything else you consider pertinent?

The methods used in the following examples are consistent with recommended approaches in the literature—active learning, play, repetition, movement, and ability to apply in real words, sentences and books. The same strategies can be used for phonological awareness skills. These stories provide examples of best practice that can be applied with many early learning skills.

Using magnetic letters, this student "wrote" the names of the characters from the Ready Freddy books that the class read during *Teacher Read* every day.

Janet

Teachers' Stories

A Multi-layered Approach to Learning Letters

(Vicky Dodge)

In my classroom I use *writers* (an old technology called Etch-a-Sketch); they are small plastic or cardboard boards with clear cellophane sheets on top that children can write on, then lift the sheets to erase their writing; they are inexpensive in Dollar Stores and are very popular with children.

As a whole class we always begin with an *ABC* review: I ask them to mark down specific letters on their *writers,* and when they finish, they place the *writers* on their foreheads facing me until they hear my response: "Yes, Bob, good!" or "Sally, have a look at which way your *p* is facing." When we first began this activity, we decided it would be all right to hold the *writers* up blank if they were uncertain, making it easy to see who was still struggling with certain letters.

When the whole class had mastered a letter and all the boards were correct, we all celebrated! I could then update the *Circle Chart* to indicate mastery. Next, we listened to a song about Peter Puppy but before starting I asked them to look at the picture that I was showing them from the book and find words starting with *p*. When the song finished, we discussed all the *p* words and also came up with others not on the page.

Following that, we did a two-minute look around the room for *p* words. When some students chose alphabet books to check the *p* word page, we listed them on the Whiteboard, putting a check beside ones that appeared in more than one book. When two minutes were up, we reviewed the list. The children were then given a sheet of 12 pictures to cut out and glue only the *p* words onto a second page entitled *My P Words.*

Once the large group activity was done, I was able to look at my chart to determine who required more practice. With a group of five, we reviewed writing *p* with various media: on the *writers,* with Play-Doh, Lego, pipe cleaners, string, and glitter hair gel. As we worked we noted the letter, its sound and its structure; we also used fuzzy felt letters showing printing directional steps. One of the children asked if we could use the *writers* to do a quick letter review. When I asked him why he said, "Because I know *p* now, so my *writer* will not be blank."

Finally, we went through the alphabet books, discussing the *p* pages together and rechecking the cut-out pictures, making sure they matched the letter.

A Whole-class Instruction Approach to Teaching the Alphabet

(Michelle Fitterer)

Before beginning our literacy centers, we gathered together for the introduction of our new letter and letter sound—the letter *g*. Excitement and curiosity spread quickly among my students, as they tried guessing what the letter would be. Drawing on the interest they had for learning about each other's names, I gave some clues about our new letter saying, "It is at the beginning of a boy's name in our class." Once they guessed the correct letter I showed a flashcard with the lowercase *g*, carefully pronouncing the corresponding sound. Immediately, my almost-readers and readers began sharing words that began with *g* and in response, I placed a dot in the *Circle Chart* for each of them.

Making words with plasticine.

For practice, I had the class repeat after me while I spoke the letter sound softly, loudly, deeply, and in other playful ways. The final whole-class activity was a letter hunt around the room, as I took photos of children proudly finding *g* on posters, books, signs, or in other print. Wherever possible, I asked each student the name and sound of the letter they had found; since this provided me with a quick snapshot of who already knew the letter or letter sound, I was able to place dots on my *Circle Chart* according to their responses. With photos of each student taken, we returned to the mats to prepare for literacy centers and a new Valentines-themed game where I could apply their learning.

The Valentine-themed Practice Game

With *Valentine's Day* on the horizon, and as an opportunity to re-teach the letter *g* in a small group setting, I introduced a Valentine-themed game as one of our four literacy centers. Before beginning the game, I retaught *g* in a similar, repetitive fashion to the whole group, then moved on to focus on children who appeared not to have learned *g* or its sound. I engaged them in our new game by using red colored paper and plenty of *Valentine's Day* stickers on one side of the memory cards. The letters I used on the game cards were *g* as well as two familiar letters *s* and *t*. Students took turns flipping over two cards to try and find a matching pair. As part of the game, they were required to say the name and sound of each letter when a card was flipped over. In addition, each student held onto a *g* card while we practiced finger tracing it. As they played the game, I was able to use the *Circle Chart* to assess whether they had now mastered the name or sound of the letter.

Later in the day, I worked one-on-one with a student who had not learned the *g* name or sound. Retracing the steps I had used during small group instruction, I retaught the letter, played the memory game, and noted the student's progress on my *Circle Chart*.

Song, Imagination and Motivation: The Alphabet

(Ruth Irving)

The following game and song was taught during a part of routine calendar time, already used for letter games, *eye-find*, and *I-find* games. Because they know they will almost always learn a new song or sing old favorites at carpet time, I based my lesson on a song to a familiar tune and actions. I am a big believer in the power of story and creating connections for the students that will help not only to jog their memories, but also to engage their whole selves with the learning.

Our letter was a new one to them, to be taught in isolation from print; in other words, they may have seen the letter many times, but they had not yet been explicitly taught *w*. I showed them a *w* card, colored red with an illustration of wind and water. Before revealing the card, I leaned in closely and spoke very quietly. I said I had brought a friend with me, telling them he might be a little quiet but had a big name, and that some might have seen him before; however, today I had a story to tell them about this friend and in fact, my friend *Wyatt* would be my helper. At this point, they were hooked.

Slowly I brought out my card; smiles broke out and I started my story of *w*, about my strong, quiet, down-up, down-up guy who loves to jump and play especially when it's wet outside; all the while I emphasized the *w* sound and made hand sweeps in the shape of a *w*. Some of the children were already copying the letter sound with mouths and hands as I spoke. I said, "Sometimes he gets into trouble a little for getting so wet, but he dries off really quickly because he is so straight and slanted: the water just runs right off him." I personified this by straightening up my own body, sitting up quickly as if I had just thought of something, and said, "He sings a song while he's jumping in the puddles." Each time I referred to *up and down* or *jumping*, I moved my hand as if drawing a *w* in the air to reinforce the story connection; two children copied it without me asking. I then said I would teach them *Wyatt's* song with his favorite sound in it.

I introduced the song to the tune of *Happy Birthday*: *wind and water were everywhere, wind and water were everywhere, wind and water went wild, wind and water were everywhere*. We swirled our hands in front when we sang *wind,* we swept our hands in a wave motion when we sang *water,* and we opened our hands at the word *everywhere.* At the word *wild,* we bared our fingers and faces like a wild animal.

I asked how many people would like to meet my friend, and I modeled looking at the card with a fake handshake, saying, "Hello *w,* my name is…" adding, "He's kind of quiet (making the *w* sound to show), but he's got such a big, strong name." I was playfully very silly and the children loved it, with everyone getting a turn as I quickly moved the picture along the rows of children so they could participate in the dramatic introductions.

At this point, I had five students who demonstrated mastery of the letter by the way they were copying the sound and repeating the letter name. I recorded a dot on my *Circle Chart* beside their names accordingly. To reinforce my observations, we played "eye-spy with my little eye a place where my friend *w* is, somewhere in this room." I noted and documented students who led in pointing out *w* examples around the room and saying the sound as well.

At the end of the lesson, I gave them blank paper except for a short line for the *w* to sit on, and they all drew the letter on the line using grey and blue to illustrate the background of wind and water. I provided modeling at the beginning and had them make the down-up, down-up in the air, first with a pencil, then with repetition of the sound.

Practicing letters in shaving cream for sensory fun!

Small Group Work: Later during learning center time, I chose five students who apparently hadn't connected with the *w* story. Using a shallow glass dish with fine, colored sand about 1 cm deep, I asked if anyone wanted to draw my letter in the sand without giving any hints as to the letter. Although two students immediately said the sound, no one came forward right away with the letter name. We drew "down-up, down-up" in the sand while repeating the letter name and sound and I recorded their efforts.

Shortly after, I told them I was about to put the sand dish away: did they want a last turn to draw the letter? Three children did and were able say both the sound and the letter without prompting. I made a note of the two other children to target incidentally later to see if they could tell me the sound or letter in a private *eye-spy.* During snack time in quiet chats, both other children were able to tell me the name and sound. I updated my records and completely filled the circle for those who had mastered the sound. I used slightly larger dots for children with whom I might want to check again at a later time just to confirm mastery.

Another little girl, Mary, seemed to follow along and take part in the whole group lesson, and indeed, I had put a dot beside her letter and sound on my sheet, with a question mark beside it. I knew that Mary was efficient about taking cues from her peers, but without their examples, she was frequently weaker in her independent work. I took the opportunity to work one-on-one with her at the sand dish to see what she remembered from the lesson. I showed her my card again, asking her if she remembered my friend. Immediately she replied *wind and water*, using the actions from the song; she knew the sound but could not name the letter.

In the sand dish, I drew a *w*, supporting her connection with the story by repeating some funny incidentals about up my friend *down-up*, giggling about how quiet he is even though he has such a big name. She said, "That's like Evangelina!" (her friend). When it was her turn, she struggled to draw the *w* in the sand. She made another unsuccessful attempt, making a kind of lower case *m*. With her hand in mine, we drew it in the air a couple of times and sang the song again. As she went off to a book center I made a note of her hesitancy for a future check-in.

A Three-step Strategy to Teach a Letter

(Wendy de Groot)

Step 1: My student teacher introduced the letter *l* using the plans and format I had earlier set up. As she taught the lesson, I observed the students' interactions with it. Beginning with a review of the letters learned to date, she took them through the accompanying songs and rhymes all of which included kinesthetic movements.

She then focused on the letter *l*, discussing its shape, comparing the uppercase *L* shape to the lowercase *l*. She talked about its straight lines and contrasted it to the curvy lines of the previously learned letter *u*. The children outlined the *l* shape through large arm movements through to smaller hand and finger movements. As they did this, she talked about the shapes our tongues and mouths made as we said *l*.

Following this she asked for words that began with the *l* sound and handed out chalkboards for printing the letter *l*, focusing on lowercase and comparing *l* to the number *one* and to other letters like *I*. She finished with a game of *Mystery Word*, a variation on the old game of *Hangman*, where one draws the number of horizontal lines to match the number of letters in a word to be guessed. She directed the children to draw three lines and gave them clues for the first letter (her word was *fun*). Most of the children quickly printed the letter *f* and those who were unsure looked at their neighbor's chalkboard and copied the correct letter.

Next, she gave them clues for the letter *u*, followed by *n*, allowing enough time for each to be copied; she discussed how we knew what letter it should have been and then demonstrated the letter formation. When the final letter for the word was written, she asked for anyone who could identify the Mystery Word to raise a hand. She continued the game with another four or five words.

The final segment of the lesson had the children moving to the tables to complete a page that pictured a lollipop and a space along the bottom to practice printing six to ten lowercase *l*'s. When completed, it was attached to their journal. The follow-up lesson required the children to draw a picture of something that started with the *l* sound and to label it by sounding out the word as independently as possible. This was typically done the following day.

While observing the students, I used the yellow circles on the *Circle Chart* (January/February/March) to identify skill mastery, and then noted the students I believed lacked mastery of the letter taught during this lesson. It was from this list that I chose the four initial students for further practice.

Step 2: The four students came with me to review the letter *l*. We reviewed the chanting song that went with the letter, including the kinesthetic movements. We

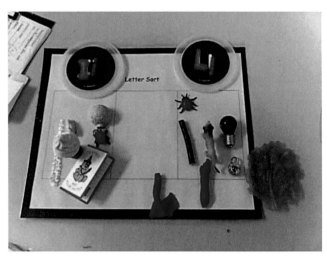

reviewed the shape of *l* and made its shapes with Play-Doh, tracing those shapes with our fingers. Using a *Letter Sort* mat with two columns, we placed the lids to Letter Sound containers (jars that hold letters and related pictures) on it. I pulled out the letters *l* and *i* and compared the two for similarities and differences; as well, we reviewed the letter *I* sound. As we put the letters on top of the matching lids, I handed the children objects from the sorting containers for identification and placement under the correct sound column. For example, they placed *light bulb* under the *l* column, and *ice cream* under the *i* column.

Subsequently, as we reviewed the objects placed in each column, I asked the children to think of a word beginning with the *l* sound. This was their ticket out the door. One child gave the word *lick* and off she went. Another was unable and when asked to identify the letter *l*, responded that it might be the letter *k*: I asked her to stay with me. A third child gave the word *light bulb*, one of the items from our shape-and-letter sorting session. The last child gave the word *lollipop* from our earlier activity.

With the remaining child I reviewed the shape and the sound of the letter, asking her to repeat the sounds of each *l* item. When we took turns thinking of *L* names, she succeeded since we have three children in our class with names beginning with *L*. I then asked again for a word that starts with *l* and she gave *lion*, one of the items in our shape and sound sort. This was her ticket out the door. I highlighted her circle on the *Circle Chart* to ensure that in future, she had achieved understanding after each lesson. She has new enthusiasm for sounding out words and printing them. I believe that with consistent support she will gain a firm foundation and achieve at grade level.

Step 3: Later in the day, I worked with a student who was also on my list of concerns. We followed a similar lesson review as I had done with the other children earlier. This child was able to make the letter shape easily with the Play-Doh, commenting that his name started with the same sound. He had some difficulty with the *Letter Sound* boxes because he was not able to identify some of the items: lettuce he identified as cabbage. When we brainstormed *l* words, he struggled, so in reviewing the items in the box and with extra support, he finally identified *ladybug* as his *l* word and received his ticket out the door.

Alphabet Action Time!

(Jennifer Schmidt)

With the whole class at the carpet, I began by printing a lower case *r* on the whiteboard and asked the children to name the letter. When many of them responded correctly, I asked what sound it made. Again, with the majority of children answering *r*, we moved on to a repetitive refrain, chanting *"r says r."*

The next stage was to identify words beginning with *r*, so I asked them to think of an animal whose name starts with the letter *r*; one student replied *rabbit*, and after everyone repeated the chant, *"r says r"* we all hopped around like rabbits. When I called, "Freeze! Have a seat. Hands up if you know another animal or bird that starts with *r*," someone called out *red bird*; after chanting and saying *rrrrrred bird*, we pretended to fly around like red birds; we repeated the pattern with *rooster* and *robot*. For my assessment, even in the whole group, I was easily able to identify students who had mastered the skill; they consistently offered correct responses.

For a small group activity, I chose five children who appeared not to have mastered the letter *r* based on my observations during the whole group game. We reviewed the letter and sound together while others were at practice centers. Recalling the words from the previous game, we repeated the chant *r says r*, while drawing *r* in the air.

Next, I introduced them to my *Letter-Sound Machine*, a crafty device I made that is supposed to tell the letter sounds; it's a crazy-looking-pretend-machine made from scraps, with a big red button on it. (It actually makes no sound at all, but that's part of the fun.)

Letter Sound Machine: Children press the button and make the letter sound. Great for practicing letter names and sounds.

The students were to place the letter card on the machine, press the button, and listen for the sound, but with no response, we puzzled over what we would have to do now. Since the machine was not working, we would have to use our voices to make the sounds instead. After each one had a turn with the machine, it became clear that one out of the five of the children had mastered the letter name and sound; one knew the name only; and three were unsure of either. I noted the degree of mastery for each on my *Circle Chart*. (At the end they suggested I take my machine home and put new batteries in it. They really believed in it!)

I Spy Game for Letters

(Kohle Silverton)

Several students still seemed to be struggling with the name and sound recognition; my initial assessment during a class discussion helped identify the specific students who would require extra practice. During center sessions that afternoon, using notes made from my *Circle Chart,* I called four children to a worktable to review the mini-lesson from earlier in the day. One of the students surprised me; she could not only quickly name and sound the letter *b,* but could even offer a few *b* words and find them. I updated the *Circle Chart* to indicate her new understanding and then continued with the activity.

Because I was not sure how effective the *I Spy* bag would be, I had made only one bag to share amongst the four children. I explained that hiding within the bag were items that all began with the letter *b*. I asked the students to predict what might be in the bag, reminding them that the items began with *b,* just like the clues the class had used for *Show and Tell*. Their four guesses were *movie, book and banana, book, Lego guys*; each child took a turn to feel the bag, look through the spy hole and identify and name one item. In order to reinforce the *b* sound, I reminded them again that all the hidden items began with that letter. They all were able to find and identify a few items for each, repeating the word with an emphasis on the *b* sound.

After the group practice, I quickly reassessed the four children using notes made from my *Circle Chart*. Two of the students had become comfortable with the letter *b,* and one seemed to have understood the concept during the group game, although his assessment was inconsistent. Because another still struggled with mastery, his *Circle Chart* assessment did not change.

The *I Spy* bag had created some excitement among the other children during center time; they had seen our small group working with it, and it had generated a lot of enthusiasm from each individual child I chose to work with. One shy, quiet boy had not demonstrated understanding in the group instruction, so I was unsure of whether he was struggling with the letter or if he just wasn't participating. Initially, he wasn't able to identify *b* or even tell me the letter sound. We practiced it together and

I explained the magic *I Spy* game. Although he could not make any predictions of the bag's contents, he did find and identify many of the *b* items within. After some practice, I reassessed to find that he demonstrated considerable progress. Possibly his shyness with the group in the beginning had kept him from offering ideas, but clearly he became more comfortable working one-to-one with me.

A Pre-K and K Integrated Approach to Letter Learning

(Nicole Kauwell)

In the pre-k room we gathered at the circle, sang the alphabet song, and I introduced the lower case letter *f*. I asked them what sound it made, and then we made it all

together. Next, we read a story from our alphabet book where almost all the words began with *f*; we then counted the number of upper and lower case *f*'s in the story. Following that, we looked at a poster with ten easy words and pictures and brainstormed other possible words such as fingerprints and freezing. I dismissed the children by showing them their name card and asking if they had an *f* in their name.

As a secondary assessment with a smaller group, I gathered a few of the older children and placed about four letters from their names on the carpet to play *Slap*: when I called out the letter, they used fly swatters to slap the letter—always raucous and a lot of fun.

With the kindergarten group at the carpet, I distributed white boards and described how to draw a lower case letter *t* (tall stick, then half way down, a short line across). Because they were sitting in front of me, I was able to see how they drew the letter and who recognized the shape. I continued until all four letters (*t, k, h, f*) were drawn: I made the sound; they named the letter; I checked each; then they erased the letter.

Whiteboard work.

Subsequently, I set up a small station at a table where I could work with three students at a time. I filled three cookie sheets with strawberry Jell-O powder and had the students reproduce letters that I called out; they were allowed to lick their fingers when they were done! (Note the book cover photo taken during this activity.) Playing *Slap* and using more upper and lower case letter matching games, I worked one-to-one with those who still needed extra practice and revised the *Circle Charts* accordingly.

A Matching, Sorting, and Cutting Activity

(Sarah Cochrane)

I am currently teaching a grade 2/3 split class but almost half of my children are reading and writing at least one grade level below their current grade. The other half is approaching, fully meeting, or exceeding grade level expectations for reading and writing. Although I knew the students who were struggling with blends and digraphs, and who had trouble with short vowels, **it had never occurred to me to assess their alphabet knowledge.**

Janet's Comment

Sarah told our university class that if she had not assessed her grade 2/3 students she would never have guessed that some of them still didn't know the alphabet; the 'experiential gap' would have remained and spelling mistakes would have become the norm in the intermediate years.

Janet

I divided my class into two groups: those who were reading at grade level (Group One) and those who were not (Group Two).

After setting up an alphabet *Circle Chart* for all students in Group Two, over the course of three days I called them individually to the teacher-table. My non-readers could not demonstrate mastery for *c, g, q, w* and *y*, with *w* and *y*.

I had the whole class divide their board into three sections: the *w* sound, the *y* sound, and *Other*. As I called out words such as *want, you, my*, the students sorted the words, based on the sounds they heard. Group One students had little difficulty with the task [but Group Two students had significant difficulty]. After entering this information on the *Circle Chart*, I worked with Group Two using a picture-and-sound sort for *w* and *y*; meanwhile, Group One students moved on to a Read-to-Self activity in various places around the room.

Read-to-Self Activity.

Small Group Picture Sort Activity: The ten students in the non-reading Group Two joined me for a picture sort. First I had to confirm that the students knew what the pictures were representing. For example, did they know what a walrus was? While the students cut out, sorted, and glued down the picture cards, I noted who was still making errors and then continued to work individually with those students. After revisiting *w* and *y,* I reassessed, documenting the students who had demonstrated mastery on the *Circle Chart.*

Clipping letters to match pictures and sounds.

Janet's Summary

There are numerous factors named in the NELP (*National Early Literacy Panel*) Report that have been proven to significantly impact future literacy success when introduced and taught explicitly in the early years. There are two factors that lead the parade towards success: Those two are the Alphabetic Principles and Phonological Awareness. *The Canadian Language and Literacy Network Research* names the same two factors as being of primary importance.

I did have my classes at VIU (*Vancouver Island University*) assess and teach Phonological Awareness skills as well; however, I chose to use the Alphabet as the Teachers' Stories section in this chapter. After all, the alphabet **is** the starting point to literacy, linked indelibly to Phonological Awareness as the next step in manipulating sounds along with letters.

The following page, borrowed from the Kelowna *Early Learning Profile*, lists the Phonological Awareness skills that, desirably, would be mastered by the end of grade 2. (Note the bar on the right side, which indicates the proposed year for instruction.)

Phonological Awareness (Grade 2)

Developmental List of Phonological Awareness Tasks

O The student understands that sentences are made up of words.
How many words are there in this sentence?

O The student understands that words are made up of syllables.
How many beats are there in this word?

O The student can identify pairs.
Do these words rhyme: cat/hat? tin/fin

O The student can isolate beginning sounds.
What sound do you hear at the beginning of *duck?*

O The student can isolate ending sounds.
What sound do you hear at the end of *duck?*

O The student can blend sounds together to hear words.
What word do you hear? *(d-u-ck)*

O The student can segment words into all their phonemes.
Tell me the sounds you hear in *duck.*

O The student can delete beginning sounds.
Say *farm.* Say it again but don't say /f/. (arm)

O The student can delete ending sounds.
Say *farm.* Say it again but don't say /m/. (far)

O The student can delete medial sounds.
Say *slam.* Say it again but don't say /l/. (sam)

O The student can isolate medial sounds.
What sound do you hear in the middle of *duck?*

O The student can substitute sounds.
What would *grad* be if you changed the /r/ to /l/? (glad)

	Grade K
	Grade 1
	Grade 2

© Page 18 from the S.D. No. 23 (Central Okanagan) Grade Two Early Learning Profile

Assess, teach and track these skills the same way our Teachers' Stories describe for the alphabet in this chapter.

Key instructions?

- Use fun artifacts,
- Dramatize,
- Encourage movement and song,
- Appeal to different learning styles,
- Practice, use repetition, use patience and practice again,
- Repeat the process numerous 'doses' for vulnerable children, and
- Celebrate! Celebrate! Celebrate!

The alphabet, phonological awareness understandings, and some glue words lead to those most important of understandings:

I CAN READ!

Tell them to "Shout it out!"

Have Fun,

Janet

P.S. The School District 23 Central Okanagan Case Study in Chapter 9 describes a set of exceptional resources belonging to the district, which will provide research, assessment and template support. I highly recommend these resources; they can be purchased through the school district web site as indicated in Chapter 9.

Learning cooperation and planning in the block learning center.

Connections: The Brain and Implications for Classroom Practice

 Janet's Introduction

Why are practice centers the best possible learning delivery mechanism for *all* children, but especially for vulnerable children? You know by now that I strongly believe we have to rely on reliable research as our "pilot ship" when it comes to making decisions about children and their learning. Some of the brain research in *Research and Recommended Books* was new to me although not surprising. The excerpts contained therein are worthy of careful examination as we consider establishing learning (practice centers) as a prime delivery mechanism for our classrooms. As you read through the excerpts you will find evidence that learning centers are a most promising structure for young learners and vulnerable readers in particular.

In summary, practice centers provide rich opportunities for the following:

- Developing neural networks,
- Providing multiple approaches to learning that meet different learning styles,
- Developing the brain's attention system,
- Engaging in conversation that promotes learning,
- Ensuring movement that integrates and anchors learning,
- Focusing on student interests to engage them,
- Offering opportunities to practice, and
- Engaging curiosity about inquiry.

When we absorb and understand the brain research introduced in this chapter, the importance of designing practice centers as our classroom's foundational organization will become apparent. Such centers are a good investment in an ideal classroom structure for students who need rich learning experiences.

Translating Brain Understandings to Vulnerable Children in School

The new science of neural understanding can be translated into exciting and practical classroom strategies and many promising implications for vulnerable children.

What do Vulnerable Children Need in their Classrooms?

Acceptance and Collaboration

Vulnerable children are different. They haven't had the experiences of their luckier fellow students. They need to work side-by-side with more literate peers so they can absorb their knowledge, support, and acceptance. Vulnerable children want to feel the same: equal and accepted! Practice centers provide this opportunity.

Learning centers: we learn from each other.

Practice and Privacy

Vulnerable children will be learning many new skills and concepts and will need more instructional "doses" than others. Practice centers provide endless opportunities in the privacy of differentiated activities where peers won't really notice that they're a bit different.

Time and Patience

Vulnerable children need expert teacher time to introduce skills that others have already learned. While classmates work at their own levels at practice centers, vulnerable children get extra-special instructional time working at comfort in their own learning style in small groups with adults.

Experience and Engagement

Vulnerable children have many experiential gaps with literacy and need to absorb new experiences quickly at a pace much faster than others. In an active learning classroom they will have as many as 20 peers eager to share language, conversations and experiences with them.

Writing center – Pirate Day – practicing "ar" words.

Motivation and Movement

Vulnerable children need to believe they can "do it." Intriguing play centers embedded with skills in a game environment work for all children. A success—and action-oriented environment where children can follow their interests will motivate children to take risks.

Joy

Vulnerable children do not need "skill and drill." They need joyful interventions, plenty of laughter, friendship, and promise—the promise of a joyful and literate future—forever.

Janet

Research and Recommended Books

Teaching Struggling Readers

(Lyons, 2003)

Facilitating Neural Networks for Struggling Children

Recent brain research shows that every child has unlimited potential for learning. This fact calls into question the notion that some children cannot learn. It also suggests that teachers who have a repertoire of ideas and techniques to draw upon will be able to trigger any one of the children's sensory maps. When one technique or approach to teaching a child how to read or write is not working, they can rest assured that another will work (p. 24).

As struggling children begin to actively and consistently initiate independent problem solving, they are able to reorganize their neural networks in more complex and efficient ways. Teachers must alter their instruction as children's competencies grow and develop (p. 25).

Every individual is always in the process of becoming … of developing neural networks. Limiting anyone, especially a beginning reader, with labels like "learning disabled," "language delayed" or "emotionally handicapped" may prevent some children from having an opportunity to reach their full potential because these labels may interfere with teachers' attitude and abilities to reach labeled children (p. 25).

Children do not all learn in the same way. Rather, individuals have unique and specialized ways to develop concepts, think, and reason. Because children have different experiences to organize their brains and each brain is uniquely structured as a result of these experiences, children must utilize many different ways or paths to learn. Therefore, it is preposterous to think that there is only one way to teach, especially something as complex as reading and writing (p. 24).

The Brain and Attention

We know, for example, that attention is much more than simply taking note of sensory information coming in from our environment. Here is what our brain's attention system does:

- Constantly surveys the environment to determine what is and is not important,
- Decides how much and what kind of sensory information is needed to complete a task,
- Allocates varied amounts of mental energy depending on task demands,

- Sustains focus when the task is not interesting,

- Determines if and when the task will be completed,

- Persists in tasks long enough to finish them despite distractions, and

- Disengages from a current task when something more important requires immediate attention, response or action.

All these aspects of attention are critical to learning (p. 26).

The research has also shown that children who have opportunities to make up a story, fantasize, and pretend while playing with an object or toy (e.g., boxes, dolls, or cars) are generally more attentive and stay absorbed in the activity for longer periods of time. Furthermore, their attention nearly doubles if they are engaged in conversation with others while playing. But when given a teacher-directed activity that is too difficult or uninteresting, preschool children disengage and become unmotivated and inattentive (p. 27).

Recent research in neuroscience has demonstrated that movement is critical to every other brain function, including language, memory, emotional thinking and learning... Movement in the environment integrates and anchors new experiences and information and connects the neural networks in children's brains so that they can learn more complex movements. Parents and teachers can facilitate learning while actively engaging children in actions that require movement (p. 41).

Differentiation and the Brain

(Sousa & Tomlinson, 2011)

Student Interest and the Brain

Attending to student interest in a classroom suggests a desire on the teacher's part to capitalize on those things a student cares about in order to facilitate learning. Attaching important content to student interests builds bridges between the student and critical knowledge, understanding, and skills. Therefore, effectively differentiating instruction in response to student interest rests on four key principles:

1. Interest recruits the brain's attention systems and stimulates cognitive involvement.

2. Any group of students at a given time is likely to have both common and varied interests.

3. When teachers know and address their students' interests in the context of curriculum and instruction students are more likely to engage with the content.

4. Attention to student interests should focus students on essential knowledge, understanding and skills, not divert students from them (p. 113).

Why Addressing Student Interests Matters

A sizable body of theory and research indicates that interest-based study is generally linked to enhanced motivation to learn and to increased achievement in the long and short term. For example, various theorists and researchers have proposed that interest-based study:

- Leads to greater student engagement, productivity and achievement,
- Generates in learners a sense that learning is rewarding,
- Contributes to a sense of competence, self-determination and autonomy,
- Encourages acceptance and persistence in the face of challenge,
- Contributes to a culturally relevant classroom for students from non-majority backgrounds by allowing them to construct meaning, beginning with their own experiences, and
- Promotes positive connections between student and teacher.

Experts in this area also note that the use of choice, novelty and prior knowledge in a particular academic context can help students who do not have strong personal interests to engage with important content in that context. For instance, academic engagement and outcomes are enhanced when students are encouraged to pick reading material that is of interest to them (p. 114).

Learning Environment

As we have emphasized, learning is supported by an environment that feels safe, affirming, challenging, and supportive to each student in that environment. Teacher belief in each student's worth and potential is a catalyst for teacher-student connections and ultimately for building a community of learners that functions something like a team—with each member drawing on the strengths of the others and contributing to their development and success. Certainly these important environmental attributes are enhanced when a teacher seeks to understand student interests and to incorporate those interests into curriculum and instruction in substantive ways (p. 118).

"A set of standards is not a curriculum any more than a sack of groceries is a dinner" (p. 119).
– Sousa & Tomlinson (2011)

All good curriculum provides opportunities for students to try out, make sense of or come to "own" the knowledge understanding and skills specified as essential. Learning will most likely be enhanced if, at least some of the time, students can try out what they need to learn in areas of interest to them (p. 119).

Process and Time to Practice

Process provides students with time to practice what they need to master. It can occur both in class and at home. To differentiate process based on student interests, a teacher might do the following:

- Provide opportunities for students to apply skills in relevant areas of interest,

- Provide opportunities for students to establish, test, or expand essential understandings in areas of interest—including areas of high cultural relevance,

- Provide models of student (or expert) work in relevant areas of interest, and

- Structure opportunities for students to share examples of ways in which essential skills and/or understandings are revealed or apply in areas of like or dissimilar interests (p. 125).

Introducing Author Debbie Diller, and Literacy Work Stations: Making Centers Work (2003)

Janet's Comment

I worked with Learning Centers (or *Work Stations* as Debbie prefers to call them), as the major organizer in my schools for at least half the day every day when I was a principal for all grades, k through grade 7. All content areas were integrated, with practice and inquiry activities provided in the centers where students worked independently. The older children worked on a contract system, becoming increasingly involved in project work as they gained more sophisticated skills. Teachers monitored centers and engaged in small group work to introduce new skills. It was one of the most inspiring and creative experiences in my career. All students thrived, including the vulnerable children.

Once we began sponsoring the *Summits on Vulnerable Readers*, I researched North American authors and speakers whose views and belief systems were aligned with the prevailing research. Debbie Diller was one of those and has been one of our most respected speakers at the Summits. Subsequently, I assigned her book *Literacy Work Stations* (2003) to my university class as the compulsory text. I asked my students to conduct a formal book review through which they would reflect on what they learned from Debbie's wisdom.

I shared one of the resulting book reviews written by Teresa Fayant with Debbie and was granted permission to publish it. I wanted my students to consider all issues related to using learning centers (work stations). Debbie's book was the most thorough resource I could find on the topic and once you read Teresa's review, I feel certain you will want to add it to your library. If you have any interest in organizing your classroom through work stations (learning centers), there is no better resource. In my opinion, this book is an exceptional working reference for all primary teachers.

Janet

A Look Inside the Book:

Literacy Work Stations: Making Centers Work

(Debbie Diller, 2003)

Book Reviewer: Teresa Fayant

Instructional Strategies

The students and their practice are the main focus of the instructional strategies that Debbie Diller discusses in *Literacy Work Stations: Making Centers Work*. That is, the focus is to give students opportunities to practice their skills, to work through deeper level thinking, to problem solve, to take responsibility and to share their learning. These aspects give the students a sense of pride, responsibility and ownership which makes the learning more meaningful, motivating them to work harder and to learn more.

The gradual release model she describes on page six, "teacher does, students and teacher do, students do" is something I already practice in my class. For the most part, this method is very effective because it allows the students to see the expectation, the task and the concept; to perform it with guidance and then to take on the responsibility independently. However, the fault in my teaching is that I often do the mini lessons (p. 12) once and assume all students will know what to do. What I've noticed is that the same students seem to have negative behaviors at literacy or math centers unless they are grouped with an adult. What this book has forced me to do is look inward at my own practice and the changes I need to make. These students who act out are often children who need multiple doses of skills and concepts. As an extension, these students obviously need more doses with the centers to know how to use them properly.

Having the students model what the centers should look and sound like (p. 11), is a great way to give them another dose of the expected skills and behaviors; when I do it in a small group I can increase the wait time that students might need in order to problem solve (p. 14) these skills and behaviors. I often have the students solve certain aspects related to social responsibility; I sometimes ask guiding questions; however, in the end I am always impressed with how the students are able to think critically about a situation when given the responsibility. Working through the skills and expectations at each literacy center allows the students the same deeper-level thinking, and in turn, I am able to see how much the students actually know related to the concept.

I have a rule in my class about not saying "I can't..." because I want the students to know they can do anything—they just might need some help. Then, once I help the students, I have them repeat what they said with an "I can..." statement. So, I really like the idea of taking this one step further and having the "I can..." lists (p. 8), at the centers as a constant reminder for the students who may need the visual reminder. Other valuable visual anchoring resources like word-walls, help boards, and student exemplars (pp. 51-65), enable students to see a variety of learning concepts displayed around the room. The visual anchors increase the student's self-advocacy and self-esteem as they problem solve, think critically and creatively apply their knowledge while instilling a sense of pride and ownership in their accomplishments.

Since students often come to me with their centers work and want to show it off, I have recently started a Wow Word Board for them to post their work. I will often encourage them to show their friends: some do, some get shy, smile and put their work on the board or in their cubby. I love the idea of setting aside sharing time (p. 21) so students can take on the role of teacher and share their work with their friends. I do something like this with the helper of the day—I have them read their favorite book to the class. I find that this has the students looking critically at books while increasing their confidence. The students love to play teacher and share what they know, so I believe this work station sharing time keeps the students accountable, while motivating them to produce their best work. The added teacher role solidifies concepts learned without adding to my workload. As such, I am very excited to add this sharing time to the class routine.

Playing with words – sight word concentration.

Lastly, it is important to have choice (p. 4) with regard to the stations themselves, the materials and activities, and the time that the stations remain in class. When students are given the responsibility of choosing what to do, they have a vested interest in the learning. It becomes more meaningful to them and, as such, they are often more motivated to complete the task. Choice also allows for differentiation within each center as students will choose what they can do, which also has the added benefit of decreasing behaviors as learning increases. The trick is to offer choice without students feeling overwhelmed. The other trick is to understand that the teacher is being intentional related to the choices that are given. I always said, "You don't get to choose nothing." We still are in charge of their learning choices through our offerings. Sometimes they don't know what they need.

Resources

In order to keep the students motivated and engaged, it is vital to fill the space with appropriate resources for learning. A few of the aforementioned instructional strategies also serve as resources for learning; for example, "I Can" charts are reminders and anchors for students of what they are able to do.

Books: fiction and non-fiction that peak students' interest, that are read in class, and are age appropriate (pp. 26-49)

- Classroom library, big book station, buddy reading, independent reading, shared reading, retells, alphabet themes, rhyme themes;

Anchors: visual aids that give students a focus, a reminder, and a reference point for their learning (pp. 51-65)

- Word walls: used to teach the alphabet, students' names, sight words, a writing aid;
- I Can charts: reminders for students of what they can do at work stations;
- Help Boards: ideas for writing, different writing forms;
- Sample work: examples of expectations of student work;

Retell Props: items that allow students to re-tell favorite stories may also be used to problem solve, or for dramatic play (pp. 66-74)

- Flannel or felt board: nursery rhyme, storybook characters;
- Puppets: reading buddies or props for problem solving;

Alphabet and Sight Word Resources:

- Magnetic letters, plastic letters, alphabet stickers, themed books, puzzles, games, picture cards, poems (pp. 75-88);

Pocket Charts:

- Alphabet cards that can be used to create words, with vocabulary and picture cards to make sentences, to re-read poems, retell stories (pp. 114-116);

Writing Resources:

- Paper of all sizes, pens, pencils, markers, sight word cards, alphabet cards, different writing samples (lists, charts, etc.), dictionaries, clip boards, dry erase boards and markers (pp. 52-59).

Work Stations

Debbie Diller describes in depth a variety of high-priority work stations for the kindergarten classroom. The stations that I regard as attractive and vital to the classroom are ones that can be used throughout the year, are easy to differentiate, simple to create, and are highly engaging.

A Classroom Library Station:

Materials: Alphabet books, books at an emergent level, copies of books read aloud in class, fiction and nonfiction books, shared readers, wordless books, pointers, highlighter tape (pp. 25-37)

- Students need to be surrounded by books that are familiar and meaningful to them, that tell stories, that teach, that help them make connections to their own experiences. The books should extend their learning and encourage them to practice the reading strategies modeled by the teacher. Props can easily be added for a retell; a puppet or a "stuffy" might be added as a reading buddy. Students can read with a peer, extending their learning in a teacher role. Taped books can be added to this center and read aloud so students can hear expression and fluency.

Classroom library with over 1,000 titles for students' own choice, plus bins with levelled books for home reading enjoyment.

A Big Book Station:

Materials: big books, pointers, bubble wands, letter cards, sticky notes, sight word cards, sticky notes, funky glasses, highlighter tape, etc. (pp. 38-50).

- Big books are a novelty for children because they provide large pictures and print that makes letter and word matching easier for students. They may practice strategies modeled at shared reading, reread the books read aloud in class, track print, or retell stories with props or dramatization.

A Writing Station:

Materials: paper of various sizes, pencils, colored pens, sight word cards, word wall, picture dictionaries, writing strips, dry erase boards and markers, samples of writing, envelopes (pp. 51-65).

- A writing station can easily be put together with an abundance of activities. At the beginning of the year this could be as simple as making lines in shaving cream, copying over letters with fingers and then with dry erase markers; it could be basic name practice and go from there to writing simple sentences or cards or letters.

An ABC Word Study:

Materials: letter tiles, magnetic letters, alphabet books, play dough, tactile cards, picture cards (pp. 84-87).

- This station can begin with matching letters in names, letter hunts, matching upper to lower case letters, picture-to-letter sound sorting, rhyming words or pictures, and move eventually to creating words, matching sight words, rearranging words and pictures into sentences.

Word work – working with sight words.

A Poetry Work Station:

Materials: pocket chart, common poems read in class, poem lines written on strips, word and picture cards, paper, crayons, highlighter tape (pp. 91-103).

- Students read class poems, rearrange them into the correct order, illustrate the poem, buddy read, fill in the blanks, and highlight words they know. This is an excellent station because poems are such an effective teaching tool for young students, and the repetition works well for learning rhyme, sight words, reading fluency and dramatic play when the poem is accompanied with actions.

Extensions and Additions to Stations:

Although there are numerous other work stations described in the book, I believe that with some careful planning many could be combined with stations mentioned previously. For example, themed puppets or felts might be included along with a book read in class to create a dramatic play addition, or to retell components to the big book and/or poetry station. Tapes of read books or poems may be added for students to hear as often as they like for expression and fluency. Multiple students may choose to work at stations reading to one another, sharing their learning or dramatically acting out different aspects. Many common kindergarten centers can have literacy items easily added to their existing resources; for example, labels and signs in the block center; menus, grocery lists, recipes, and get well cards at the house center; and plastic letters and alphabet glitter at the sand and water table. (pp. 104-125).

What to Remember

Students learn best when activities are hands on, engaging, and meaningful. Learned behaviors and concepts increase dramatically when students are involved and invested in the learning process. When creating the work stations there are activities to consider in order to keep the students' attention while they explore and expand their literacy skills: playing games, making something, talking with a partner, telling a story, or doing something new (pp. 1-10).

Learning becomes meaningful when students are given ownership in decision-making. They should help decide what they would like to practice, what materials should be included or changed. Choice in activity allows for differentiation and a variety of learning styles. However, with choice comes the risk of overwhelming the students with too many materials. Behaviors will increase when students have too many choices or are unsure of the expectations. Therefore, each skill or task needs to be modeled by the teacher and linked to the teaching. Gradually transferring responsibility to the students increases their chances of success.

Another way to ensure appropriate behavior is to explain and model any new materials with associated tasks or activities; expectations must be made clear each time activities are added to a station. Time is kept fairly short and activities remain open-ended to so that time is used efficiently. When first introducing stations, five to ten minutes might be enough, but with a little practice and by incorporating the previously mentioned aspects, students should be able to work up to 15 to 20 minutes quite quickly and be fully engaged during that time.

Why Small Group Instruction?

Small group instruction is very important, as it allows teachers to see their students and their abilities more clearly: distractions are limited, students are more accountable for the task at hand, and as such, they are able to remain focused for longer. In addition, smaller numbers may set students at ease when encountering a new activity or concept. Small groups create a comfortable environment, allowing students to take risks and accept new challenges. Also, with smaller numbers students can be grouped according to their skills and abilities. This affords more time for extra doses of practice for those vulnerable learners, as well as flexibility for those who have easily grasped a skill or concept. In the same regard, the teacher may group children based on a specific social skill that certain ones need to practice. The small group component not only permits other students some increased, independent practice time, but also makes these practicing students more accountable to completing the tasks. Finally, fewer students in a group facilitates closer observation with regard to assessment; the teacher will note areas of strength and areas that are requiring greater doses for concept attainment; thus, teacher planning and preparation becomes more effective since her instruction will serve the needs of the individual students more accurately (pp. 5-122, 127-137).

Students are engaged in an alphabet recognition game called Roll a Letter. Students use a 30 sided die and roll to fill in a square on a bar graph. They fill in a square for every letter they roll. When one letter column is filled that letter wins.

Assessment

It is important to note that literacy stations provide students with an opportunity to practice their skills: they are not for assessment. However, there are some insights that can be gained from watching the students during their centers practice time. This small-group practice time lets the teacher observe the students more closely, and often a simple checklist can be used to keep track of the information gained.

While observing students, it is important to notice any problems arising at stations or between students; the situation presents an opportunity for both the teacher and the students. The teacher must look inward at what may have caused the problem, asking a variety of questions. Was the task modeled sufficiently? Did the students become bored? Are there enough materials, too many? Are they organized and easy to use? Is there a help board for students? Is the task or activity meaningful for the students? A problem at a center may be the perfect topic for a mini-lesson the next day. Students then problem solve for a solution with guidance and the ensuing discussion serves to benefit any other students who may have been struggling.

A Synopsis

Debbie Diller's book is an excellent resource for teachers, whether they are just starting out or are experienced veterans. Her book is easy to read and understand as she clearly explains the necessity of literacy stations, and the logistics supporting their usage. All too often, early primary teachers struggle with incorporating the most effective learning into their program. Frequently, teachers add academics at the expense of play, a choice that is detrimental to all early learners, especially those most vulnerable. Debbie does a wonderful job of explaining how play and literacy are intermingled; she offers a variety of strategies to incorporate literacy and meaningful play into the program, using materials that are usually readily available. Her strategies allow the students increased practice time at the students' skill level, solidifying and applying their learning. After reading the book, I have already implemented a few of her strategies such as the I Can charts, help boards, buddy reading, mini lessons and sharing time. I cannot wait to see how my students will grow as strong, confident, willing learners. This book is an excellent read and I strongly recommend it to my colleagues.

Teresa Fayant

Janet's Comment

I recommend two of Debbie's other books as important resources for work with learning centers:

Spaces and Places: Designing classrooms for literacy (Diller, 2008)

Practice with Purpose: Literacy work stations for grades 3-6 (Diller, 2005)

In Debbie's well-informed books you will find everything you need to know about establishing a learning-center system and working with vulnerable readers in small groups.

Janet

Teachers' Stories

The Intentional Teacher and Learning Centers

Janet's Comment

Intentional teachers can tell you exactly why they have set up each learning activity in their classrooms. They know its purpose; they know what they expect students to do while they engage in the center activity; they anticipate outcomes; they understand developmentally what the fit will be between the child's needs and the resources placed there; they can match the offerings to the mandated curriculum. Intentional teachers must be highly organized. Embedded within their playful, busy classrooms is a high degree of structure.

At the same time, intentional teachers understand that young children learn best in a playful environment where they can interact with peers, make choices, experiment, and celebrate their individuality. Remember what the research in this chapter tells us about the developing brain and its needs. There is much to consider when creating the ideal classroom. My university class students had already explored the importance of the Learning Environment as a play setting described in Chapter One. Next, I asked them to explore how the learning environment, as well as the play and skill development, could intersect in a necessary but invisible way.

With this focus in mind, I assigned my students to their roles as intentional teachers and gave them the task of designing three different kinds of centers. I wanted them to achieve a heightened awareness that, even when we are designing play centers, through the resources we place there, we are affecting decisions that children will make about the options available to them. The goals we set, the resources we make available, the instructions we provide, the discussion we generate, the links we make between and among centers, will all affect the experiences our children have: we need to be conscious of this process. I asked them to design and implement the following:

1. A teacher-directed center that is skill-oriented and will achieve a curricular expectation;

2. A child self-directed center for child exploration, inquiry, and discovery; and

3. A center that promotes and accommodates both of the above. While the teacher's goals are achieved, there is room for children to explore as well.

As you create your centers, ask yourself: what are my intentions? Careful planning and implementing of these intentions will result in greater success for your vulnerable children: they need to experience joy in their interventions.

Janet

Examples of Teacher-directed Centers

Literacy Centers

Literacy centers provide students with opportunities to work and learn independently while providing teachers with time for small group instruction. The main purpose of literacy centers is to help encourage students to become confident emergent readers. As teachers, we deal with many levels and ways through which children learn in our classrooms. Different literacy centers allow all students the opportunity to succeed with literacy. My *Vancouver Island University* students designed the following practice centers:

Write Around the Room: Children use clipboards and pencils to write words they see in the room. The teacher may have high frequency words visible; also, theme-related words or pictures could be presented on charts that the students can see at a quick glance. Some may label objects in the room so the students are aware of how the words are formed. **This activity gets the students moving, practicing their letter writing and challenging their hand-eye coordination.**

Magnetic Letters: The students make words using their magnetic letters on their magnetic boards without any help. The teacher is easily able to assess letter recognition, phonemic awareness and work on word families—all in all, a great center for building vocabulary. By manipulating the letters and playing with words, students come up with familiar ones like sight words, names of peers or theme-study words.

Listening Center: Students listen to a book that is being read to them on a CD player. Wearing headphones so as not to disturb others, students follow the words and move through picture-walks with the book. When finished, they write or draw a picture of their favourite part in the book. Many

These students chose to go to the listening center during our daily center time. An assortment of engaging stories are available to choose.

teachers have the students present their ideas to the rest of the class once they are back together as a group. The teacher assesses the students' ability to listen to a story, recall and record what happened on their paper, and present their favourite part to their peers, all the while working with letters and words and improving their oral language skills.

Pocket Chart Poems: Students are given a poem, usually one with a classroom theme. Then they are given the same poem, except this time it is on sentence strips written out in full lines from the poem or in single words, depending on the level of the students. Next, the children recreate the same poem by inserting the strips in the right order in a pocket chart. Once the poem has been completed, the students practice reading it aloud; this same poem usually remains in the pocket chart centre for at least a week. The intention here is to have the children play with word order and pay attention to upper and lowercase letters; oral language becomes a factor when reading it aloud.

Alphabet Center Outdoors: Find Five

Materials: one deck of alphabet cards, outdoor environment, playground equipment

- Each student draws five alphabet cards from the deck at random. Then they race to place their cards next to objects whose initial letter sound name matches their cards. When finished, they draw one new card each until the deck is gone. Following that, we go together on an alphabet walk to check if the sounds match the words of the objects they are found next to.

- By using the alphabet cards in this way, students build their knowledge of initial letter sounds, their vocabulary, and their awareness of objects in their playground environment. All these skills support early written exploration and will transfer to writing tasks when students begin labeling images and composing stories.

Seek and Sort Center:

Materials: four sorting trays, sorting cards (color, texture, size, shape), forest

- Student may have their own sorting trays or they may work cooperatively. To start, they draw a sorting card to direct their collecting and then seek out objects from the forest to sort into their tray according to like characteristics as determined by their cards. For instance, a sorting tray organized by shape might have round objects like fir cones and rocks in one section and triangular objects such as leaves or blades of grass in another section. This builds on skills taught during prior sorting tasks and object explorations through science and math lessons over the school year.

- This activity challenges students to use multiple senses in exploring object characteristics in the natural environment. It also builds sorting skills by requiring them to transfer specific scientific and mathematical knowledge gained from previous activities to their present exploration. Similarly, students will continue to build their knowledge of concepts of color, texture, size and shape; an extension of this sorting challenge could be in using multiple cards in a single tray.

"Our World" Center:

Materials: world maps, travel brochures

- The goal is to provide a means of fostering cultural awareness and respect for one's own culture, as well as the culture of fellow classmates. This center is set up in a corner of the classroom with lots of wall space and flags hung from the ceiling to mark off the area. There is a bulletin board where children or parents could post photos of their travels or the places they are from and a world map with the areas of ancestry and travels. The class might gather here for social studies lessons based on topics raised by children about their culture, neighborhood, city, or country.

- During center time, without direct teacher supervision, the children may cut and paste to create cultural collages, or likes and dislikes from travel magazines and brochures, or create their own flags or crests as outlined by the teacher. This center serves to solidify learning that has taken place over a period of time (after a unit on First Nations culture, children could create a mini book on what they learned).

Alphabet Tray Sorting Center

Materials: Sorting trays, alphabet letters, found objects

- The goal of this center is for students to use letter-sound correspondence (phonemic awareness) to sort objects into a tray. This provides students with the opportunity to experience print in a kinaesthetic way. Alone or with a group, students practice monitoring, revising, and reflecting on their decisions about where they chose to place the objects in the tray. To challenge and encourage them to extend their thinking, one may ask them to organize the objects into their own categories and explain their reasoning.

These students are engaged in a fun letter recognition version of Snap. One student flips over a letter card while the other student says the letter and hammers a Tee into the letter ... FUN!

- This literacy center can be put together using a few trays from the dollar store, along with some objects existing in your kindergarten classroom. In the bottom of each compartment, place a card with the sound or letter you would like your students to practice. After gathering a collection of objects beginning with that letter or sound, place the trays on tables or in a designated area in the room. Choosing objects that connect with their interests, such as sports, dolls or movies will encourage them to participate.

- The main activity here is to have students, either individually or in groups, sort objects in the trays into categories chosen by the teacher. To extend learning, ask students to sort the objects into their own categories and have another student try to guess their sorting rule.

This student is intent on finding out which letter will win!

A Roll-A-Letter Center:

Materials: die with lower and upper case letters on them, paper graph of letters

- The purpose of this activity is to increase letter recognition. It requires sheets of lower and upper case letters displayed as a graph, one letter-die per student and some crayons. Every time the students roll a letter, they colour in one cell of that letter's column and becomes a game of chance to see which letter is rolled the most. This activity can also be used to practice and assess knowledge of letter sounds since each time they roll a letter, they must say that letter sound.

A Zoo Stamping Center:

Materials: stamping letters, ink pads, cards of word families

- One very popular, teacher-directed center I created is Zoo Stamping. We use a program called Zoo phonics in our classroom to introduce the sounds of the alphabet through animals and actions. For example, Allie Alligator snaps her jaws and says "a." Once the children have learned all the sounds and signals, we introduce a merged alphabet where the letter overlays the animal picture. As we practice our word families, the Zoo Stamping center gives the children an opportunity to practice building words without yet requiring the skills to print the alphabet.

- Along with one stamp for each letter and animal, there are ready-made cards of word families (-at, -en, -op) and four or five words for them to stamp on strips of paper with non-toxic stamp pads in three colours. Once the children complete their word family, they read the words to the teacher and then proudly put it in their "back and forth" folder to take home to read. Extension activities include adding to the word families, making up their own words or making cards to decorate.

A Story-Telling Center:

Materials: felt board, favourite stories, video capacity

- Another teacher-directed center I use is Story Telling. As a follow-up activity for a story we have read and dramatized, this center encourages oral language skills as the children retell a story using a felt board, puppets or props. I purchased felt story kits specific to a story, for example, *The Mitten* by Jan Brett and had the children make puppets on popsicle sticks, which we did for *The Gingerbread Boy.* For *Goldilocks and the Three Bears,* I set up stuffed animals and kitchen furniture.

- The children love it when I am their audience. Other times we share with the class, big buddies or video their story-telling on an iPad so they can watch themselves. Of course, the process is more valuable than a polished performance: children love to have an audience!

Examples of Self-directed Centers: Child Exploration, Inquiry and Discovery

A Castle-Themed Dramatic Play Center:

Materials: Local businesses for scraps/donations, old costumes/clothes/jewellery from home/friends, thrift stores, costume/toy stores, dresses, crowns, armour, shields, (foam) swords, wands, heeled shoes, jewellery, castle, sheer fabric, sequined or glitter pieces

- The aim of this center is to demonstrate engagement in drama activities; explore and imagine stories by taking on roles and use speaking and listening when engaging in exploratory and imaginative play. Since this center can be quite extensive, set up a large cardboard castle in the corner with two or three bins of costumes and props. If it's a major theme, other decorations such as fancy-looking drapes or sparkly "chandeliers" could be hanging up around the room.

- As this center is mainly self-directed, it is impossible to predict what will come out of the students' imaginations. Some of the more standard activities I see are "playing castle" with princesses and knights, kings and queens or battle-themed scenarios, always with carefully set guidelines on appropriate play. Other indirect uses could be reading a book in the castle, building additions like a moat to create the scene or painting a picture of the castle scene.

A Construction Center (Straws and Connectors):

Materials: Online (www.Roylco.com, www.strawsandconnectors.com), toy and thrift stores, other teacher or parents' donations: any building mechanisms or even a mixture of different types of building toys will suffice.

- The goal here is to describe properties of materials, to demonstrate techniques for performing manipulative movement skills and to participate cooperatively in groups. I recommend investing in a set of colorful and exciting Straws and Connectors (Roylco®) and placing it in an open bin so that students can see the colors when choosing a center. Add pamphlets with suggestions about what students could build as well as instructions on how to build some things. They may need a little direction or just enjoy the challenge of trying to make using instructions.

- Many students choose to connect the straws to make a tall structure. Some just connect them randomly with no specific idea in mind, or suddenly discover they are actually creating a shape, then use their imagination to turn it into something entirely different. Other students may have a goal to create a structure they have designed in their head or have seen in the instructions.

An Observation Study Center:

Materials: four large magnifying glasses, four collection bags, forest environment

- Students will have their own magnifying glasses to make observations when exploring the forest environment either cooperatively or independently. Collection bags allow students to return to the classroom with items of particular interest to share under our large magnifying glass table. They are free to explore as they feel inclined and may choose to share their observations with their peers. They may also engage with students in other centers, using their special tools. If students are challenged to self-direct their exploration, encouragement rather than direction may be provided. Such challenges will be debriefed as a class.

- Because this activity is intended to provide tools to support the students' natural curiosity about their world, few restrictions or expectations will be placed on them here. This activity not only encourages inquiry and discovery, but also supports seeking and sharing new ways to expand their exploration. It is likely that this activity will look very different for each student as it evolves and as the environment changes with the seasons.

A Photo-journaling Center:

Materials: Two child-friendly digital cameras, outdoor environment

- This activity encourages students to record their learning and engagement in a tangible, lasting way and to record and share their observations with ease. Students will work in pairs to explore the outdoor environment and record the exploration by taking photographs using simple digital cameras. While initial instruction will be necessary on how to use the cameras, students will be free to compose and capture images of their choosing. They may photograph other students and the environment as they find it, or they may choose to make creations and then photograph the products of their work. The key: the camera will be their cooperative journal. They may take turns using it, but they share responsibility for what it produces. Later in the week, they can each choose the photo they are most proud of to share with the class and email to their parents.

- In addition, explaining their chosen pictures will help build oral language skills, connect school learning with home and bring our Outdoor Center explorations into the classroom.

Exploring with Magnets Center:

Materials: an assortment of magnets, magnetic objects, non-magnetic objects, recording sheets

- My goal is to engender students' curiosity in the effects of magnets on different materials. The center is located at our science table where an assortment of magnets and materials such as paper clips, dolls, wooden blocks, hot wheel cars, pencils, scissors, coins, keys, kitchen utensils, art supplies and food items are arranged for students to explore. Recording sheets attached to clipboards and pencils are available to note discoveries of items attracted or not attracted to the magnet.

- The object is for students to immerse themselves in experimentation with different materials, then let them freely roam around the room. If the weather permits, we extend the activity outside to explore magnetic forces on the playground and around the building.

A Sink or Float Center:

Materials: tub, water, assortment of floating and non-floating objects in trays, recording sheets

- For the Sink or Float exploration center, my goal is to help students discover through experimentation what makes one object float and another sink. I set up a clear Rubbermaid water-filled bin on the science table along with an assortment of materials such as plastic recycled containers, cutlery, elastic bands, chalk, felt pen, pencils, scissors, paperclips, bananas, apples, carrots, pomegranate, a hair comb, a small doll and a plastic salamander. Near it I place an "I Wonder If" tray. Science *Sink or Float* observation and recording sheets attached to clipboards are available for

predicting and recording which objects would sink or float by simply circling the letter S for sink or the letter F for float. It should be noted that the recording sheet has a few assorted objects listed but that the majority of the sheet has room for the students to choose what they want to test. Students are encouraged to roam the room looking for interesting objects to test.

A Nature Center:

Materials: a tub, a collection of environmental objects, miniature toys to stimulate thinking

In this picture you can see students playing in the center. One boy recorded his experience in his journal as a story about a miniature dinosaur that was alive right now and lived in our class.

A Group Weaving Center: *Materials*: a loom frame constructed or purchased, ribbons, lace, ribbon, yarn, bark or other creative additions, baskets, knitting needles

- The goal of this center is to invite children to experiment and explore with new tools. The loom and its materials, ribbon, lace, or yarn, encourage children to create representations. Furthermore, this center transforms into a cultural exploration area. Hands-on materials near the loom teach about local Aboriginal peoples; for example, pieces of cedar bark may be woven into the loom, inspiring students to use traditional resources in a new and creative way.

- A loom can be purchased online or created after a quick trip to a hardware store. Place the loom on a table with or without chairs around it although you may find that children prefer standing while weaving. Collect various sizes, colors, lengths and textures of yarn, string, lace, or ribbon and place these in baskets or containers on the table. Strips of bark and other natural materials might also be included. Students may wish to weave the materials using their fingers, but paperclips and knitting needles would provide options for students with different learning styles.

- The main activity at this center would be weaving materials into the loom. Without reducing the child-directed nature of this center, one can provide suggestions or images nearby to demonstrate the many ways a loom can be used. For example, pictures of designs and patterns found in looms around the world may encourage students to create their own complex representations. I have also seen an artist weave with thin strips of paper covered with messages, greetings or names of people.

A Drama Dice Center:

Materials: large foam die with labels pasted on them

- The intention for this center is to encourage students to extend their thinking through dramatic play by combining unusual props. By rolling dice with different characters, settings or emotions pasted on their surfaces, children may be inspired to see things from different perspectives. Although the teacher has created the dice, it is the students who are making the choice to roll, select and combine the characters and props they will use during play.

- This Drama Dice Center complements and builds upon the dramatic play area found within kindergarten classrooms. Over-sized, large foam dice will work perfectly for this activity. It is the teacher's choice of how many dice to include, as well as what themed images are pasted on the surface of the dice. Ideas may include characters, settings, emotions, occupations or animals. For example, one student may roll a witch who is happy and works as a fireman. Images may be found online and then attached to the dice using masking tape. Introduce the activity to your class, or simply place the dice near your dramatic play area and watch what unfolds. Another idea is to have the dice include characters from stories that you have been reading. Furthermore, to interest the children in using the dice, have them brainstorm ideas about what props and characters *they* would like to see included.

- It is not uncommon to observe children acting as a doctor, pet or mother figure during dramatic play. I feel that including themed dice alongside a costume trunk encourages them to extend their thinking and develop more complex characters during play. Students may also be encouraged to combine props in unusual ways and make connections to the stories they have heard in class.

Examples of Centers that can be both Child Self-directed and Teacher-directed

These will be centers that offer several choices: to choose something the teacher proposes, or try something they would prefer to do, or a combination of the two.

Outdoor Centers:

Materials: nature books, animal habitat books, an outdoor natural forest

- My approach to this assignment arose from two key considerations. First, we share a classroom with limited space for displaying new and exciting centers, and we are similarly challenged with the storage of resources and materials. When considering the design of six new centers, I realized that it was important to develop easily implemented ideas.

- Second, I was particularly inspired by our discussion of ways to bring the outdoors into the classroom. My background is in environmental education and yet I felt my exploration of our natural environment was inadequate this year. Typically, our outdoor investigations were limited to structured whole class tasks driven by specific curricular expectations.

Outdoor Center One: Home Building:

Materials: books of animal homes, pictures of structures in the natural environment

- Students work cooperatively or independently to design and build homes using natural materials found in the outdoors. However, the expectation is that they continue to explore new ways of building and new types of structures. Books of animal homes and photographs of structures are provided for their reference. For instance, since we have been exploring animal homes in our current classroom curriculum, we might soon create a challenge that is focused on different animal homes such as nests, burrows and caves.

- This activity encourages students to use available materials to explore the creatures in our local environment and to help them understand how animals and humans actually create their homes. It also enables students to extend their thinking about homes and structures: a popular recess activity is always "fort building!" Cooperation and planning, of course, become a natural component of such group activity.

Outdoor Center Two: Hiders and Hunters:

Materials: Eight colored beanbags in zip lock bags, two blindfolds, playground, forest

- Two of four students are "hiders" who are responsible for hiding the eight beanbags. The other two students wear blindfolds to cover their eyes during the hiding. While they are discouraged from peeking, they are encouraged to listen for clues about where to look. Once hidden, the hunters are responsible for hunting for the hidden treasure (the beanbags). When all of the treasure is found, the two pairs switch roles. If the hunters find the search too challenging, the hider can give clues such as to look up, look left, look right, look down. This kind of support can be teacher guided as well.

- This activity builds observation skills through a simple task: the brightly colored beanbags develop the students' ability to recognize colors and structures that best conceal the treasure. When blindfolded, students also develop their listening skills and awareness of their environment. Since the job of the hiders does not simply end with the hiding, the game builds memory skills. The responsibility of hiding, hunting and guiding allows students to explore and discover these skills through their own creative inclination.

A Sensory Table Center:

Materials: a large tub or old plastic pool, multiple objects depending on the teacher's intention (see description of possibilities).

- As a water table: the goal is for children to explore the properties of water and observe how different objects and materials react to water (sink or float, absorb, flow). As the objects are changed throughout the year, the focus of the learning changes. One week there might be cups and funnels for estimating, measuring and pouring. Another week there might be sea creatures for imaginative play. The water table would be used for color mixing, bubbles, ice rainbows (colored water on crushed ice) or creative exploration with toy sea creatures and seaweed.

- As a sand or rice table: Measuring, estimating and pouring are the goals at this center, as well as investigating the properties of rice or sand compared to water. Children may treasure hunt by digging or using magnets. The center is also used for creative exploration using toy turtles and frogs and river rock. It becomes a great place for finger painting when water and sand are removed.

A Blocks Building Center:

Materials: multiple types of blocks and mixture of building materials

- The block center allows the children to explore mathematical relationships through play. Spatial awareness, proportions, patterns, geometric shapes, counting and sorting are all examples of what may engage children as they explore and experiment. Social skills are also practiced as children work together and share materials to build structures. This learning can take place through independent play and construction and can be extended through teacher-directed lessons. Using paper and writing utensils, the children design and plan their ideas or make a drawing of what they created in order to share it with others later. The block centre is available daily for self-directed inquiry and occasionally used to reinforce mathematics and literacy through teacher-directed activities.

- I allocate a large area for the block centre so the children can design and build grand structures or cityscapes. A

Recreating buildings—pictures of architecture buildings were posted around the classroom.

good chunk of time is required here in order to complete designs. Providing many sizes and types of blocks allows the children to experiment with combining different sizes, shapes and textures of materials.

Dress Up and Dramatic Play Center:

Materials: Superhero books, cape materials as described, fabric craft materials, garbage bags, masks, others as listed: Superhero ABC storybook written and illustrated by Bob McLeod, white garbage bags to cut open and use as capes, masks bought from dollar store, ribbon, foam letters, glue, scissors, permanent markers, staplers, single-hole punch; permanent dress up capes in the classroom are made out of thrift shop women's skirts or acquired second hand. Scarves and blankets also make wonderful superhero capes.

- The goal is to facilitate the connection between literacy skills, letter recognition, oral language and creative skills. Listening to, reading, rereading and then using the book "Superhero ABC" is one springboard for dramatic play ideas. As well, if they choose to create their own super hero cape, artistic thinking and fine motor skills such as cutting, printing and gluing are addressed. I am particularly conscious of making this center appealing to boys.

rubberboots and elf shoes

SUPER HERO CAPES
rubberboots and elf shoes

- I set it up using tables close to the carpet area. The students have already been introduced to the book, heard the story and had opportunities to read the book on their own. Several copies of the book are at the table along with the craft supplies needed to create masks and capes. Once this is completed, the children move to the carpeted area to engage in dramatic superhero play in their capes and masks.

A Bag Painting Center:

Materials: large sandwich bags, gooey substances as described, Q-tips, paintbrushes

- The goal of this center is to encourage students to experiment and explore using traditional materials in a new way. From a child's perspective, the fun is in discovering how to create art with different substances. The teacher may have students write letters of the alphabet in the paint or have students combine different colors as a science experiment.

- Fill large sandwich bags with a thick substance and tape three sides of the bag to a tabletop or counter including the open side. Children draw on the bag forcing the material in the bag to move, thus creating images. Change the type of substance in the bags to keep your students engaged; use paint, cornstarch and water, or naturally occurring materials. The bright colors and hands-on nature of this centre motivate students to explore. Add different tools for students to use other than their fingers. Objects that may work well include Q-tips, paintbrushes, toothpicks, or straws.

- Students enjoy drawing pictures by themselves, taking turns guessing the images that their peers have drawn, or mixing and discovering different color combinations. Alternatively, a teacher can direct students to focus on a single purpose such as writing the letters of the alphabet, demonstrating their knowledge of numerals, or drawing a variety of shapes and lines. Whether the center is teacher- or child-directed, the main goal is still being achieved: to encourage students to experiment and explore using familiar materials in a new way.

This little girl began writing the alphabet on her own because she had lost interest in moving the paint around.

Only a small amount of paint is needed.

Styrofoam Hammer Center:

Materials: Styrofoam, golf tees, small hammers

- The goal of this center is for students to be creative using unusual props as well as to have an opportunity to play with words in a kinaesthetic mode. Literacy and numeracy concepts are learned through the use of real tools such as hammers and golf tees and students may see this as an optional time to explore and create art with such simple objects.

- Warehouses and other "big box stores" will donate the Styrofoam needed for this centre. Letters, numbers, and pictures can be drawn on the heads of colored golf tees that are then hammered into the Styrofoam to make words or stories or art. Students might also pair up and call out the numbers or letters that their partner should hammer.

The Painting Center:

Materials: easels, paint, brushes, pencils

- My goal is for the children to be stimulated to stretch their thinking. Obtain a two-sided easel covered with newsprint and trays to hold brushes, pencils, felts and containers for five colours of poster paint. Give the children artists' smocks to wear while creating and listening to classical music. The only direct guidelines here are that upon completion, their masterpieces should be bright, beautiful and titled.

- Skills that come into play include story telling, color blending, types of lines and pictures that we have done as a class in directed drawing booklets. Often I see influences from illustrators in the picture books we have previously read together. I like to put out picture books with the final pictures sealed off with elastics. If they have no ideas of their own, they may predict the ending and paint it, then share it with the class. Completed paintings are hung in the classroom to dry and be showcased before they are sent home.

 ## Janet's Summary

Janet's Ten Lessons Learned

Lesson 1: Start small if you are just beginning: one center at a time, one activity in each center, simple instructions for the children, orderly routines, one step-at-a-time. Success breeds success. Take the next step when you are ready.

Lesson 2: Assess, teach and track. If you don't make the literacy skills your prime target, it will be like "shooting in the dark;" you will miss the most vulnerable children.

Lesson 3: Make skills invisible in a play-dominated environment. Some teachers prefer to separate the play centers into another part of the day. I don't. I like to mix the centers so children get breaks naturally in their work; however, it's entirely up to you.

Lesson 4: Be intentionally balanced. Carefully plan your centers, always seeking a balance between skill and play orientation, indoor and outdoor activities, and big and small muscle workouts.

Lesson 5: Make research your driving force. Monitor new publications, especially those reporting the latest brain research and adapt your classroom practice to it. I have found that when I have an articulate summary and can quote sources (like *The NELP Report*), teachers will accept new concepts and possibilities. Too many professionals reference "research" but cannot quote sources or sources are not comprehensive.

Lesson 6: Schedule literacy all day in the earliest years. Integrate other curricular subjects into literacy experiences. Nothing else matters until they can all read and write.

Lesson 7: Keep your administrator informed. Insist on services to vulnerable children. Provide documentation, data and evidence concerning needy children and about how you are coping. Advocate.

Lesson 8: Engage some families in safe small ways even if it is hard work. They love their children but don't know what to do. They can make a big difference if you show them the way.

Lesson 9: Partner with colleagues. Plan together, laugh and cry together, share resources and centers—platoon. This is a big and important job. You'll be better together! Remember to have fun too.

Lesson 10: Never give up on vulnerable children. Some of them didn't have a chance until they met you. Now they are getting lucky! Remember they just need more "doses" than most.

Janet

Learning to match sounds with letters and names.

Practicing our letters by stamping them in Play-Doh.

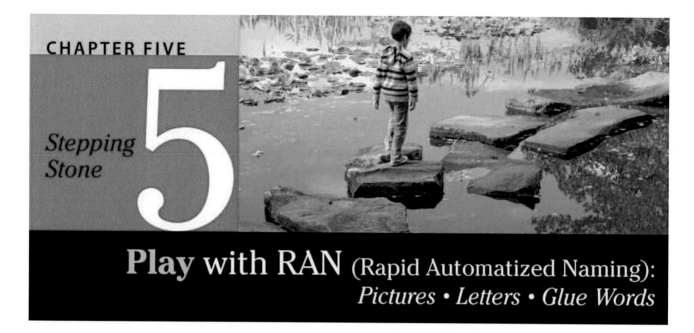

The Importance of Automaticity in Reading: A Sight Word Renaissance

 Janet's Introduction

The truth! I will still be in my sixties when this book is published. When **you, too,** have spent 40 years in the education system you will have seen many trends, ideas, programs and innovations come and go—many of them a waste of time and money! At the same time, too frequently I have seen valuable aspects of literacy programs vanish. The teaching of sight words was one of those casualties for a couple of decades when "whole language" dominated classrooms in the 80s. Now the research is clear that sight words (also known as high frequency words and sometimes referenced as immediate word recognition skills) are an essential foundation for fluency and comprehension. I call them the "glue words" because they glue our organic words and thoughts together. It just seems so simple to me. The most recent meta-analysis (The NELP Report, 2008) presents a scientific proposal as to why this might be true: It is brain and cognition related.

Janet

The NELP (*National Early Literacy Panel*) Report, 2008

The NELP report identified *Rapid Automatized Naming* (RAN), as being one of the strongest predictors of future literacy success in later grade levels. Rapid Automatized Naming (RAN) measures how quickly individuals can name aloud objects, pictures, colors, or symbols. Variations of RAN time provide a strong predictor of their later ability to read and are independent from other predictors such as phonological awareness, verbal IQ, and existing reading skills. Importantly, RAN of pictures, letters and symbols and words can predict later reading abilities even for pre-literate children.

One of the prevailing theories about the link with reading ability is that RAN and reading ability both depend on general cognitive speed of information processing and the brain's ability to do so. This implies that paying attention to RAN in the early years is an important contribution to cognitive processing. The opinion of numerous experts, authors and researchers in the literacy field implies that developing speed in the identification of sight words could have a major impact on a child's fluency with reading and that the relationship of RAN and reading will be stronger if sight word reading speed is measured by discrete presentation. Using the discrete testing method, participants are shown symbols individually. In discrete RAN testing naming speed is measured. This consists of the mean time from presentation to articulation.

The importance of teaching sight words to all children has been a dominant and consistent research-based message for four decades even though we, as educators, have considered the topic to be debatable. Now the research has become profound with the advent of brain research.

 Beginning with one of the first definitive pieces of research on the frequency of certain words in the English language (LaBerge & Samuels, 1974) to the NELP (*National Early Literacy Panel*, 2008) we learned that ensuring children have a solid base of sight words at an early age accelerates their reading progress. Controversial professional debate has centred on the instructional practices we use to ensure sight word mastery—specifically how we use "flash cards." If used in a "drill and skill approach" I agree we may put undue pressure on children which could result in a negative self-image. If we use flash cards in a motivational game-saturated environment, however, presenting children with words commensurate with their reading level, there will be no problem—and that's our job as professionals, to determine the appropriate timing and strategies for each child.

We know that most children who have had a rich literacy upbringing will absorb sight words readily and often in one "dose;" however, we know that vulnerable children may need many exposures with playful practice experiences to achieve the same results.

It's a No-brainer!

I was intrigued by this part of the NELP report. I have had so many passionate and argumentative debates with "whole-language" converts over the years who refused to acknowledge that there is a place for memory work in the early learning years—especially when it comes to sight words. Why would we even contemplate not teaching sight words to five-year-olds? We want them to read. Sight words comprise up to 75% of reading material in books and on the Internet. As "kids" would say: It's a no-brainer! The response is usually about how memory-work may be too arduous and negate the joy of reading. The solution is GAMES!

Consider this adult educator's viewpoint:

Timothy Rasinski, in an editorial comment *Word Identification Involves More than Teaching Phonics* in *Reading and Learning to Read* (Vacca & Vacca, 2012) makes an important point about links between adult and child game behaviors:

"I have found that word identification instruction seems to be most engaging, authentic, and effective when it feels like a game for students and teachers. Think of all the games that we play as adults that involve words in one form or another – Scrabble, Boggle, Scrabble Slam, Crossword Puzzles, Up Words, Wheel of Fortune, Buzz Words, Taboo, and so on. If adults love games that involve words, why wouldn't students? Indeed that is what we have found. Making words, word ladders, word sorts, word bingo, developing word walls, and the like, all have the feel of a game that makes the students want to engage in their study and play with words" (p. 226). – Timothy Rasinski, 2012

From an academic perspective, consider this expert viewpoint. McGill-Franzen emphasizes the importance of the connection between automaticity, sight words and fluency, which, of course, inevitably results in enhanced comprehension. She distinguished between the terms *sight words* and *high frequency words*—terms often used interchangeably in *Kindergarten Literacy* (McGill-Franzen, 2012).

"Even the most wonderful, verging-on-nonsense children's narratives have a coherence of ideas, of course, and these gems of meaning can't be comprehended unless a child can read each word – and read them fast, fast, fast. Why? The more words that a child immediately recognizes, the easier it is for him to swiftly find his way across the line of print in order to construct meaning. Immediate word recognition is called *automaticity*. Automatic word recognition is fast and effortless: It is a necessary condition for fluency, although fluency is more than automaticity.

Words that are recognized automatically without analysis are called *sight words*. Words that appear frequently in our reading materials are called *high-frequency* words. Typically high-frequency words are learned as sight words simply because students see them more often" (p. 115).

From a child's perspective, consider this viewpoint as witnessed through my eyes:

I have a compelling memory of an obese, silent, young boy who had been diagnosed by a regional children's hospital as cognitively impaired. He lived on a remote island where I had been consulting with the teaching staff. His teacher loved and nurtured him, including him in all activities. He was two years older than the other kindergarten children but didn't yet speak. When we began our sight word practice-center routine he was, of course, part of the group—no segregation here. Because he was generally passive and unresponsive to prompts, any indication of cognitive response was a cause for celebration.

Several months later I was visiting and monitoring progress in his classroom and I noticed him in his usual quiet space where he felt safe and comfortable. As I was leaving the classroom, I heard a strange but riveting noise from his direction. I turned. He was making eye contact with me—highly unusual. He moved his head indicating he wanted me to come closer—also highly unusual. As I approached, he looked down at the three flash cards he had ordered on his desk, concentrating on them intensely. He read *I am happy* in a stuttering but forceful and guttural way. What happened next was the best part. His usually sombre, big round face burst into an expression of exuberant happiness and pride; his smile blazed with delight; his eyes shone.

"I can read," he said. My heart filled to its brim—I had never heard him speak. Now he was reading. Sight words, organic words and the cycle of success in action! Now you know who inspired the cover picture on this book.

Response to Research

Since I started this journey, determined to find the path to literacy success for vulnerable children, I have become increasingly aware of the need for educators to respond to compelling research. I have become intolerant, therefore, of some teachers' resistance to assessing, teaching, and tracking sight word mastery.

In the face of scientific evidence, as well as "on the ground" success there are no excuses left. Consider the following: our pilot sites (Chapter 9) have been working with hundreds of vulnerable primary children on developing sight word capacity. We taught these children the first 10 sight words and began to create stories from their own memories and experiences: We added sight words in clusters of ten as they achieved mastery and their stories became more sophisticated.

Consider this example of the power of sight words:

One child's organic words (from his/her own experience) were: *monster, closet, screamed, babysitter.*

The complete story was subsequently dictated by the child and scribed by the teacher:

> *There was a monster in my closet. I screamed. My babysitter chased it away.*

We counted the sight words (underlined): **Nine**

We counted the organic words: **Four**

Without the sight words there would have been no story! With a combination of sight words and the child's organic words, we have a reader and a writer.

The Significance of Sight Word Teaching, Learning and Practice

Sight word instruction is as important to fluency and comprehension in reading, as water is to ducks. For vulnerable children, the link is more important since knowledge of even a few words can result in a kindergarten child being able to pump a fist in the air and celebrate "I can read!" while fellow students pump their fists too in celebration of achievement. (Make this a powerful peer ritual in your classroom.)

Over 90% of kindergartners are developmentally capable of learning two words (*I* and *can)* by memory, remembering *jump, play, sit,* and *hop* with clues from their drawings; then creating their own books: "I can _____(jump, play, sit, hop)!" These are their first experiences with reading and writing, which they can share with very proud moms and dads. This is a FIRST moment in the never-ending cycle of success that they will never forget. They have joined the world of literacy.

Janet

Research and Recommended Books

Wikipedia: Dolch List Reference

What is the Dolch list?

Wikipedia (2014) is the source of the following definition and lists of sight words by grade level. While there are other high-frequency words lists available, my preference has always been the Dolch list. Once we begin sight word acquisition, assessments and tracking it seems sensible to stay with the same list on a classroom, school or district-wide basis. You will note in the following lists that there are grade designations assigned to words based on the degree of difficulty. While I recommend working through the words in this order, I feel strongly that we should encourage students to learn as many words as possible as quickly as possible, since a child's ability to read with increasing degrees of difficulty and fluency is directly connected to sight word mastery (as well as the other factors such as decoding ability).

I recommend a focus only on the 220 "service" words and ignore the noun list. Instead, as described in the introduction, I recommend using each child's organic *Key Words* for nouns, a more motivating and meaningful experience. *Key Words* are words that children generate from their own personal interests and experiences such as family names, pet names, place names, events or movies.

The Dolch word list is a list of frequently used English words compiled by Edward William Dolch, a major proponent of the "whole-word" method of beginning reading instruction. The list was prepared in 1936 and was originally published in his book *Problems in Reading* in 1948.

Dolch compiled the list based on children's books of his era. The list contains 220 "service words" that have to be easily recognized in order to achieve reading fluency in the English language. Even today, between 50% and 75% of all words used on the Internet, in schoolbooks, library books, newspapers and magazines are included in the Dolch basic sight word vocabulary.

Although some of the 220 Dolch words are phonetic, we encourage children to learn these words by sight to enhance fluency; hence the alternative term, "sight word." The list is divided according to the grades in which it was intended that children would memorize these words.

Dolch list: Non-nouns

Pre-primer: a, and, away, big, blue, can, come, down, find, for, funny, go, help, here, I, in, is, it, jump, little, look, make, me, my, not, one, play, red, run, said, see, the, three, to, two, up, we, where, yellow, you.

Primer: all, am, are, at, ate, be, black, brown, but, came, did, do, eat, four, get, good, have, he, into, like, must, new, no, now, on, our, out, please, pretty, ran, ride, saw, say, she, so, soon, that, there, they, this, too, under, want, was, well, went, what, white, who, will, with, yes.

1st Grade: after, again, an, any, as, ask, by, could, every, fly, from, give, giving, had, has, her, him, his, how, just, know, let, live, may, of, old, once, open, over, put, round, some, stop, take, thank, them, then, think, walk, were, when.

2nd Grade: always, around, because, been, before, best, both, buy, call, cold, does, don't, fast, first, five, found, gave, goes, green, its, made, many, off, or, pull, read, right, sing, sit, sleep, tell, their, these, those, upon, us, use, very, wash, which, why, wish, work, would, write, your.

3rd Grade: about, better, bring, carry, clean, cut, done, draw, drink, eight, fall, far, full, got, grow, hold, hot, hurt, if, keep, kind, laugh, light, long, much, myself, never, only, own, pick, seven, shall, show, six, small, start, ten, today, together, try, warm.

Toward a Theory of Automatic Information Processing in Reading

Decades ago, LaBerge and Samuels (1974) alerted us to the significance of high frequency words. Their research revealed that 90% of all the words that people read are made up of only 5,000 words.

Beginning to Read:
Thinking and Learning About Print

Adams (1990) makes the first step obvious! He reports that the following 13 words are 25% of the words children find in early literacy experiences. These words should be first on the list to learn: *a, and, for, see, she, in, it, is, of, that, the, to, was* and *you.*

Early Intervention for Reading Difficulties: The Interactive Strategies Approach

Scanlon et al. (2010) challenge us to stretch our expectations of children instead of relying on dated and limiting curriculum guidelines: "Because knowledge of high-frequency words provides children with so much access to reading materials and allows them to be strategic in learning new words, setting higher expectations for sight word knowledge is probably in the children's best interests" (p. 228).

Reading and Learning to Read

(Vacca & Vacca, 2012 – 8ᵗʰ ed.)

Vacca and Vacca provide us with a technical definition for rapid word recognition and emphasize that learning by "sight" is only one of the important ways that children recognize words and caution us about limiting sight word instruction to flash cards. Children typically use many different cues in word solving:

Popcorn word wands: students search for matching words in books or around the classroom.

"Word recognition suggests a process that involves immediate identification. Immediately recognized words are retrieved rapidly from *lexical* memory. Word recognition is sometimes referred to as *sight word recognition* or *sight vocabulary*. These terms suggest a reader's ability to recognize words rapidly and automatically. In this chapter we use *immediate word recognition* to describe rapid recognition. Keep in mind, however, that the process of immediate word recognition is far more complicated than merely recognizing words on flash cards. When a word is retrieved rapidly from memory, the process is often triggered by the application of letter-sound knowledge. Learning to read words rapidly involves making associations between particular spellings, pronunciations, and meaning by applying knowledge of letter/sound relationships. Skilled readers use the strategy of immediate word recognition on 99% of the printed words that they encounter… Immediate identification of words is the result of experience with reading, seeing, discussion, using, and writing words" (p. 224).

The implication is clear. Teaching phonics, phonological awareness, sight words, print awareness, word study and other literacy skills is best accomplished when taught simultaneously in an integrated, contextual way.

Literacy Development in the Early Years: Helping Children Read and Write

(Morrow, 2012)

Morrow proposes a systematic process for teaching sight words while emphasizing the importance of context and supplementing the teaching with centre activities, games and playful activities:

- Words are said aloud and used in a sentence.

- A sentence is written on a chalkboard or flip chart and the sight word is underlined.

- Features of each word, such as the letters or its similarity to other words, are discussed. The teacher points out regular or irregular patterns the word may have.

- Children are asked to spell the word aloud, spell the word in the air with their finger, and write the word on paper.

- Children chant the letter as they spell words.

- The teacher has a high frequency word box. While sitting in a circle, each child has a turn to pick a word, say it, use it in a sentence, and show it to the group.

- The words can be written on index cards, similar to their very own words and stored with the child's other cards.

To ensure that children are acquiring sight recognition of high-frequency words, they should be tested on their ability to read them. The teacher should ask them to identify the words with flash cards and find them in context within passages to read (p. 150).

He is very proud that he is learning to make sentences..

When Readers Struggle: Teaching that Works

(Fountas & Pinnell, 2009)

Fountas and Pinnell link the significance of learning sight words to the needs of vulnerable readers. This confirms our field research: Vulnerable readers can learn sight words just like all other children. They simply need more exposure and multiple "doses."

"Proficient readers have learned many words: but more important they have developed powerful systems for learning words. They are able to problem solve "on the run," while reading for meaning. Struggling readers generally have a lower repertoire of words that they can recognize effortlessly and their word solving is inefficient, slow, and tedious. Sometimes they passively move through text not even attempting to solve words that are hard for them. With a low repertoire of words, the reader has difficulty monitoring and correcting reading. Fluency and comprehension are affected… In this Chapter, we explore ways of helping students build a core of words they recognize automatically, including many high-frequency words, as well as how to help them develop systems for learning words" (p. 261).

Students use white boards to write letters, sight words or begin to construct sentences.

They emphasize the importance of using writing to help children know high-frequency words in detail, and that it is "important to write high-frequency words quickly and automatically, using appropriate directional movements." They suggest frequent and playful practice exercises on large paper, whiteboards and creative writing materials with playful instructions such as:

- Write it here.
- Write it again.
- Write it quickly.
- Write it big.
- Write it smaller.
- Write it faster.

"Knowing a large number of words that can be written without effort contributes to fluency in writing, leaving one free to pay attention to the content and solve new words" (p. 316).

Teachers' Stories

Engaging Sight Word Games:
Teacher-Designed and Teacher-Tested

Janet's Comment

Our VIU (*Vancouver Island University*) classes reviewed extensive research on the importance of sight words in literacy development. We discussed at length the importance of a play-based approach to learning sight words as opposed to a skill-and-drill approach using flash cards. At the same time we recognized that there is a role for RAN (Rapid Automatized Naming) as identified in the NELP report. As an assignment, students were asked to research ideas electronically and create games that would engage their children in playful ways, then document the children's response to the game. One of the criteria for the assignment was that resources would be readily accessible and inexpensive. Teachers brought their games to class for demonstrations with colleagues—an enjoyable and informative session! They were also asked to try other teachers' games and propose variations or extensions that worked in their classrooms. A word of advice: The Internet is LOADED with great **sight word games.** Just use these three search words and you will have multiple choices!

Janet

Game 1: Green Eggs and Ham

(Michelle Fitterer)

Materials:

- Words: it, in, at, an, he (your choice),
- Green and pink foam/poster board (x2) for eggs and ham,
- Paper plates (2 packs of 10),
- Rubber spatulas (x4),
- Glue & scissors,
- Sticky notes or paper and tape (to place words on back of eggs and ham).

*All of these can be gathered at the dollar store.

Green Eggs & Ham: flip the eggs or ham to discover a sight word and give word that rhymes with it.

Rules:

1. Spread the eggs and ham over a table or carpeted area with the sight words facing down; each student will have their own paper breakfast plate and spatula.
2. Students take turns flipping over **one** egg or piece of ham to reveal a sight word.
3. In order to add this piece of food to their 'breakfast' plate they need to be able to read the sight word.
4. If a student flips over a piece of food with a plus-1 on it they are given a bonus flip; similarly, if a student flips over a piece of food with a minus-1 on it they have to put one of their food items back into the pile.
5. The game ends when there are no eggs or ham left in the pile; then the students can count how many eggs and ham they will have for breakfast.

Extensions:

Word difficulty can easily be increased when mastery is achieved. After a student flips over a food item and reads the sight word, he can be challenged to name a word that rhymes with that sight word.

Teacher Reflections:

The smiles on the four students' faces while they were playing the game told me that they were having fun. If a student could not recognize or sound out the sight word then another student would step in to help them out (providing the beginning sounds). Their imaginations lit up when I showed them the cover of Green Eggs and Ham, by Dr. Seuss, and I told them that we were having it for breakfast today.

Students counted and compared how many eggs and pieces of ham they had compared to that of their peers, and created patterns with their eggs and ham. They told me they loved the game and did not want to stop playing!

Students liked calling out the sight words even when it was not their turn, and this took away the much-needed practice for the struggling readers in the group. Sometimes it looked as though they were confused about whose turn it was, and had difficulty being patient as they waited for their turn. There was some confusion with what they had to do with the plus-1 and minus-1 cards. **One of the things I learned was that I had to teach how to play any game rule such as cooperation, taking turns, and celebrating each other's success.**

The main learning for me was just how easy it is to incorporate sight words into a fun and interactive game. Describing the game in a way that connected to their prior knowledge—showing the cover of Dr. Seuss' book and igniting their imaginations about having breakfast—was an important first step to hook their interest. As a result, the students were eager to keep playing the game when it had finished. With the few sight words that I included in this game, I was able to gain a quick understanding of who did/didn't know these words; furthermore, whether they could produce a word that rhymed with the sight word.

It was also interesting to see the responses of children who did not know the sight word—wiggling in their chair, calling out a different word that began with the same letter, or not trying to sound it out. By the end of the game, I noticed that the students who mispronounced some of the sight words at the beginning (*and* instead of *an*) were now identifying them correctly. What a wonderful feeling to see this progress so quickly!

Game 2: Hop On Pop-Scotch

(Margie Radigan)

The game was based on the Dr. Seuss book, *Hop on Pop*, which focuses on the -op word family. Words used in the game included *-op*: top, hop, pop, crop, prop, cop, plop, flop, shop, chop, stop, mop, sop, slop, drop, plop.

Materials:

- Copy of *Hop on Pop* by Dr. Seuss,
- Sidewalk Chalk,
- Sidewalk or concrete area,
- Paper,
- Pencil, and
- Bean bag or a small stick/stone as a marker.

Rules:

1. After you read *Hop on Pop* with your students, brainstorm a list of all the "-op" words you can think of (it is okay to refer to the book if need be). Review the words with your students, sounding out each one as you go through your list.

2. Use chalk to draw a traditional 10-square hopscotch board on the cement. The squares should alternate: one square and then two

Students enjoy this game based on the Dr. Seuss book, Hop on Pop, and variations of the game using more traditional hopscotch games added to their learning and fun!

squares side-by-side, and then one square as in a traditional hopscotch game). You and your students can make multiple hopscotch games to be used simultaneously.

3. In each square, have a student print one or two of the "-op" words from the list using the chalk.

4. Now it is time to hop! Play this hopscotch just like the traditional game only with one important difference—when a student tosses her marker onto a square and begins to hop through, before she skips over the square with the marker, she must make up a sentence using the word (or words) in the square. For example, if her marker lands on a square that says, "drop," her sentence could be something like, "I hope I don't drop these cookies on Pop!" Encourage the children to be creative with their sentences!

5. On her way back through the hopscotch board, to finish her turn, she must make up a new sentence using the same word or words.

6. If a student hesitates or loses her balance while trying to complete her turn she can have another chance after the next student has a turn.

7. This is a great chance to model sentence structures so it is a great opportunity to play along with the students.

"In gym class that day we put these words out on mats for hopscotch. They were playing, yet practicing their words. They loved it. They didn't always say the words but I didn't want to pressure them. It was nice to have the word "I" as part of the group of words as all of them knew it." – Alison Kimmerly

---

Extension:
Introduce new word families or other sight words into the hopscotch template. There are endless possibilities for play-based literacy learning!

Teacher Reflections:
This was a great activity to add to my Dr. Seuss collection as March 2nd marked what would have been Dr. Seuss' 109th birthday and the activity dovetailed nicely into my weeklong Dr. Seuss celebration. To introduce the activity I read the story to my class after lunch and then we did an -op word brainstorming activity where we listed all the op words. We came up with 16 words!

Earlier in the year I had introduced the game of hopscotch to my students to play during their recess breaks, so I did a quick review of how to play and explained that we would be going outside to create our own -op word hopscotch games. The students were numbered off into six groups of three and one group of four and then they got down to the task of drawing the seven hopscotch games with ten connected squares. They then took turns printing the -op words in the squares. The final task before beginning the game was for the students to search the playground for their individual markers to play the game. Then the fun began—it was a good plan to have reviewed the traditional hopscotch game using numbers so that they were comfortable with the rules prior to me modelling the new game when the students had to create sentences using the -op words. I recently had a new student join our class from China and he had never played hopscotch before.

In some of the groups I observed some students copying the sentence structure of their peers, which I accepted at the beginning. After a while I decided to rotate all of the #1s in each group to a group to their right while all of the #2s switched to the group to their left. This helped to provide a variety of creative sentences using the words.

I would like to introduce this activity to our big buddy sessions as the big buddies could model more varieties of sentence examples for proper use of the words being learned. It was a fun activity that I will definitely do again using other stories.

Game 3: Glitzy Word Bottle

(Shauna Buffie)

Materials:

- Words: and, then, they, this, some, over, until, why, what, when, were, too, two, again, also, make, we, mom, dad, sister, me, I, can, so, above, come, came, jump, made, went, to, there, it, one, for, word, first, he, she, be;
- Word bottle recording sheet (http://tunstalltimes.blogspot.ca/2011/07 /discovery-bottles.html) or just create your own form so children can record their words;
- Bottle labels;
- Printed words;
- Three empty plastic bottles;
- Packing tape;
- Pom poms;
- Glitter and sequins;
- Rice (dyed with food coloring – optional).

Word or letter bottles: helping to make letter bottles and then having friend go try it out and see how many letters she could find.

Rules:

1. Shake the bottle and record the words on the word bottle-recording sheet. Shake as many times as needed. This is an individual activity that can be done beside another person or alone.

2. The game/activity ends when the bottle-recording sheet is full.

Teacher Reflections:

After showing the children what to do with the game/activity, they easily caught on and were anxious to play. I put this out during the morning as part of their "small job" time, when they choose something of my choice that I had placed on the tables or carpet. Some of them enjoyed this so I would take it out again at "big jobs" which is when they can choose a centre activity. I found that because of the paper/pencil aspect of it, the girls were more apt to choose it during "big job" time on their own. Many of the children helped one another out and worked together to find the words and see that their classmate got it recorded on the word bottle-recording sheet.

One of the issues I encountered was that when it was introduced, everyone wanted to be the first to play. I found issues with how I put together the bottles that I would change the next time. Mixing sparkles in with the sequins makes the words harder to find and read. I would also print off two copies of each of the word sheets for each bottle and glue them back-to-back so that there was no blank side on the back of the word card.

Some children learned new sight words; for others, it reinforced words they already knew. Some children simply enjoyed finding a word and copying the letters to record it on their sheet, helping them with letter recognition and fine motor skills; some enjoyed shaking up the bottle and were excited to find a word and have a friend help them record their finding. I learned that I need to make more of this type of activity available to keep sight words fresh, new and engaging.

Game 4: Scrambled Eggs

(Rose Boulton)

Materials:

- Words: Pig, big, jig, wig, cat, fat, the, is (Your choice—use any rhyming or sight words you are working on—make sure the rhyming words are on different coloured eggs),
- Eight or more plastic egg containers in different colors,
- Permanent felt pens,
- A basket to store them in, and
- Copies of the booklets read in class (optional).

Rules:
1. Begin with scrambled eggs (taken apart) dumped out of the basket.
2. Partners take turns finding a match (pig/pig) and assemble the egg.
3. Read the word aloud to your partner to see if they agree and put it back in the basket.
4. When all eggs are matched, scramble them and begin again.
5. For round two, find rhyming words and assemble eggs (pig/wig). Note: This time the top and bottom halves of the eggs will be different colours.
6. Read the rhyming words aloud to your partner. Note: there will be some words left over that do not rhyme.

Teacher Reflections:
The students enjoyed playing this game and were quick to catch on to the two rounds of matching and rhyming words. Students who could not yet read the words were able to match them and then work with their partner to sound out the words. The fine motor skill of assembling and scrambling the eggs was also fun for the kids. Originally, I used erasable marker to write the words so I could reuse the eggs but it rubbed off on their hands. Now I will use a strip of electrical tape to write on with permanent felt so I can continue to change the words we are using.

Scrambled eggs: children were challenged to find rhyming words and connect the eggs.

Game 5: More Scrambled Eggs Recipes
(Teresa Fayant)

I like the scrambled eggs game but modified it slightly making my own egg recipes.☺

Game: ABC Scramble

I made this version because I have a few junior kindergarten students in my class and I wanted them to be able to play a version of the game. They weren't ready for sight words. It would also work for any students who still need more doses of the alphabet.

Materials:
- Egg carton,
- 12 colored plastic eggs,
- 4 or so small paper plates,
- Paper scraps with the alphabet letters on them (divided into the eggs).

* You can use the store paper ones that are for art collage, or large ones cut out of newspapers to expose the students to different fonts.

Rules:

1. Students are given a paper plate and then choose an egg and break it on their plate.
2. They identify the letter name and the corresponding sound in order to keep them. If not, the letter(s) are placed back in the egg (if one or some are identified they can keep them and put the unidentified eggs back).
3. The winner is the student with the most alphabet letters on their plate once all the eggs have been cracked.
4. Have the students say a word that begins with that letter.

Teacher Reflections:

A version of the Scrambled Egg game for junior kindergarten engaged the students in identifying the alphabet.

* Note: I played this game with my junior kindergartens the same day I played the scrambled eggs game with my kindergartens, because I wanted them to have an egg game too. We did not leave the letters out; I did not take out paper plates. We simply cracked the eggs and dumped them on the open flat side of the carton so they didn't fall. The students loved it! They were able to identify the letters and think of words, and by immediately cleaning them up and choosing again we picked some eggs a few times and thought of new words each time.

Game 6: Who am I?

(Heather Marshall)

Materials:

- 10-12 target sight words on blank index cards or cut tag board so that each player has a set of the same words,
- A detective costume: hat, coat, magnifying glass, and a mystery mask.

Rules:
- The "detective" spreads her/his cards on the table/carpet so that all the words are visible.
- The "mystery-maker's" cards are in his/her hand but hidden from the "detective."
- The "mystery-maker" starts with "Who am I?" and gives clues to the word on her/his top card: Example: My first letter is P. I have 6 letters. I don't have the letter A.
- The "detective" has to identify and read the sight word to keep the card.

Extension:
Have a pile of animal cards face down. If the detective gets the sight word she/he can then turn over an animal card to reveal an animal. The detective has to make an oral sentence using the sight word and the animal.

Game 7: Lunchtime Surprise
(Michelle Fitterer)

Teacher Reflections:
This might be my new favourite addition to our lunchtime routine. After I have dismissed them for their morning recess, I walk around and hide a sight word in their lunch kit. Of course, I am strategic with which words I place in which lunch kits (based on ability level). The kids rush in from recess as they cannot wait to see which word I have hidden in their lunch. As one can imagine, this creates a very loud start to our lunch, but they are engaged and reading sight words! They compare, share, and read each other's words. Once they have begun eating their lunch, I do a quick whip around that sounds something like:

"I spy a word sitting near by—it begins with 's' and rhymes with tree—who has this word?" (they love this riddle part I throw in).

The student with the word "see" raises her card, reads it aloud and then uses it in a sentence.

One day, I thought that I would speed up the process and skip the sentence part. Well, they just would not accept that at all! They loved making up sentences to go with their sight word. The repetition in this activity is lovely—they are exposed to 15-20 sight words in one sitting. Best of all, they are having fun in the process!

Game 8: Calendar Silliness

(Michelle Fitterer)

Teacher Reflections:

This game is a different take on the traditional format of RAN (Rapid Automatic Naming). I found that when I simply flipped the cards up one at a time and had the children say the word they saw, only a third of my class was engaged. What is more, this third of the class had already mastered these words and was not the group I was really targeting with this exercise. One day this idea came to me right in the middle of teaching calendar.

I began by showing them the flashcard with a sight word on it. For example, the word "like."

We practiced a few times and they would say it only when I held it up—pretty basic.

Then I began using it in a sentence. "I **like** Gipsy because she is cute. I **like** Mr. Cowan [my husband] because he makes me nice lunches." I connected the sentences to my real life, or the lives of my students (they loved this). I held the word up in the air for them to say as I was saying my sentence.

Then things became great fun and a little rambunctious! I know two things about my kids: they love chanting and they love interrupting. We have been working on this,

but why not draw on their strengths? So, I began telling a story: "Once upon a time there was a little girl who walked (then I would hold up the sight word card) and they would yell **"LIKE,"** which would interrupt my story. I played along and pretended they were being awfully rude interrupting my story. Then I would begin again, switching out words as needed. Needless to say, all of my kids were extremely engaged. I loved it and they loved it!

Game 9: Playground Scavenger Hunt

(Michelle Fitterer)

Teacher Reflections:

Every day that we have Literacy Tubs I pray for the rain to stay away, so that I can use the outdoors as one of my centres. I have had my kids doing hopscotch outside as one of their centres. It has evolved over time from ABCs to word families, and now to sight words. After they complete their hopping they do one lap of the playground and begin again. They love this, but were in definite need of a change and a challenge.

Tyla found a "T" in the k's outdoor scavenger letter hunt.

That morning, it took me no time at all to prep this literacy centre that I had been thinking about the night before. I found five pieces of construction paper in my art bin; wrote a five-word sentence on each; cut up the words; and I was done! The sentences integrated the sight words we had been working on:

I like mom and dad.
The cat is so little.
I can jump up high.
I see the big car.

Before the literacy centres began, I hid all the cut up pieces around the playground; assigned each student a color; and then sent them off looking for their five pieces. Once they had found all five, they brought them back to our classroom door and began trying to form their sentence. We referred to this as "breaking the code like detectives." We helped each other and I provided scaffolding, such as:

"Does a sentence begin with an uppercase letter or lowercase letter?" or "Oh, I see a period here. Where should this go?"

After we had made all the sentences, we read them together and then I had the kids hide the pieces of paper for the next group. They loved this activity. Think of all of the literacy skills embedded in this one literacy centre! The only tricky part about it was making sure the kids didn't hide their words and make it too hard for the next group to find.

Game 10: Based on the Card Game SPOON

(Heather Marshall)

Materials:
Based on four players:

- 1 deck of word cards (slightly bigger than a regular deck of cards); four copies of each word per deck. Use ten different words for a total of 40 cards per deck.
- 3 white spoons, one less than the number of players.
- 1 red spoon (a white one coloured with red permanent marker).

Rules:
Goal: to achieve four of a kind (four of the same word) and sneak a white spoon without anyone noticing if possible. If you are the one left to pick up the red spoon, you have to make up a silly phrase or sentence with a word from your hand.

1. There is one person chosen at the start to be the dealer and "card picker upper."
2. She deals everyone four cards and then places the deck face down beside her.

3. Each player must only ever keep four cards in his hand, so when the dealer draws a card from the top of the pile, he decides whether or not to keep the card (in case it matches any of the existing cards in her hand) or passes it on to the next person. If he does decide to keep it, he must still pass a discard from his hand so that he only has four cards remaining after the switch.

4. Each player picks up the card that is passed along, and decides which card she will pass along to the next player. It goes around in a big circle, but players must be encouraged not to get too speedy. If a player collects all four cards of one word, she then sneaks a white spoon onto her lap. If another player notices the spoon disappear, she too picks up a white spoon and the rush usually triggers an attempt to take the spoons.

5. Whoever is left with a red spoon has to say a silly sentence with one of the words from their hand (if he already has two or more of a word, he uses the word he has the most of). The winner, the person who took the first spoon, must show everyone his four matching word cards and tell everyone the word.

6. The next player is now the dealer for the second round. The spoons are placed back in the middle of the table and new hands are dealt.

The fact that the game is to match words means that children can still play even if they are struggling to read the sight words, since many children can tell words apart by the look or the shape of the word even if they don't know yet what they say.

Teacher Reflections:

I had previously assessed the class and chosen four students who were able to identify only one or two sight words and seemed unsure of even those answers. Note: I had not done much explicit teaching of sight words before the third term because we have such a strong oral focus for the majority of French Immersion Kindergarten. I have been writing morning messages and pointing out sight words for those that are ready but was not surprised that my weaker students had not picked up on the sight words.

I started with ten sight words. We made no progress at all for the first, painfully long game, which I finally abandoned. This time we used only five sight words and I made sure the look of them was different. We had also been directly working on sight words in our song, morning message and in isolation for the last few days.

The children enjoyed the game and two of the students were able to master the five sight words in isolation and find them in our song. Another student, Lizzy, could get three out of five and find them in our song but only retained one when I retested her the next day. The last student has been uninterested in print and books throughout the year and I needed to work with him identifying what a word **is** before sight words would make any sense. I made Lizzy the "expert" and she taught the rest of the class to play the game, two students at a time. These multiple "doses" helped her to recognize and retain all five of the sight words. She got flustered when I asked her to write them but could easily identify and copy them from a list.

It is important for vulnerable students to learn some sight words so that they can experience success with reading and see themselves as readers. The fifty most common sight words make up a large percentage of text in the books they will be exposed to for reading. Automaticity with these words will make their reading experience easier and therefore more enjoyable and repeatable. The more they read, the more "doses" they get!

Game 11: Go Fishing

(Alison Kimmerly)

Materials:
- Dr. Suess Book: One Fish Blue Fish, Red Fish, Blue Fish,
- Fish cut out of foam,
- Magnet pieces,
- Doweling or long sticks, and
- String.

Attach the string to the wood and put a magnet on the end of it to create a fishing rod. Cut out foam fish and put magnets on them. On the back of the fish write down different sight words.

Rules:
1. The children go fishing and say the words on the fish they catch.
2. If they could say the word they get a point; if they couldn't say the word they lost a point and had to put the fish back.

Teacher Reflections:
Overall, I had a great experience and ended up with two games. I would say the hardest was managing the rules of playing a simple game. The highlights for me were watching the children play and get excited about knowing the words. It is so nice to have games that I can take with me as a teacher-on-call.

Game 12: Integrating Charts and Sight Words

(Teresa Fayant)

I regularly do an activity for oral language production: I put pictures up and students tell me what they see, adding descriptive language. Therefore, it was a logical transition to an "I see…" chart story using sight words. I included some of the sight word descriptors we had been using (color words - big, little) and some picture cards that would be a good fit with the descriptors.

Having the sight words on the pocket chart was great for my vulnerable learners: They were still learning the concept, increasing their practice and reading time without getting hung up on copying out the words.

I taught this station in a mini lesson, but what I noticed was that it was difficult for more than two students to work at the pocket chart, so for the larger group of five I had the students make their sentences at the carpet, then as they read it to me they would put it on the pocket chart. I then used it as a work-station with two students during literacy centres.

Theresa is pleased that she can identify "butterfly" and say the word.

As an extension, I allowed some students to write their sentence on a strip and put it up on the board. I will be keeping this as a literacy workstation and allowing students to read their composed pocket chart or written sentences with the class during sharing time.

It is important for vulnerable students to learn the first fifty words, because many of them are sight words that are straight memorization. These words, when students are fluent and automatic, add to the students' comprehension because they are not spending valuable brainpower trying to decipher the words. In addition, these are the words most commonly used in emergent readers, so reading skill, confidence and fluency improves when these words are used.

A Five-day Experiment with RAN (Rapid Automatized Reading)

Janet's Comment

We discussed the RAN (Rapid Automatized Naming) research in our VIU (*Vancouver Island University*) class acknowledging that we were uncertain how to apply the research in a meaningful way in primary classrooms—specifically related to sight word memory. The NELP Report recommends that additional research needs to explore and identify how teachers might use RAN in classroom practices to support rapid memory retrieval so I suggested there may be class members who would like to try an experiment. I invited them to complete their own research in their classrooms and report back to us about their experience.

Wendy decided to accept the invitation and submitted the following report. The results are worthy of note—the children made significant gains.

Janet

Experiencing RAN with Sight Words in the Classroom

(Wendy de Groot)

Materials:

- Graphs to track progress,
- Word and letter cards, and
- Timer.

Plan and Process:

I decided to try RAN with some of my students in the hopes that it would help "cement" recent learning of Letter Names and Sight Words.

I used a version of discrete testing as described in the NELP report. I used individual cards and timed the articulation of the card. I found it difficult to time the articulation for each individual card (pause time between seeing the card and identifying it) so I instead documented the end time (how long it took to identify the entire stack of cards). The students that I chose knew the information so it was not a matter of seeing if they could identify the letters or words—they could already [and this is important as the purpose is to speed up the time for word recognition not to teach the words].

I introduced RAN to my students individually and asked if they would participate in an assignment that I had to do for my teacher "Janet." I explained that they would be my "guinea pigs." They thought that was cool and all agreed.

I chose Taylor and Jada to participate in the Sight Word RAN study. Both girls had recently mastered List #1 of our Sight Words and were working on learning List #2. On Monday (the first day of the study) I reviewed List #1 words with the children. I played a short game of *Slap Down* with the words, a version of the *Green Eggs and Ham Game* described earlier. I laid out five of the word cards and called out one of them. The child had to "slap their hand down" on the word that I had called. I quickly exchanged the word they had identified with a new word so that they were always searching among five cards to find the word. Of course when we got to the end of the deck, we ended up with four, three, two and finally only one card. They loved this game!

I finished with the RAN testing and recorded the time that it took to identify the entire List #1 word stack. I recorded the time and told them that we would be meeting each day to review the words and find ways to identify them even faster.

Experiencing RAN with the Alphabet in the Classroom

I chose Lucian and Avaya to identify the letters of the Alphabet they had recently mastered. Lucian identified uppercase letters and Avaya identified lowercase letters. I repeated the same steps as above (Taylor and Jada) and both children were thrilled to be "guinea pigs."

We met each day for just a short while at varying times of the day. Each time we met we reviewed the cards, played *Slap Down,* did a search "in text" for the words or letters from Level 1 and Level 2 books and then a "mock" un-timed test.

Results:

On Friday, the final day of the study, we did the same activities but this time I recorded the times. In all cases the children had improved times.

Student	Monday	Friday
Taylor (Sight Words)	27.51 seconds	21.05 seconds
Jada (Sight Words)	39.89 seconds	17.48 seconds
Lucian (Uppercase Letters)	83 seconds	51.23 seconds
Avaya (Lowercase Letters)	46.39 seconds	29.30 seconds

Children's Response

I had a strong sense on the Monday that my students were so keen to be part of this learning exercise and have one-on-one time with me that even if the study did not really follow the protocol of the RAN experiment, my students would still benefit. I was right! Not only did they improve their time, I wish I could have measured the visible improvement in their confidence.

My little Avaya just bubbled with enthusiasm and an "I am so smart!" attitude. My Lucian was even more amazing. I had earlier in the year been worried that he might have some kind of learning delay. I was also a little nervous about having him participate in the study because he had only recently mastered letter/sound identification. But I am so glad I included him! He sits taller, pays attention and puts up his hand in discussion time. I noticed this in just one week of RAN practice. Previously I was noticing him slouching, covering his mouth, not making eye contact and certainly not participating. His parents have been really supporting him at home too. Combined with our *Home Reading* program and daily work, we have made a big difference for him!

Jada and Taylor who participated in the sight word RAN made terrific gains as well. Neither girl lacked confidence to start, but I would say are really feeling confident now and I am noticing a big leap in their writing at Journal Time. They are both showing much more independence.

My Learning

I confirmed that RAN is valuable for my students to assist in cementing their learning. I chose average to low average students, and this strategy was very successful in improving rapid recall of information. I saw first-hand that this improvement affected how they viewed themselves as learners and even improved other areas such as writing.

Summary

I plan to use this adapted form of RAN in the future as part of my regular program to assist with cementing knowledge for my learners. I am planning to set up a series of activities that my students can do regularly with Buddies or grade 7 helpers that will be similar to this in the hopes that I can reach more of my students through RAN, though perhaps not as concretely as the one-on-one work with me [their teacher] achieved.

Janet's Summary

No Glue (Sight) Words: No Stories!

The research, stories and experiences described in this chapter could lead us to the following conclusions which can then be used as operational principles in classroom program design.

Games, Laughter and Fun with Sight Words

- Games are the preferred way to motivate students to engage in their study and play with language.

Sight Word Expectations, Flash Cards, Context, Explicit Instruction

- We need to set high sight word expectations in the early years. Early learners can never learn too many sight words too soon.
- There is nothing wrong with the use of flash cards to practice automaticity, as long as context experiences are included as well. However, learning by sight is only one of the ways children arrive at immediate recognition skills. Reading, seeing, discussing, using and writing words must be introduced in tandem.
- Vulnerable children will need to be taught sight words in formal ways and will need multiple experiences with the words before developing automaticity;

however, most children are developmentally capable of learning many words in their kindergarten year.

- Framing the learning of sight words in the context of purposeful reading experiences is essential. Harvesting sight words from shared reading and writing experiences is an important strategy that will help children make meaningful connections.

- Linking new sight word learning with beginning level books helps children make the transition from seeing themselves as emergent readers to experiencing the joy of book reading.

Spelling Sight Words

- Children should be learning to spell sight words correctly as they are learning to write them; this will be an important contribution to general spelling ability.

Word Study Linkages and Sight Words

- Integrating word family studies into sight word knowledge development will propel reading and writing progress forward in a meaningful way.

Automaticity and Rapid Automatic Naming (RAN) using Sight Words

- Children need experiences that encourage automaticity in their ability to read sight words quickly, automaticity being one important contributor to fluency and enhanced comprehension.

Engaging Families in Games with Sight Words

- Engaging families in word play games at home to reinforce classroom successes will significantly contribute to their child's reading development.

Assessing and Tracking Sight Word Progress

- Assessing and tracking each child's progress through sight word knowledge is important for informing instruction. The link between the quantity of words children know and their growing ability to read increasingly difficult material is undeniable.

Impact on Pilot Sites

Armed with these new insights we have made sight words a central part of our pilot sites (that target over 90% literacy success for all children). Sight words are posted on word walls and in personal dictionaries. Organic words (from the child's experience) are listed in the back of their journals or in boxes of personal card sets. Sight words are learned in context and harvested from their own stories. Practice is essential, especially for vulnerable children who require more exposure to master these new words. Practice is woven contextually into play and games either through board games or contests and accompanied by much excitement, joy and success.

We extended these practices, backed by significant research studies that encourage us, especially for the vulnerable children who need extra "doses" to close the experiential gap. We divided the Dolch (1948) list into envelopes of ten words (on tag board or recipe cards) beginning with the simplest words and provided them to children as they were ready, in increasingly difficult stages. Sets of ten words were placed on large rings as they were mastered by each child and become the raw material for games and a reference set for writing. When the ring was full of mastered words they proudly took them home to demonstrate success to thrilled parents, then started a new ring with more challenging words. Some added their own organic words from their stories to the ring too; others kept their own words in journals or boxes for reference.

In one classroom we created stations of sight word games, supervised by teachers and teacher assistants, LA (Learning Assistant) teachers and administrators. For 60 minutes each day children rotated between stations; each station was organized into groups of sight words based on the child's mastery level. Adults adapted the games to the group's sight word level. The room became a cacophony of laughter and sounds of delight as adults and children celebrated progress together. At one station, children had to find their sight words in newspapers or books; at another they dug into surprise bags to find the ones they knew; at another, they copied the word on small whiteboards. We made sure they always used sight words in a sentence and found them somewhere in the room or in books as well—context, context, context!

Most kindergarten children can master over 50 sight words by the end of the year, some 100 or more. The sooner they learn all 220 service words, the faster they will be reading books and writing stories. We have evidence that this is possible. I witnessed it in an aboriginal community where over 80% of the children had been identified as vulnerable at the start of their kindergarten year. In our case studies (Chapter 9) we found repeated evidence that learning the sight words early accelerates reading and writing success in kindergarten and beyond. One rule dominates: the learning has to be perceived by the children as FUN AND GAMES!

Janet

After classroom shared reading time, these students read a book together.

6

Stepping Stone

Schedule Shared Reading and Writing
(5 Times a Day)

Part 1: Shared Reading

Janet's Introduction

Dear Janet:

Well, I have officially become a more CRAZY and FUN teacher, now, as a result of learning more about Shared Reading. I am much more PLAYFUL now! I have embraced the idea of props and artifacts in a big way. At first, I thought it was "gimmicky" and silly to suggest using "reading glasses," "witches fingers" and thematic "pointers." I thought the children would just fool around with them and break or lose them, but then, as I saw in my colleagues' presentations and discussions, more and more people were ACTUALLY using these ideas so I decided to give it a try.

Kathleen Lougheed-Mercier

Isn't this a priceless quote? Kathleen is my "poster child" for the power of Shared Reading and Shared Writing! She wasn't a "believer" in the beginning. When I was teaching my last fabulous class of kindergarten teachers—many with 20 years experiences—I spent the first half of the course reinforcing, demonstrating, proving, practicing, and insisting that we pay attention to the importance of essential literacy skills as the prime focus in every early learning classroom and I was unapologetic about it. If vulnerable learners don't get a running start at catching up on the experiential gap between them and the "luckier children" they won't have a chance to become literate.

Now, I didn't say that's all they would do in September when school starts, but I did need to know that my class understood that this was our highest priority. Gone are the days when snuggling up for a warm and fuzzy story to quiet the class down was good enough. Now that we have scientific evidence about the importance of the early years, we have to be intentional teachers. We must do everything with purpose; there is not a minute to lose for these children.

The NELP Report identifies Shared Reading and Shared Writing as one of the seven most important factors that will have the greatest impact on future literacy success. I, therefore, considered it worthy of a significant school professional development, university class study and follow-up classroom assignments to practice the priorities identified in the research, and reflect on its meaning for their future practice.

I wanted my colleagues to understand that Shared Reading and Shared Writing events can become the most joyful part of the day, beginning on day one in September; but they must have significant purpose. I used the following PowerPoint to introduce my class to the prevailing theories and related suggestions for practice.

Our New Song:
It seems that every day I have a new student making that big jump to putting their sounds together and truly be reading! My new addition to Shared Reading is that I sing a song "All the readers in the room throw your hands up!" And every single student "raises the roof." I love it!

Michelle Fitterer

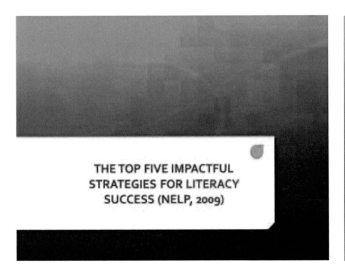

THE TOP FIVE IMPACTFUL STRATEGIES FOR LITERACY SUCCESS (NELP, 2009)

THE TOP FIVE:
IMPACT ON Future LITERACY SUCCESS

+ Alphabet Knowledge
+ Phonological Awareness
+ Rapid Automatized Naming (RAN)
− High Frequency Words
+ Shared Reading and Writing
+ ALL IN A PLAY-BASED ENVIRONMENT EMPHASIZING ORAL LANGUAGE.

WHAT IS SHARED READING (Writing)?

+ ...originated in New Zealand (1979) to replicate the bedtime story experience –called the Shared Book Experience.

+ **Common Elements: (Rog, 2012)**

1. Enlarged print and illustrations with all children;

2. Modeling of reading by teacher;

3. Repeated reading for comprehension, fluency and focus on print features.

What is the **Purpose** of Shared Reading?

+ Shared Reading: **SKILLS and CONCEPTS** in **CONTEXT!!!**

1. Exposes children to the joy of reading;

2. Entice them to want to be readers;

3. Children practice systematic and explicit instruction about print – text features, sounds, phonics, phonological awareness, high frequency words, build comprehension skills such as predicting/connecting, story text structures;

4. Children begin to think, act and see themselves as readers.

Venues for Shared Reading

+ Big Books

+ Poems

+ Posters

+ Nursery Rhymes

+ Shared Writing

+ Projected Print

What do **Teachers** Do?

+ Select or writes the text;

+ Model fluent and expressive reading;

+ Think aloud about their own reading processes;

+ Use techniques to point out print concepts, skills, HF words, alphabet knowledge, phonological awareness, patterns, new vocabulary, connections.

+ Make the experience **FAST-PACED, INTERACTIVE, AND MULTILEVEL!**

What Do **Children** Do?

+ Observe;

+ Gradually participate through multiple readings;

+ Gradually engage in group reading as they become comfortable and familiar with the text.

+ Begin to understand the connections between explicit instruction in skills and concepts, and

+ *"Every student can take something unique from the experience depending on his or her stage of development and level of engagement."* (Rog, 2012)

When do you do Shared Reading?

"Every Opportunity You Have!!!

+...five times a day?"

Leslie Mandel Morrow (2012)

The *Shared Reading* Assignment

I then gave them the following assignment, which was challenging. I asked them to conduct several readings over the course of a week. I did this for several reasons:

1. I had been noticing in my research that there was a renewed focus on the potentially important effect that "repeated readings" can have on children; children repetitively reading the same text and hearing the same text over and over, and the positive impact this can have on a child's progress over time if applied in appropriate ways;

2. I wanted my students to practice applying repeated Shared Reading experiences in different ways so they could see the potential and power of focused and carefully planned Shared Reading experiences; I wanted them to feel the depth of possibilities;

3. I wanted them to understand that skills, while they need to be taught, must be integrated meaningfully into real and exciting experiences with engaging books: Then children will understand that there are joyful outcomes connected to the hard work of learning essential skills.

4. I separated the assignments on Shared Reading and Shared Writing although I believe when teachers become skilled at each process, they can be effectively integrated: At this early stage, however, I was most interested in my students focusing on becoming skilled in each process separately.

5. I am a true believer that we all work harder when rewards are in sight: Multiple Shared Reading and Shared Writing experiences every day can be satisfying rewards for children when we do it with enthusiasm and for their pleasure!

ASSIGNMENT 5 (a) SHARED READING

Note: Assignment 5 (b) will be a continuation on the topic of Shared Writing.

SHARED READING

Where the Rubber Hits the Road! Where Skills make Sense!

Shared Reading is one of the literacy experiences that have the greatest impact on future literacy success. For this reason we will spend the next two classes focusing on this topic.

In Preparation

- Read the articles on Shared Reading distributed in class;

- Choose a book that lends itself to the experience (it should have many sight words in it, great pictures, and an exciting storyline);

- Find a class with which to use it;

- Choose a selection from the book–an exciting piece–and print it on chart paper (so you can bring it to class, otherwise you could use a smart board or overhead). In Shared Reading the children need to see some of the text so they can participate;

- Practice the text to build expression;

- Find some artifact(s) to bring to class related to the topic of the book to build excitement; and

- Plan a follow-up activity that could be put in a center or used as a class activity after the reading(s).

Tip: Make Shared Reading time a special event–use snugglies, blankets, pillows, hand-holders, treasures, squeeze balls–something that signals this is a special time and is only used during Shared Reading (to signal intimacy with you and with books).

I propose at least three readings of the book (if possible) on different days.

First Reading: For Joy and Pleasure and the Love of Reading

Focus on pure pleasure—cozy and comfortable—no reference to skills although you can use predictions and discussions about pictures that create a feeling of child involvement. Use your props or artifacts as an enhancement. Insert drama if appropriate. The whole purpose of the first reading is to build excitement about books and for you to model what great reading looks like. Emphasize that you are modelling for them that this is how they will be reading soon! That's why they are working so hard on letters and words. (No chart yet.)

Second Reading: A New Focus

Read the story again (or a part of it if it is too long). When finished, put up the chart of an excerpt from the story. Tell them you want them to see how much they have learned about reading. Play games getting them to point out things you have already taught – letters, sight words, punctuation, commonalities with their names, etc.

Third Reading: Another New Focus

Before you read, see how much they can remember. Read the book again and have them check to see if they are right. Ask for alternative scenarios. Return to the chart excerpt. Read it several times, a sentence at a time, asking them to join in reading each sentence for those who can—no pressure again—you want them to realize that they are becoming readers just like you. For those who do not participate, don't worry, they are learning too. Add character studies here: children can act out different parts of the story.

Follow-Up

Introduce a follow-up to the story. Put it in a center as an activity, or put an activity in each center related to the story, or plan a whole-group activity connected to the book.

Documentation

Please provide a two- to three-page description of your experience indicating:

1. Your plan for the three readings,

2. Your props or artifacts,

3. What worked best,

4. What you struggled with and therefore what you learned,

5. Your perceptions of the children's experience and learning,

6. Your follow-up activity,

7. Your plan for future Shared Reading experiences: frequency and scheduling in the day, type(s) of book, questioning strategies, integration of previously taught skills,

8. Your perception of the value of Shared Reading,

9. How Shared Reading will change your practice (if at all), and

10. Your innovative new ideas as a result of this assignment.

You will be invited to tell your story in class for the benefit of your classmates.

Cheers, Janet

Janet's Comment

When you read the results of the assignment in the Teacher's Stories in this chapter, there will be nothing left for me to explain! My class were wizards at this assignment and reported having a wonderful time with many rewards, for themselves and their children. Teacher Kathleen describes how the experience affected her: "Since the three Shared Reading sessions, the children are ON FIRE about their ability to read, find sight words, letters and print features in our big book, and also, in the books in their personal reading baskets!"

Janet

Research and Recommended Books

Impact of Shared Reading Interventions on Young Children's Emergent Literacy Skills (Chapter 4)

(National Early Literacy Panel Report (NELP), 2009)

Whether it is a parent reading a picture book with a toddler or a teacher reading a book to a class of preschoolers, shared reading practices are widely recommended to promote language and other skills related to early literacy development. Shared reading activities are often recommended as the single most important thing adults can do to promote the emergent literacy skills of young children. The *National Early Literacy Panel* (NELP) examined the effects of interventions that primarily, or entirely, focused on shared reading... Consequently, the NELP studies provide comparisons of some kind of intensified or improved effort to read to children with the usual kinds of shared reading that children commonly experience... Overall, the evidence supports the positive impact of shared reading interventions that are more intensive in frequency and interactive in style on the oral language and print knowledge skills of young children (pp. 153-155).

Reading Essentials: Emphasize Shared Reading (Chapter 9)

(Routman, 2003)

In shared reading, a learner—or a group of learners—sees the text, observes an expert (usually the teacher) reading it with fluency and expression, and has decided to read along. In the optimal learning model, shared reading is an ideal way to demonstrate and support what good readers do. The teacher not only makes reading visible and explicit for students but also provides scaffolding so that students will be successful. Shared reading is also powerful because it helps students and teachers bond; students are partners in an enjoyable process and see themselves as ultimately capable. Furthermore, research indicates that shared reading typically improves reading achievements (p. 130).

In kindergarten, grade one, and early grade two, shared reading focuses primarily on enjoying and re-reading new, familiar, and favorite text. As the teacher progresses word by word and line by line with a pointer or a sliding piece of paper, students join in visually and/or orally. These repeated readings build confidence, fluency and word familiarity as well as provide practice in phonemic awareness and phonics. Once students have read a text through a few times, shared reading texts are ideas for word work (p. 131).

Teaching Literacy in Kindergarten

(McGee & Morrow, 2005)

Researchers have also demonstrated how shared reading, and a related type of reading called *Finger Point* reading, supports children's concepts about print, especially those concerning letters and words (Ehri & Sweet, 1991). *Finger Point* reading occurs when children point to printed words, one by one, left to right, across the page while reciting a predictable text from memory. Not all children in kindergarten can *finger point* read, although they improve during the year. At first, children memorize the text (this is called *Memorized Pretend* reading), but they do not point at the printed words. They merely sweep across a line of text with their hands without even attempting to point to individual words. Later, they do point to individual words, although they do not match those words with the answer words they are saying. Children who learn to *finger point* read demonstrate higher levels of print and phonemic awareness (Morris et al, 2003). In summary, the purposes of shared reading techniques are to help children achieve the following skills: initially, to recognize alphabet letters and associate sounds with letters; secondly, to develop phonemic awareness skills such as identifying rhyming words or words with the same beginning sound; thirdly, to acquire print concepts, including book orientation, print directionality and also concepts about letters and words; and finally, to learn *finger point* reading.

The common element in shared reading, whether reading from big books or regular-sized books, is that children are invited to read the text along with the teacher, (which is not the case in interactive reading). Teachers will select alphabet books, books with language play, predictable books, and appropriate big books to use in shared reading. Children need to be able to see the alphabet letters and alphabet books, but do not necessarily read the text. Thus, regular-sized books can be effective for shared reading when the letters are large, although Big Book Alphabet books can also be used. Similarly, children do not need to see the text in order to gain the benefits of the shared reading of a book with language play, especially when the intention is to develop phonological or phonemic awareness such as identifying rhyming words or finding two words that came with the same phoneme: children need only to listen. Therefore, teachers can use regular sized books, but again, Big Book formats may also be used; in contrast, when teaching print concepts, teachers should use Big Books or enlarged charts. Children have to be able to see the text and observe as the teacher points to words, left to right, across the page (p. 74).

Literacy Development in the Early Years: Helping Children Read and Write

(Morrow, 2012)

The shared book experience is usually carried out in a whole class setting, although it works in small groups as well. During this activity, teachers not only model fluent reading, but they also help children develop listening skills, since during the reading, the children are asked to participate in some way. Shared book reading often involves selecting a Big Book designed so that everyone in the group can see the pictures and the words clearly while it is being read. If the book is a new one for the class, the children are asked to listen during the first reading. If it is being read for the second time, or is already familiar, immediate participation is encouraged. Often the teacher uses a pointer during the reading to emphasize left to right progression with younger children and the correspondence of spoken and written words. Children's participation could include chanting together repeated phrases in the story, stopping at predictable parts, and asking children to fill in words and phrases or reading key words special to the story. Shared book experience might include *Echo* reading: the teacher reads one line and the children repeat it. Big Books with regular-sized copies of the same book should be available for children to use independently after the first Big Book reading. Shared book readings can be taped and made available in the listening station, an activity that provides a familiar and fluent model for reading, with good phrasing and intonation for children to emulate. Research indicates that shared book reading contributes to the acquisition of reading and writing; it also enhances background information, giving a sense of story structure while familiarizing children with the language of books (pp. 213-214).

Reading and Learning to Read

(Vacca & Vacca, et al, 2012)

Shared Reading

The teacher and the class of beginners partake in the reading and re-reading of favorite stories, sounds, poems, and rhymes. Butler (1998) recommends the use of shared reading as a way of creating opportunities for children to learn what a book is, what an "expert" reader does with a book as it is read, and what makes a story a story. Taberski (2000) claims that the use of shared reading in her classroom, "offers numerous opportunities to show children what reading is all about" (p. 128).

Consider the following steps when sharing books with early readers and writers.

1. Introduce, talk about, and read a new story:
   - Show children the cover of the book and invite discussion of the illustration "Ah, what does the illustration and the cover remind you of?" "What do you think this story will be about?"
   - Tell children the title of the story, invite further predictions as to the stories content;
   - Read the story dramatically. Once children have experienced the joy of hearing the story, invite conversation, "What did you enjoy about the story?" "Where are the characters like you?" It is better not to overdo the discussion with lots of questions. Accept the children's personal reactions and responses and support their efforts to express their enjoyment of the story and to talk about the meaning that it has for them;
   - Encourage children to re-tell the story in their own words. Allow them to use picture clues and assist them as needed;
   - Re-read the story, inviting children to participate in some ways by refocusing on repetitive elements, or chants, and having them join in with you. Keep the emphasis on meaning and enjoyment.

2. Re-read familiar stories. Once the children have become familiar with several stories, ask them to choose a favorite to be re-read;
   - Strive for the children's increased participation by creating re-along opportunities;
   - Create book experiences to build children's book knowledge. For example, as you read, point to the words in the text and demonstrate skills such as page turning, and directionality —left to right, top to bottom;
   - Teach children about book conventions—front and back cover, title and author page, pictures to support the story;
   - Make children aware of written language conventions—words, pages, spaces between words, the use of capital letters in proper names or at the beginning of a sentence, punctuation marks, quotation marks to indicate dialogue between characters.

3. Develop reading skills and strategies. As children progress in the sharing and re-reading of favorite stories, teach them literacy skills and strategies—recognizing letter/sound relationships in words, using context to identify words, building a site word vocabulary, developing oral reading fluency, comprehending meaning.

4. Encourage independent reading;
   - Develop a classroom library of books that have been shared and reread many times; and
   - Encourage students to read favorite books on their own and with others.

Catching Readers before they Fall

(Johnson & Keier, 2010)

Shared reading with children

Don Holdaway (1979) introduced shared reading, an interactive reading experience, as a way to imitate the typical bedtime story. The purpose of shared reading is to make text accessible to all children, allowing them to experience what it feels like to be a proficient reader. It is a time for us to teach about the reading process and serves as a gateway to guided reading and independent reading. Enjoying of the story is important and children are encouraged to participate in the shared reading experience. If we want to support children as they build an effective reading process system, then we must show them what it looks like when a proficient reader is using his or her system. Shared reading provides us with a place to do just that. There is an opportunity for teachers to "provide a solid foundation for reading and writing. At the same time, it fosters a sense of community as children collaborate to talk, think, listen, and join in on the reading" (Parkes, 2012). This is especially beneficial to our most struggling readers as they are guided by a teacher in putting together an integrated reading process system and are part of a community of readers.

… The teacher does the reading and encourages the children to join in on a refrain of some other known part of the text. While the first reading may be done for enjoyment, repeated readings provide multiple opportunities for the teacher to model a reading strategy, skill, or behavior as the children are supported in a low risk setting. Teachers think aloud to help children see what goes on in the head of a proficient reader. A focus for a shared reading lesson could include, but is not limited to the following (pp.74-75):

- Comprehension strategies such as visualizing, questioning, activating schema, monitoring and correcting, and predicting at the word level or the text level;
- Concepts about print such as voice to print match, left to right reading with return sweep, reading the left page before the right, and punctuation and what it means for the reader;
- Meaning, structure and visual sources of information to solve words and comprehend;
- Searching and gathering information to support word solving or comprehension;
- Word work and work study analogies;
- Fluency;
- Non-fiction text features, such as italics, graphs, diagrams, and bold print;
- Non-fiction text format such as cause and effect, and questions and answers; and
- Genre studies (pp. 74-75).

Teachers' Stories

Bringing Real Life into Writing

Resource: *Little Chicks* by Mary DeBall Kwit

(Vicky Dodge)

First Read: Focus on Joy

Our focus in class right now is spring and the farm.

- I asked the children the day before to bring in any items that reminded them of the farm. Students brought in blankets (with farm animals on them), teddies, plastic toys, books, pictures, photos, drawings, fur/feathers (bunny, wool) and DVDs. As a class we shared what each student had brought. I had extra items ready for those students that could not bring something. I brought in live ducklings; the chicks are not hatched yet, otherwise, it would have been a chick!

- We talked about eggs and chicks. Again, I had five different kinds of eggs to compare—size, shape, and colour. After that, we made predictions about which egg the chick on the front cover of the book would have come from.

- Before I read the book I asked the question, "This book reminds me of you. Can you tell me why when we finish the book?"

- Once the book was read the students answered the question:
  - "Because we are young like chicks and we are just learning."
  - "Because we have mothers like the chick does."
  - "Because our mom helps to take of us."

- Once the answers were given, I redirected my question, but this time I told them to think, instead, of how they read. "This book reminds me of you and how you read. Can you tell me why I think that?" I gave them some time to think about this question and I told them that I would ask them again when we re-read the book.

- Before we finished our first read I asked one more question: "What things did I do that all good readers should do?"
  - "You used good sound when you read."
  - "You showed us the pictures."
  - "You showed excitement when something was happening."
  - "You changed your voice for different characters."
  - "You looked at us."
  - "You didn't read too quickly."

Second Reading: Comprehension and Glue Words

First we did an A/B partner re-tell.

- I showed "A" partner a picture and they had to describe to their "B" partner what was happening in the picture. Then I picked three "B" partners to tell the class what was happening in the story. As a class we decided whether the stories told about the picture made sense to our story. The switching back and forth between partner "A" and "B" continued until both had described three different pictures.

- We then looked at part of the story on mounted chart paper. As a class we choral-read the story. Once we had finished I asked the students my question again, "This book reminds me of you and how you read. Can you tell me why I think that?" The first response I heard was, "Because we are like chicks, we are learning to read for the first time and we need help to know how to do it properly. It was like when the Broody Hen showed the chick how to scratch for food—you are showing us how good readers read." Well, as I told my student, I could not have said it better myself!

Using a pocket chart to highlight key words.

- We then looked at the passage on the chart paper and we circled the sight words that we knew in each line. We decided that we were going to pick the top five words that showed up the most often. Our sight words we picked were: *is, in, and, the, on.*

Third Reading: Reading, Predicting, and Practicing

In a circle we went around and re-told (out loud) the story one event at a time in the same order as the book, helping each other if we got stuck. Some students were not sure but all participated and wanted to help those who got stuck. We then re-read the story to see if they were right. Many students were reading (from memory) with me even though the part of the story was not on the chart paper. We then talked about how they would change the story. Would they change the middle or the end? Would other characters in the book talk as well, or have a bigger role in the story? Before we finished our third read we revisited the sight words that were circled on the chart paper and read them aloud again.

Follow-Up Activity: Chicks Hatching from Egg with Sight Words

The students made paper chicks hatching out of eggs on a large blue sheet of paper. Once their chick was made they wrote the five sight words that occurred most often in the passage on their eggs. As a class we counted out loud, that there were three of each of the sight words on the chart paper; therefore, they had to write each sight word three times on their egg.

My Experience and Learning

Overall, the students were fully engaged for all three readings and for the activity. The readings never took longer than thirty minutes so the children were able to stay focused. When making the paper chicks I had everything cut out for them so they were able to put them together fast and spend more time writing their sight words. The students told me that they liked reading the same book over again and they wanted to do it more often. I have done this in the past but need to do it more often, especially now that most of them are emerging as readers. Even my lowest readers enjoyed the success of being able to read the book and are choosing it for silent reading time.

I find that I am explicitly teaching what I want the kids to know and that they are responding positively to it. I feel stronger in my accountability when teaching this way: I can defend it or show progress to anyone that may walk into my room at any given point with concrete examples. I have seen the importance of sharing reading more and more, especially over the past two years. Continuing and building on students' skill levels is so important when learning to read and I believe that Shared Reading gives them this opportunity.

Shared Reading as a Vehicle:
Shared Reading Sessions will help me teach about text features, concepts of print, phonemic awareness, sight-words and punctuation. Frequent Shared Reading sessions will build a feeling of community and cohesiveness in the class as the children join in the reading and become inspired by each other's abilities to "read" along. Through multiple readings of a shared book, they can build their own personal reading skills in the comfort and safety of a situation where everyone is invited to join in if they are ready, yet those who just want to watch and listen are allowed that freedom.

Kathleen Lougheed-Mercier

A Substitute Teacher's Story

Resource: *Pete the Cat – I Love My White Shoes*

(Alison Kimmerly)

As a teacher working on call (substitute teacher) I always make sure I have a few books I know children will love. I have started a collection of *Pete the Cat* books. The children love them and will read them over and over again. There are also many activities available online that links to the *Pete the Cat* stories. Most of the books come with a song, which is so much fun! The book I am using for this assignment is *Pete the Cat – I Love My White Shoes*. This is one is my favorite and in my opinion has the best song. Also, the children absolutely love it!

First Read: Singing, Motivation and Punctuation

I bring my *Pete the Cat* stuffed animal and show the children the book. I usually let the special helper hold Pete while we read. To make things fair, the other students can find a classroom stuffed animal to sit with them. After introducing the book we talk about what the book might be about and what they think will happen. I show them some of the pages and make sure they see an exclamation mark and ask them if they know what this is? We talk about it and model how we change the way we talk when we see exclamation marks. I then continue to read the story. This story is so much fun and it is easy to add enthusiasm.

As it has repeated phrases, the children end up saying some of the words with me. Once we have read the story I say something along the lines of: "Wasn't that such a fun story to read? Boys and girls, did you know there is a song that we can sing to read this book? Do you think you would like to hear it and see if we can read the book with a song?"

The children usually reply with a big "YES!!!!" So of course we put the song on and follow along with the book and they love it! We all end up bouncing around while we sing the song and read the book. Often the children ask to listen to the book while they are eating or playing centers.

Pete the Cat comes to visit.

Second Reading: Sequencing and the Packet Chart

It is very easy to read the whole book. I tried this in one of the classes I was in this week and I put part of it up onto the pocket chart. This made it easy to change what Pete stepped in and what color it turned his shoes. Later we could use these in a sequencing activity.

Oh no!

Pete stepped in a large pile of…? Strawberries! (Blueberries! Mud! Bucket of Water!) (These all had pictures attached to them.)

What color did it turn his shoes?

RED , BLUE, BROWN, WHITE but now they were WET.

Did Pete cry?

Goodness, no!

"He kept walking along and singing his song."

Since we had talked about exclamation marks the first day, when we read the story, I had the students find them in this section of the story. We then reviewed what exclamation marks mean and practiced what it sounds like when we do or don't use the exclamation mark. This was really fun and the children loved showing their excitement. The class had been talking about the letters *r* and *s* so we circled all the *r*'s and put boxes around all the *s*'s. We also used fun pointers to point to the words as we read them. There are four times in the book that use the phrase, "He kept walking along and singing his song," so four students took turns with pointers.

Third Reading: Sequencing and Predicting

We talked about the order of things that Pete stepped in. We then did a sequencing activity as a class using the words with pictures of the different things he stepped in (strawberries, blueberries, mud and a bucket of water). After re-reading the story we talked about other things he could have stepped in, such as, "Oh no! Pete stepped in a large pile of watermelon? What color did it turn his shoes?" As I said this, I filled it in on the Pocket Chart. The students all shouted, "PINK." We brainstormed different things and what color they would turn Pete's shoes.

With this class I did a *Pete the Cat* literacy art project. Everyone created their own *Pete the Cat* wearing shoes of their color choice. We did this as a directed art project using construction paper and glue. Using different pre-cut rectangles and squares I modeled to the students how to cut to make their own *Pete the Cat*. The last thing they did was create shoes for Pete. Once they had finished their cat, they added a sentence strip: I love my _____ shoes. They had to fill the color with their own printing. First they did it with pencil, then traced over using a colored marker to match the color.

Reading with a friend.

I have used this story to create a Big Book as a class where each student creates one page. They have to draw Pete stepping in a large pile of something and fill in the blanks: Pete stepped in a large pile of _____. What color did it turn his shoes? _____. Once a big book is made it can be read during Shared Reading as well as added to the classroom Big Books for children to read during Literacy Centers. Children love this activity and think it is so much fun to re-read.

My Experience and Learning

To me Shared Reading has always been an important part of the day in primary classrooms. So many things come out of it and it can take you in many directions. With *Pete the Cat*, we also talked about the moral of the story: "No matter what you step in, keep walking along and singing your song—because it's all good." Most importantly it is fun! I find that often children don't think they can read, but my modeling with them and doing it together as a class, they all of a sudden build up their confidence. My favorite thing is when a child asks me to borrow one of my books during reading time or centers. Then they show me how they can read it and they are so excited about it.

Partner reading.

The practice of Shared Reading is one that I see myself including in my classrooms no matter what the age level or content. It is valuable and applicable for building on a multitude of skills and strategies and for scaffolding and supporting learning in a way that naturally targets a variety of students and interventions. Shared Reading is a component of my teaching that will continue to be a priority as a crucial element of learning for my students.

(Link to some resources for *Pete the Cat*, as well as the songs: www.harpercollinschildrens.com/petethecat)

Making an Intimate Event out of Shared Experiences

Resource: *Sheep in a Jeep* by Nancy Shaw

(Michelle Fitterer)

First Read: Enjoyment

My goal for the first read was to create an exciting, comfortable atmosphere for our Shared Reading times. We discussed what Shared Reading was, what it would be like and why it was different from other story times. To create a special experience I closed the blinds and turned off the lights; gave each student a special reading buddy; and allowed students to get sweaters or blankets to use while lying on the mats. Next, I brought out some props, a toy sheep and red jeep to stimulate their interest in what our first story would be about. There were many laughs and predictions throughout my dramatic performance of a sheep driving a jeep. We completed our first read through, where we would only stop briefly to make further predictions and share connections to the story. To end the lesson, I informed the class that I would be placing some toy sheep and other vehicles in a center for free play.

Second Read: Skills, Sight Words and Print Awareness

Before completing the second read we set up the comfortable atmosphere just as we had done the day before. I explained that there are two reasons why I love to reread stories: for pure enjoyment and to help me become a stronger reader. During the first read it was easy for my students to tell that this was a rhyming story. In response, to strengthen their skill of identifying rhyming words, I had them tap their nose every time they heard a word that rhymed with "jeep." This helped engage my students, especially those who complained that they had "already heard this story before." Afterwards, I showed them the chart paper with a small passage from *Sheep in a Jeep*. Immediately, they began trying to read the passage and were excited to spot some of our sight words. Volunteers circled the sight words from our word wall, then we took part in choral reading of the text. Our focus was on reading left to right, return sweep, and keeping an eye on different types of punctuation. We celebrated with clapping and high-fiving in acknowledgment that we were becoming "good" readers.

Third Read: Comprehension and Predicting

The next day, we began our third read aloud with some volunteers retelling different parts of the story. After a read through of the story, I got them to rub the tops of their heads to "wake up" their imagination. I flipped through the book enthusiastically and explained that I enjoy creating "what if" scenarios to create an alternate ending. They turned to a partner to finish this sentence stem: "Jeep goes splash! Jeep goes thud! Jeep goes deep in _____." The conversation was full of laughter and very interesting ideas—squids, ice cream, cats, lava, or a portal (to name a few). We ended this lesson with several reads of the chart. They especially loved it when I demonstrated what **not** to do when reading (reading backwards and from bottom to top).

Fourth Read: Celebration

For our final, celebratory read of *Sheep in a Jeep* we went out to our school's field and read it on the grass, and then played a game of "What Time is it, Mr. Sheep?" After coming back inside, we practiced reading the excerpt a few more times in preparation for our performance in front our buddy class. We

Reading with a big buddies or big brother.

wanted to share the passage to show them that we were becoming "good" readers. As a final celebration, our big buddies joined us in a choral read of the chart excerpt. We plan to post the chart paper on a wall where it can be re-read to build fluency.

My Experience and Learning

What worked best for me throughout the Shared Reading process was having a detailed plan that outlined my goals for every reading. In this way, I felt confident that I could maintain my students' interest during the repeated readings of the book. Using a short passage to practice fluency also worked well for this group. By the end of the week most of them had memorized the entire text and they were absolutely glowing with confidence.

Many of my students are now beginning to use expression when they read and recognize different types of punctuation. I discovered that my students' energy, engagement and attention span varied depending on the time of day a Shared Reading lesson was presented. In response, I will create a consistent routine for when we take part in Shared Reading. I believe that my students learned or strengthened many literacy skills during the week. Identifying sight words, directionality of print, return sweep and different types of punctuation are only a sampling of the skills we revisited.

This week has been filled with new learning and positive experiences with Shared Reading. Firstly, I know that my teaching practice has changed; I cannot wait to

begin another book with my class. As I reflect on my experience I am left with an overwhelmingly large sense of guilt that I had not started this reading experience with my students earlier in the year.

I cannot contain my excitement about the growth I saw in both my students and me. Not only did they all participate in the choral reading activities but also many of them enjoyed reading the chart excerpt during free-play centers! Interestingly, I felt that the Shared Reading process brought our class together more tightly as a community of learners. We can reflect on the laughter, learning and experiences we shared and

Recreating the book *"Jack and the Beanstalk"* that was read at Shared Reading time. This was completely spontaneous during reading time.

celebrate our growth towards becoming "good" readers. Furthermore, I did not realize how many lessons and activities could stem from one story.

My plan for future Shared Reading is to establish a consistent time each day for this special experience; to continue to explore a book over repeated readings; select books that draw on the interests of my students; and weave essential literacy skills through my lessons. The possibilities seem endless when it comes to Shared Reading, and my students and I are headed for one very exciting journey to strengthen our reading skills!

Integrating Drama, Technology, Imagination and Teacher Collaboration

Resource: *Rosie's Walk* by Pat Hutchins

(Shauna Buffie)

This is a book I have not read for a number of years. My kindergarten, grade one and two colleagues felt the same way and thought it would be worth revisiting with all three of our classes. We collaborated on ideas and decided that we would all work on it at the same time in each of our classrooms.

First Read: Drama, Sequence and Sight Words

The children were gathered on the carpet with rest mats, some had "stuffies," a few were on beanbag chairs and a few on sensory cushions to best meet everyone's needs. From a big book I read the story through without stopping so that the children would get the flow and rhythm of the story. It is a simple and short text so at that same sitting we read it again, this time adding actions with our hands and bodies for the words *across, around, over, past, through* and *under* while seated.

I had a pocket chart up of pictures, without text, showing the sequence of the story for the children to refer to. We then moved around the room pretending to be Rosie the hen and the fox retelling and acting out the sequence of the story and paying attention to the selected words. Later that afternoon I projected *Rosie's Walk* (http://www.schooltube.com/video/13e5b71bb3663c832b4b/Rosies-Walk) through the computer as I have a ceiling-mounted projector and screen. The children particularly enjoyed the music and movement of the illustrations. The text pops up for each page and each word is highlighted as it is read.

This was followed by a simple cut and sequence small book that had the selected words as well as *home* and *"What a good day for a walk."* Again, this highlighted movement and direction words. The children read together with a partner once finished. They then took the book to share with their family so that they were able to retell the story at home.

Second Read: Drama and Comprehension

We re-read the big book again at the carpet pointing out the text with most children joining in aloud with voice and hand/body actions. They were excited to follow along as they knew the story quite well and knew what was going to happen next both with the text and the illustrations. There was much discussion after reading.

Third Read: Writing Own Variations

I projected images from the story as they worked on coloring their pictures. Many had copies of the book beside them as they worked (I had several regular-sized copies in the classroom) and many were very engaged in trying to match the colors to what was projected on the screen. The final project that is ongoing and will take about a week to complete is their very own book following the pattern of Rosie's Walk using all of the words. The children were completely engaged and excited about this project. This is a sample of the text that a child who struggles and needs support created:

> *Kade the fluffy kitten went for a stroll.*
> *Across the wiggly bridge.*
> *Around the lost temple.*
> *Over the snowy mountains.*
> *Past the red house.*
> *Through the green jungle.*
> *Under the grey cave.*
> *And got back in time for warm milk.*

My Experience and Learning

The Shared Reading with the big book and the projected story were both very successful. The children enjoyed the text and illustrations and were very proud that they could remember and re-tell the sequence of the story. They liked acting out the story with one another and took the paper-and-pencil tasks very seriously and worked carefully to complete their tasks with enthusiasm. They most looked forward to taking their completed books to read to our principal, as she values their learning and encourages their visits.

Word work station.

I believe Shared Reading is extremely valuable. It is what I like to do most often on a daily basis in my classroom. I like being able to model reading in an energetic, interactive and fun way. It builds the confidence of my non-readers as they become familiar with the story and then can "read" it again along with the class or on their own. The research supports that it builds confidence, fluency and familiarity as well as providing practice, phonemic awareness and phonics for the children. I could not imagine a classroom without a lot of Shared Reading built into the schedule several times a day.

Janet's Summary

Shared Reading

This quote from Kathleen summarizes the experiences of Shared Reading and why the NELP Report identifies this is one the important factors in achieving literacy success.

Reading with a Buddy, even a 'stuffed' one, is always fun and produces giggles and smiles. This student is reading the story of Chester to our class friend, Chester.

"This week, we set a class goal of having FIVE Shared Reading experiences EVERY DAY!! We have a special place marked on the white board: a number 5 over a rectangle. Each time we do a Shared Reading (all eyes on the text), my 'student of the day' puts one coloured magnet in the rectangle; we look to see how many more reads we need to do. When we have four magnets, the next read is a BUTTERFLY magnet! Then we celebrate with a song. Any more Shared Readings are bonuses!! It is a good visual motivator to remind me to do a LOT more reading WITH the students."

Janet

Part 2: Shared Writing

 ## Janet's Introduction

An Excerpt from Shauna Buffie's Assignment:

"She returned the next morning with Pete who had casts on his legs and a hospital wristband that read:

Pete the Cat
Medical Issue: Broken Legs
Surgery: March 24, 2014
The Royal Queen's Hospital

…This is when the excitement began! The children were so engaged in looking after Pete and his broken legs that we could not leave him alone for a minute all day. That night they asked Mrs. Stevenson [our principal] to take him home with her again. She took him to her doctor that day to have him checked out but later that evening he got into all kinds of mischief at her house. He swung from the chandelier, slid down the banister, swam in the hot tub, unrolled toilet paper, spilled flour, had milk and cookies, brushed his teeth, and was tucked into bed with a bedtime story and his other stuffy friends. She took photographs of Pete getting into mischief so when he returned with her the next morning, we put the pictures up on the projector as she shared the adventures of Pete the Cat's evening in her home. The class was beside themselves with enthusiasm and loved listening to the stories being shared about each photograph."

Now, that's what I was looking for when I gave my class their Shared Writing assignment. This excerpt is from teacher Shauna Buffie's response to the assignment! Enjoy the rest of the wild and wonderful adventure that she (and many other adults) had with her class in the Teacher's Stories section. You won't believe it! (I went right out and bought the full set of Pete the Cat as well as stuffed Pete for my own future use and inspiration.)

Before the assignment, I shared some of the latest thinking from the research and from credible authors through a PowerPoint, in-class activities and discussion.

Janet

Research and Recommended Books

Writing Essentials

(Routman, 2005)

In shared writing, the teacher and students compose collaboratively, the teacher acting as primary scribe for apprentices as she demonstrates, guides, and negotiates the creation of meaningful text, focusing on the task of writing as well as the conventions. Text can be short and completed in one session or long and written over several weeks.

Shared writing builds on what the teacher has already modeled through writing aloud and is the important scaffold that students need in order to attempt their own successful writing. While shared writing can be done in pairs, in groups, or as a whole class, I use it most often with the whole class. I make sure the topic is engaging to students, and then I keep a lively pace throughout the lesson. The classroom, with all the children in front of me, is easy to manage and I relish the opportunity to have every child participate and shine (p. 84).

For all learning, but especially for our English language learners, challenged learners and economically underprivileged students, shared writing helps provide the rich oral language modeling that stimulates literacy development. Shared writing taps into students' interests. When work is interesting and students see and value its purpose, they are motivated to work harder... Shared writing is a safe context in which struggling learners can shine. Students who are weak in organization, structure, and form, are often strong in ideas, receiving validation for their ideas in front of their peers, building students' writing confidence, a necessary prerequisite for becoming a writer (p. 85).

Working together in shared writing.

Teaching Literacy in Kindergarten

(McGee & Morrow, 2005)

Shared and Interactive Writing

Shared writing is an activity in which teachers help children cooperatively compose a message that is to be written on enlarged charts. As teachers write the message, negotiated with the children, they talk about what they are doing such as moving over to leave a space for the next word, or listening to beginning sounds to identify which letter they will write. When the message is completed, teachers help children re-read the chart. Eventually, this shared writing moves into interactive writing, in which children write some portions of the message while teachers write other portions.

Purposes of Shared Writing

Shared writing demonstrates a great variety of concepts about print including that writers communicate ideas that can be written, generate ideas for writing by talking, change ideas and refine their language, and consider sequence structures. Children learn that print is written from left to right and from top to bottom in lines of text and that words are composed of letters (Parkes, 2000).

Shared writing can also be used to help children recognize and write alphabet letters. Before writing a word, teachers can tell children what letter they will write. After writing a word, they can have the children name the letters in the word. Later, when children can recognize several alphabet letters and have some directionality concepts, shared writing can be used to demonstrate the *alphabetic principle* (the awareness that printed letters and words are related to spoken sounds and words) and thus help children learn letter-sound relationships (pp. 79, 82).

This kindergartener is writing about a polar bear on an ice floe.

Catching Readers Before They Fall

(Johnson & Keier, 2010)

Community Writing: Writing With Students

Community writing is a time to write together as a class, or in small groups, with all students' contributions given consideration. The writing pieces are generated from authentic talks, shared experiences, or inquiry-based projects. Children may share the pen with the teacher while composing the text, (also called *interactive writing*), or the teacher may write while the children orally compose the text (also called *shared writing*). Andrea McCarrier emphasizes the community aspect by saying, "As collaborators in the process, students become a "writing community" with the support of skilled teaching and making decisions together as they move from ideas to oral language to messages they want to write" (2008, p. 67).

Group or community writing

Community writing pieces are often read and reread *while* composing and *after* completion. The finished pieces are used as familiar text for children to practice putting together an effective reading process system. When writing pieces, children are given many opportunities to practice strategic reading and writing actions and skills:

- Saying the word slowly,
- Listening for sounds,
- Copying out parts of words,
- Putting spaces between words,
- Writing strong leads or endings,
- Including a beginning, middle and end,
- Using dialogue, and
- Rereading,

- Checking and confirming,
- Linking back, (making analogies with words while spelling),
- Self-monitoring, and
- Using text structures of various genres.

In the context of community writing, the students not only learn about letters, sounds and how words work but also about decisions writers make such as what to include, how to best structure a sentence to make a point, or how to organize thoughts on a topic… Community writing can be done in all subject areas, as long as it comes from an authentic shared experience and is surrounded by a great deal of conversation.

Learning to Write and Loving It

(Trehearne, 2011)

Modeled and shared writing, interactive, writing and independent writing are key instructional approaches used to scaffold learning. These approaches allow for a range of assistance from extensive support (modeling and shared writing) to limited support (independent writing). Although it is difficult for teachers to "get it all in," especially in a half-day program, integration definitely does help.. Hand in hand with all the writing approaches go all of the approaches to reading, word work and phonics… Oral language activities that incorporate lots of rhyme, rhythm and song while supporting the development of phonological and phonemic awareness also support writing development. Many writing experiences occur in joyful, playful situations at centers.

Getting the Most Out of Morning Message and Other Shared Writing Lessons

(Dacruze-Payne & Browning-Schulman, 1998)

What is Shared Writing?

Shared Writing is writing with students. It is a way of introducing students to writing *through* writing. When teachers write with students they can make visible what is often invisible. By seeing and hearing an experienced writer write, students begin to understand the connections between oral language and written language. They observe concepts about print in action. They realize that writers can record ideas in a variety of ways and forms; they recognize that writing serves different purposes.

Shared writing can serve as a tool for helping students accomplish an activity they can't yet do on their own; it can bridge the way to independent writing (p. 8).

Working together to write in the missing letters.

What does Shared Writing look like?

Shared Writing lessons may take almost any form—recounting shared experiences, innovations on stories, making lists, writing procedures, letters, observations, messages, newsletters and more. During Shared Writing, a teacher and students talk and decide about what they want to write together. There may be an intended focus, but the content and construction of the message often unfolds as they talk. As the ideas are negotiated and decided upon, the teacher may act as the primary scribe or invite the students to share the pen (p. 8).

Janet's Comment

I highly recommend this book, *Getting the Most Out of Morning Message and Other Shared Writing*, by Payne and Schulman, published by Scholastic. I used it as a guide to create this PowerPoint for my class.

Janet

Grade 1 Readiness:
Someone popped into my classroom at the end of the day and I decided to share some writing samples with her. She exclaimed that my kids were writing more than the Grade 1's down the hallway! It reassured me that we are well on our way to being ready for Grade 1 next year!!! - Michelle Fitterer

SHARED WRITING

*Getting the Most Out of Morning Message
and Other Shared Writing*
Payne and Shulman
Scholastic 1998

Frank Smith (Writing and the Writer) said:

"Writing is learned by writing, by reading, and perceiving oneself as a writer."

What is shared writing?

- "…dancing with a pen." New ZealandMinistry of Education

- Writing **with** students
- Introducing students to writing through writing
- Making visible the invisible
- Understanding the connections between oral and written language
- Observing print concepts in action
- Helping children participate in an activity they can't yet do on their own
- Bridging to independent writing

8

What do you need to consider?
Many Things!

- Purpose for writing
- Skills to be developed
- Level of teacher support required
- Number of students (whole class, small group, individual)
- Who will do the writing (teacher, teacher and students)
- Recounting shared experiences, innovations on stories, making lists, writing procedures, letters, observations, messages, newsletters … and more
- Content and construction unfolds as you talk it through
- Ideas are negotiated and decided on
- Teacher is primary scribe but pen is shared

8

---

20 minutes, one day or over several days!
Think about SETTING THE STAGE…

- Circle time daily news
- A two-week diary of a project
- A SPECIAL area in the classroom – an easel, a smart board, an overhead projector, a special table
- A message home
- Letters to anyone they can think of – news events, radio and TV shows, producers of social media games

8

WHAT DO YOU DO?

GETEXCITED!!!
Decide on the topic together - or not - but
TOGETHER:
Discuss content, format and where to begin.
Compose word by word.
Reread the message up to each word over and over.
Stop to talk about sounds and sight words.
Discuss spaces, capitals, punctuation etc.
Turn over the pen for individual letters or words.
Encourage predictions.
Reference and integrate other instruction in the week.

Why Use Shared Writing?

CHECK THE RESEARCH ON SHARED READING!

...a basis for thinking, talking, reading, writing ,and listening
...helps them explore language and build understandings
....opportunities to construct and organize ideas

Demonstrations by an adult and peers – over and over and over again!

Teachers demonstrate that:

- Writers communicate ideas and thoughts on paper.
- Thought processes occur as you write.
- Talking about experiences can elicit ideas.
- Writing can communicate ideas.
- Writers use different ways to plan what to write (brainstorming, drawing, graphic organizers).
- Writers draft ideas (ways to start and end, expand ideas, and use interesting language).

10

Teachers demonstrate that:

- Writers use strategies such as rereading to check, confirm, or add to writing.
- Writing can be changed and refined.
- Sequence is important.
- Writers need to understand concepts about print.
- Conventions of written language are tools writers need.
- Strategies help determine correct spelling.

10

OTHER GREAT IDEAS

- Create their own Shared Writing Center as a choice
- Make a big book of all your morning messages for reading and rereading and revisiting as a class or at a center.
- Write all shared writing on overheads, then put them in protective folders to reread as a center.
- Learn to read nursery rhymes together then rewrite them with creative twists.
- Compose the texts for wordless books.
- Use shared writing to cover content areas by including informational webs or diagrams and labels.
- Develop a home program for shared writing using the handout.

The Shared Writing Assignment

Once we had completed the Shared Reading Class we moved to the topic of Shared Writing. Most of my class members were well experienced in the primary grades: Some reported that Shared Writing was a daily activity in their classrooms—Morning Message and class-created reports on projects and poems. I had a different agenda:

1. I wanted to get my colleagues out of their daily groove to further explore magical thinking in their classroom writing.

2. I wanted them to infect their children–even at the kindergarten level–with a lifelong love of the writing process.

3. I wanted them to feel the natural connection between joyful Shared Reading and Shared Writing with children, one that is structured on a solid base of foundational and essential literacy skills.

4. I wanted them to understand that all of this magic happens at once: Children learn skills; children read what they can noticing the skills within their reading (with our help); children write what they can using the skills they know—scribbling, drawing and adding words as they are able; and the cycle continues and is accelerated by the experiences we, as teachers, provide them.

5. I wanted them to experience the power of teaching children how to rely on each other to cooperate and collaborate as they share a pen with their teacher and with others.

6. I wanted them too, to find ways to make this a safe experience for vulnerable children who may not ready for writing, but must be included as early as possible so they can experience the joy of knowing that they can be like everyone else and that they are supported in their learning by their peers.

You will see how much of this they achieved when you read the *Teacher's Stories*.

ASSIGNMENT 5 (b) SHARED WRITING

I gave them the following assignment.

Where the Rubber Hits the Road! Where Skills Make Sense!

I want you to choose a picture book that you really like; it inspires you in some way—the art, the characters or the message. With your children create the story that you think goes with the pictures. If you choose a book that does have words I want you to cover the words so the children can't see them and make it a problem that they have to help you with: Together you will have to write your own story to replace the one that is lost.

Telling her own story about the bear.

Teachers' Stories

Results of the Shared Writing Assignment

The Most Amazing and Creative *Pete the Cat* Event!

Resource: *Pete the Cat* by E. Litwin

(Shauna Buffie)

Poor Pete with Casts on his Legs

Plan and Process

In our classroom we have a reading bin full of books about *Pete the Cat* (Eric Litwin) as well as a couple of *Pete the Cat* stuffed animals. We have read and re-read the *Pete the Cat* books many times together as a class, as well as by choice individually or with friends. Our *Pete the Cat* with his yellow coat stuffy has been so well loved that recently his legs were coming unstitched and were literally hanging by a thread. We wrote a note to our principal Mrs. Stevenson asking her if she could please help to fix him. Several students took the note and Pete and delivered them both to her in her office. Mrs. Stevenson took him home that night and kindly had him stitched up. She returned the next morning with Pete who had casts on his legs and a hospital wristband that read

Pete the Cat
Medical Issue: Broken Legs
Surgery: March 24, 2014
The Royal Queen's Hospital

This is when the excitement began! The children were so engaged in looking after Pete and his broken legs that we could not leave him alone for a minute all day. That night they asked Mrs. Stevenson to take him home with her again. She took him to her doctor that day to have him checked out but later that evening he got into all kinds of mischief at her house. He swung from the chandelier, slid down the banister, swam in the hot tub, unrolled toilet paper, spilled flour, had milk and cookies, brushed his teeth, and was tucked into bed with a bedtime story and his other stuffy friends. She took photographs of Pete getting into mischief so when he returned with her the next morning, we put the pictures up on the projector as she shared the adventures of Pete's evening. The class was beside themselves with enthusiasm and loved listening to the stories being shared about each photograph.

And so it began, each night for several nights in a row, Pete began going home with Mrs. Stevenson and each morning the children would be anxiously awaiting her visit to the classroom with Pete and new photos of his adventures. He went out on dates with her and her husband, visited the fire hall and physiotherapist, all the while continuing to get into all kinds of mischief. *Pete the Cat* then came home with me for a couple of nights where he again was up to no good.

Since then he has had sleepovers at several other children's' homes where he continues to misbehave and have outings with their families. All of the families were fully engaged in our fun and sent in a memory stick or e-mail photos so that I could show them the next day and have the children orally share their stories.

Most recently, a *Shaw Cable* worker on a truck saw my principal taking pictures and asked what was happening. When she explained, he wanted to be involved and took Pete with him to work for a whole week where Pete made a new friend, the *Shaw Bear* stuffy, who now lives in our classroom with us. How exciting to receive photos each day from a member of the community who has no connection at all to our classroom and has randomly asked to be involved! Pete continues to go on adventures with family.

This was not at all planned but just something that happened and because of the aliveness and excitement level of the children, I pushed other plans aside and decided one of the activities I would engage the children in would be to begin writing and compiling a book of Pete and all of his adventures. For several days in a row, we would brainstorm on chart paper words and ideas that we would need to write about the adventures he had had the night before. We would share the pen at the chart paper. The children could then choose a photograph of Pete on one of his adventures and glue it onto a paper that had a spot for the photograph and a spot for writing.

Pages the children wrote for the book.

The more independent children used some of our Shared Writing on the chart paper to write about the picture that they had chosen that day. For some children, I would share the pen with them to get their ideas written down to be included in the book. Other children needed me to help write their words in a highlighter first for them to trace over. Each child has now written several pages for our shared book. The writing pages and new photographs of Pete are put out as a daily choice activity for those that wish to continue writing more pages for our book.

Flat Pete?

Another activity that I created was a mailing of *Flat Pete*. Usually each spring we read the book *Flat Stanley* by Jeff Brown. Based on the character in the book we would then mail our own *Flat Stanley* out on adventures. Because of our engagement with Pete it seemed appropriate to create a *Flat Pete* and mail him out. The children colored their own *Flat Pete*, then an envelope was sent home to be addressed and mailed to someone they knew. Together we created a letter to go into the envelope with Pete. We then stuffed our envelopes with *Flat Pete* and a return envelope and our letter with the following request:

"I am mailing my Flat Pete to you. Please help him to have some adventures. After 10 days, send him back (envelope enclosed) telling me where he went. Please take some pictures of Pete on his adventures, or pick up some postcards and send them too. I will be excited to see what he does. I hope you and Pete have a great time!"

Then we took a walk up the hill to the end of the block to the mailbox. We are now waiting, as our *Flat Pete*s should start to return to us within a couple of weeks [March, 2014].

Flat Pete travels everywhere!

The Children's Response and My Learning

This experience reinforced how important it is for children to be excited about their learning. I knew I had created the magic when one little girl who does not speak often came up to me and whispered in my ear, "But why, Ms. Buffie, does Pete only come alive when he goes with Mrs. Stevenson or you? Why don't we ever see him come alive in our classroom too?" Every child in the classroom was fully engaged in the Shared Writing experiences around *Pete the Cat*. It allowed them to work at their own level. It allowed me to share the pen with all of them to begin with, when we wrote our ideas each day on the chart paper, but then allowed some to take that shared pen experience and take a safe risk and try it on their own.

The Potential Power of Wordless Picture Books for Budding Authors

Resource: *Follow Me* by Nancy Tafuri

(Margie Radigan)

Plan and Process

For the Shared Writing assignment I chose the book *Follow Me* by Nancy Tafuri. The story takes place on the seashore and since we live on the east coast of Vancouver Island, I thought it fitting to offer an opportunity for the students to make personal connections to living near the ocean. I also chose this book because it had beautiful illustrations of local sea life. *Follow Me* is a story without words, which outlines the experiences of a curious young seal pup as he ventures away from his mother to explore along the seashore. The pup comes into contact with crabs, seagulls, sea otters and various tidal pool creatures that co-exist in his seaside habitat.

Janet's Comment

This is one of the most beautiful picture books I have seen from an artistic perspective. It is worthy of being a coffee table book in any of our homes or classrooms.)

Janet

The first reading occurred prior to our regular [Language Arts] routine Monday morning. I invited the students to join me at the carpet where we reviewed the variety of Shared Writing activities that we do regularly. I asked them to think of all the ways we share the pen during our school days and, with some guided support, the students recalled the following: Daily Morning Message, writing notes to invite our principal and counselor to join us for a Virtues pizza lunch that the students had earned, creating a class promise and co-creating the menus for our restaurant center.

More recently, we wrote to the *Nanaimo Food Share* (NFS) and to the *World Wildlife Foundation of Canada* (WWF) explaining that we were learning how we could help the polar bears in Northern Canada as they struggle with the melting of the sea ice.

- First reading: prior to introducing the wordless picture story, I explained that we would read the story in silence. With the use of body language and facial expressions, I made notice of the key focal points on each page to the students.

- The second reading occurred after lunch that day, at which time we walked and talked through the story making predictions, thinking out loud and sequencing the events as they unfolded across the pages.

- The third reading occurred the next day when the students were invited to begin retelling the story. We first discussed the importance of a title because titles have the power to make us more curious and wanting to know what the story may be about. The students were invited to share their ideas for the title and they chose to title the story, With Me.

The Children's Response

Reflecting on how the students responded to the Shared Writing experience, I asked a staff member to videotape parts of the weeklong, Shared Writing activities. When viewing the footage later I was amazed by how engaged the children were from the beginning when I turned the pages silently; during the brain storming of what was happening at the beginning, middle and end of the story; and during their collaborative writing and retelling of the story.

During the third reading experience the children were encouraged to co-create the story based on their personal background knowledge and creative observations. They engaged in a rich dialogue based on their observations of the setting, characters and how the character showed emotions. The students experimented with sorting the picture story into three categories: beginning, middle and end. During this reading one student raised his hand and asked, "Is the seal pup a boy or a girl?" I responded by turning the question back to the students and **they** decided that the seal would be a boy.

My Learning

It is my opinion that introducing wordless picture books as a basis of storytelling provides a powerful opportunity to encourage children to read and to write. This is an important skill because it assists the students to observe how authors tell stories (even stories without words) and it empowers the students to see themselves as writers. During center time, I asked for volunteers who would be interested in illustrating the pages of our book. Four keen artists volunteered to get together to plan about who would do which page and what key traits they would draw to portray the meaning of our shared story.

These students decided to make cards for their friends and family.

Shared Writing can be used for a multitude of purposes, from creating stories, writing letters, creating birthday cards, sending notes to the office, inviting another class to attend a special celebration, writing to ask for more paper towel or hand soap from our custodian, to writing thank you letters to our big buddies.

Shared Writing activities also provide me, the teacher, with a context through which I can introduce, address or reinforce concepts of text, the conventions associated with the English language as well as reinforce the key phonological awareness skills, the use of punctuation, prefix/suffixes, sight words, rhyme, and segmenting. For example, through conversations with my students (prior to, during and after the writing experience) I can explain the focus of the writing task such as *ing* endings and punctuation. The students can add dialogue, feelings and expressions while they explore language: naming objects, adding adjectives, adverbs, nouns and verbs. For this assignment, I focused on emphasizing the importance of finger spaces between words and the directionality of letters: the left-to-right, top-to-bottom orientation of the English written language.

In closing, most of the students can reread or retell the story that we interactively wrote this week, which illustrates the point that they "own" this piece of writing. This rich, interactive storybook experience is a powerful and valuable strategy to captivate and motivate young students to see themselves as readers and writers.

These students are collaborating on a story.

A Teacher Leaves her Comfort Zone: What Results!

Resource: *The Colors* by Monique Felix
(Michelle Fitterer)

Plan and Process

Day #1: To set the stage for the Shared Writing process I set up a comfortable and calm learning environment with low lighting, optional seating, and cozy blankets or pillows. As well, before beginning the first read of our picture book, we reviewed how our brains work best and how "calling out" can interrupt the learning process for our classmates, especially during visualization activities. This brief conversation set very clear expectations for our first read of *The Colors*. The final step before reading was for my class to warm up their imaginations (tickling the tops of their heads), so that they could read the pictures to tell a story in their minds. As I flipped through the story I refrained from adding any words and simply used facial expressions to convey how the mouse might be feeling on his journey. Throughout the read, my class only needed subtle reminders to stay focused; the children were engaged until the final page!

Day #2: One could sense the buzz of energy that arose the following day when I pulled out *The Colors* and revealed that we would be adding thoughts, words, and feelings to the story for our second read. In preparation for a brainstorm that would follow the read aloud, I had colored markers and a piece of chart paper ready to go at the carpet. My plan for this read-aloud was to narrate the story page by page and integrate my students' ideas where possible. We paused several times to highlight elements of the story (characters and/or problems) that were missed during the first read, as well as to discuss the mouse's emotions throughout his journey.

To conclude this read, we brainstormed a list of words that we might use in our Shared Writing the following day. Immediately, they made the connection that we would need bullets to make our list, so the special helper placed a column of dots down the chart paper. While we co-created our list of words I made sure to reinforce their understanding of the connection between oral and written language. Chunking words, sounding out letter sounds, and writing and re-reading words with correct directionality were all a focus of this piece of Shared Writing.

Day #3: For our first Shared Writing experience (of a book), my class came to the conclusion that it should be **six** pages long, because this was how old many of them were and it was their favorite number. As a result, we focused on two images for each of the beginning, middle and end of the story. Using our list of words from the day before, we began to share the pen and write our story. In advance, I had photocopied and enlarged several images from the book to guide us through this process. As ideas were being offered I would call students up to the chart paper to record letters, sight words, or punctuation based on their ability (ensuring success for all). I encouraged the rest of the class to re-read the text and watch for finger spaces, capital letters and the correct spelling of our sight words. This helped sustain their interest in the *Shared Writing* process when it was not their turn to share the pen. In one sitting, we were able to create our story.

Day #4: To illustrate and complete our Shared Writing I had volunteers paint the blown-up images from the book, co-create a title page and number the pages, as well as sign their names as the authors of our story. When it was complete, I modeled how to read through the story with expression and fluency–paying careful attention to punctuation. They were so proud and excited that we visited our librarian to read her our new story. *Mouse's Adventure* now rests in our classroom library of big books where its pages are already fraying from being repeatedly read and enjoyed!

Children's Response

I couldn't have asked for a more wonderful response from my students! Firstly, many of them made the connection that Shared Reading and Shared Writing were very similar. As we had already established a comfortable atmosphere and clear expectations for Shared Reading, the class understood what and why we were taking part in Shared Writing activities. The most exciting response from my class was when I brought out the completed product during our family reading time. They couldn't wait to get their hands on this giant book that we had created together. It is not uncommon to see up to four students gathered around reading our class effort, *Mouse's Adventure*.

My heart glows when I see them pointing to each word as they read the text from left to right and with return sweep! During quiet reading times throughout the day, my vulnerable learners will rush to snatch up our big book to read to our class pet named Cuddles. This is especially exciting because these learners often avoid reading activities by going to the washroom or wandering aimlessly around the classroom. Finally, the cutest response from one my students was when he attempted to squeeze the big book into his tiny reading bin! The whole class erupted in laughter over the funny sight.

My Learning

I often preach that you learn the most when you make mistakes and experience new things out of your comfort zone. This Shared Writing experience proved to be one of those moments! What surprised me the most was how comfortable I felt with Shared Reading in comparison to this week's assignment on Shared Writing. I am discovering that I need more time and practice with releasing the amount of control I have during a writing activity. For example, I froze when students began firing suggestions and words at me to write down on the chart paper. I wanted to honor everyone's suggestions, but knew that it would be impossible to include *every* sentence or word that was offered. What is more, I had to constantly remind myself not to add transitions or conjunctions to improve flow to the piece of writing. As in many classes, I had the added challenge of managing complex behaviors of the students who became disengaged when they were not sharing the pen. Having the class monitor the writer and reread the text to check for finger spacing, punctuation and spelling worked well to engage most students.

Regardless of the discomfort I was feeling throughout the Shared Writing process, the outcome was successful and rewarding for both my students and for me. We were able to review and apply our understanding of print concepts and phonological awareness while we wrote the beginning, middle and end of the story. What is more, this exercise has inspired my class to create mini-books in our writing center during free play. It is wonderful seeing them transfer their learning from our whole-group lessons and apply it in a new situation. Shared Writing is another literacy activity that encourages students to see themselves as readers and writers. What may have been my biggest learning from this experience is to share the pen more often and to relax! Now, when I plan a Shared Reading lesson I will always leave open the possibility of a Shared Writing activity to follow.

Summary

It became clear to me quickly how naturally Shared Reading leads to powerful Shared Writing experiences. It is necessary to have a clear vision and plan before beginning, so that I can feel calm and confident throughout the Shared Writing process. In this short time I have realized how powerful the outcome has been for **all** of my learners. In the next few weeks, I intend to draw on the recent excitement about the *Don't Let the Pigeon Drive the Bus* series, and create many classroom books! Like Shared Reading, I will include Shared Writing experiences in my short- and long-term planning, as I feel it has strengthened my teaching practice!

Writing: Their Least Favorite Activity? Not Any More!

(Michelle Fitterer)

Seat work (journal writing) used to be my children's least favorite activity. The moans and groans would begin as soon as they walked in and saw the "shape of the day." For several months, I was stumped and wondered *why* they detested writing and drawing so much. Rather than putting the blame on them and what appeared to be a lack in motivation to write and do seatwork, I began to reflect on what I was doing and how I could change to suit their needs. After a guest speaker, Ann George, spoke at our university class, it all became clear. I was putting too much pressure on them to complete their journal in that **one** sitting. I saw myself encouraging everyone to draw their picture and then quickly add labels or a sentence or two. There was no feeling of a relaxed atmosphere. This has all changed.

Ann George proposed that they could work on their journal several times throughout the week to get to their finished product. She also said that her journal writing classroom time is LOUD, that she allows kids to get up and help others with spelling and sounding-out words. I was so caught up in the final product and trying to be like other k classes, that I was creating a stressful environment for my kids.

Now, if you walked into my room when we are working on our journals, you would hear jazz music playing over our sound system; the room would be alive with conversation; kids would be sounding out words and sharing ideas with others; you'd see kids counting their fingers to determine how many words there are in their sentence they are about to write; then there would be my two EA's (Education Assistants) and I walking around supporting students with phonics and segmentation. I let my class know that when I work on a drawing or piece of writing that I sometimes needs several days to finish it. This has helped them relax when we have to close our books and move onto another activity. They no longer feel like they have to scramble to finish their work. Ahhhh, how proud I am of myself for changing my writing routine to suit my students' needs. I am even more proud of my students and the work they are producing.

Janet's Summary

Teacher Kathleen provides an insightful summary of how essential skill and sight word learning combined with Shared Reading and Shared Writing experiences brought literacy life for her most vulnerable children:

"I think I am starting to remember how to PLAY again thanks to this project—not just PLAYING during Free Play Centers, but learning how exciting and fun it is to integrate literacy into play and to integrate play into literacy learning! The children LOVE to play *Green Eggs and Ham* [sight word game] every time they have a chance. As a result, one of my weaker alphabet students read ALL TEN of his sight-words to his Mom after school yesterday, AND my group of "most vulnerable" students informed me yesterday at the Writing Work Station, that they were NOT ready to rotate stations after 15 minutes and they wanted to KEEP ON writing in their books. I gave everyone an extra five minutes, but they were still intent on their work, so I rotated everyone else and left those five at their table. Now that's motivation!"

I highly recommend the book *Using Picture Books to Teach Writing With the Traits* by Ruth Culham, published by Scholastic. She explores, as in her other books, ideas, sentence fluency, organization, word choice, voice, conventions and presentation. The book also has an annotated bibliography of more than 200 picture books with teacher-tested lessons.

She says, "After adding picture books to my toolbox, my students' writing improved. Their work got better all the way around–and they had more fun creating it. Finding that picture books could be used to teach writing to students of all ages was one of my greatest, most delightful discoveries."

Janet

Writing a story about Pete the Cat.

Learning the joy of reading early.

CHAPTER SEVEN

Stepping Stone 7

Involve Families: Practice and Celebrate

From Birth to Vulnerability?

 Janet's Introduction

Vulnerable children often have vulnerable parents. That is a reality we must keep foremost in our minds as we work with these children. My dear friend Clara used to say to her staff who complained about vulnerable children: "Parents didn't keep the good kids in the closet: They sent us the best ones they have."

At the birth of our firstborn child, we knew that "anything could be" with our precious new arrival. Whatever our image of success—from leader of our country to premiere ballerina—we imagined years of laughter, happiness and joy ahead. Whatever dreams we contemplated as we examined the miracle of those perfect little toes, we felt we were cradling great potential in our arms.

"Anything could be" promise.

There isn't a parent who has watched her two-year-old toddler and not felt with great conviction, that here was a child who was something really special, a child more wonderful than any other two year old she knew; something about her child made her shine brighter than all the others. As they take their child to the first day of school, parents are optimistic but naturally somewhat apprehensive. How will their child adapt socially? Will the child be a successful reader and writer?

So many parental dreams are shattered when teachers take over responsibility for their children five days a week, seven hours a day. We can only imagine how it feels to be those parents when, after just a few months of school, they are asked to a special meeting at school to hear news they can't or don't want to believe. Their child is biting other children or bolting for the door at every opportunity – running away somewhere, maybe even home; or their child cries frequently, retreats under tables, is inconsolable; or their child resists sharing toys with other children and bullies others to obtain a prime toy; or their child doesn't seem to respond to even the simplest instruction or request, perhaps resorting to bizarre behavior, barking like a dog while hiding under tables. Resolving such problems means we need parents' support and cooperation. We ask questions: Could there be a hearing problem? Would the parents agree to psychometric testing, or to see a specialist, or a school counsellor? Would the parents be willing to keep him at home for half the day until he learns to cope with a large group of children and classroom routines?

Grandpa reads to his grandchild who is loving the story.

These are true stories told by my university students who are experienced, practicing teachers. From their viewpoints they too were stressed and worried for the safety of the child exhibiting these behaviors, as well as for the other 24 children in their care who were at risk. Some children demonstrated violent tendencies; the teachers were frustrated that they couldn't implement the motivating activities they had planned due to the attention demanded by the challenging children in their care; they were angry that the school system was ill-prepared to provide additional adult resources in their classrooms in order to make the situation more manageable. A common and understandable conundrum is that most of us don't know who our kindergarten children will be until they arrive at our school door, nor do we know how they will adjust to a large group of children until school is underway. How can we plan for them?

How did that glorious and hopeful dream fade between birth and age five? How did these children become vulnerable? Although no harm was intended in the following situations, vulnerable learners were the ultimate outcome. In one instance, economic issues dictated both parents having to work; they couldn't find qualified care, and the child suffered secret abuse from a caregiver. Other parents were school dropouts: books were not a priority in their homes. A hearing deficit went unnoticed in one child. Another had undiagnosed autism but was just on the margins of the spectrum. Immigrant twins from Syria were still trying to adjust to the North American culture after escaping crowded refugee camps. Some children were just plain hungry. Some children were puzzles. They came from middle-class and upper-middle-class homes but manifested no apparent reason for the challenges they seemed to face. In one case study, I discovered that a child in an upper middle class home entered school language-delayed despite being bilingual; her nanny was an immigrant and spoke almost no English!

Teachers and Parents: Working Together for Vulnerable Children

We all have in mind the best for our children and, whatever our circumstances, we do what we can to help them realize their potential. Working on building a strong team relationship is the best investment we can make in moving vulnerable children forward. What do we learn from the research and leading authors?

Positive Solutions: Professionals Must Set the Stage!

We are the professionals. We can set the stage for a cooperative relationship that can only result in a true partnership. Our staff at Northridge School excelled at working with parents of vulnerable children and we had many such children! In order to create those cooperative relationships, we must begin the minute we meet the children. I am happy to share some of our best strategies with you.

Building Relationships with Parents: Ideas!

- Ned, our kindergarten teacher, visited every registered kindergarten child's home in June. He brought a surprise bag of summer reading, and donations from local dollar stores. He took pictures of the child, parents and himself together with a promise of a welcoming school entry in September.

- The entire staff agreed to call every parent in the first three weeks of school to report something positive about their child's experience. They took pictures and sent them home every week for every child. Volunteer parents made this task easy. Staff called five parents every week to ask how they were feeling and I was able to provide substitute time to relieve them. In this way every parent received a call every month. Email has made this easier but nothing takes the place of direct voice contact. We logged the phone call contents to use as references later or to pass them on to the school counsellor or other staff for follow-up.

- We invited parents to form a cadre of volunteers with over 100 people joining the ranks; the motivating difference was that they could volunteer for the category that interested them most: classroom game tutoring, game-making as requested by staff, photocopying, sharing special talents like dance or yoga or painting, and reading with individuals in the library. They became our goodwill ambassadors in the community.

Parent volunteers built a reading loft, used for many activities.

- If we heard inaccurate gossip about the school, I would phone the parent(s) to set the record straight, gently and kindly. If I believed there was any truth in the stories, I dealt with it internally. In this way, parents and teachers became accountable, and we were able to deal with issues before they became crises.

- We had a graphic artist develop a school "happy note" that we could send home spontaneously. Teachers kept a record of frequency so that they could ensure all children and families received reinforcement every month.

- We recorded children reading or finishing a project and sent the evidence home.

- We designed checklists of critical skills, sent them home and asked parents to keep track of skill development over the course of the year as we kept them informed.

- As principal, I volunteered to attend coffee parties in the neighbourhood to discuss school topics that interested parents. I knew that was where school issues were frequently discussed. It was fun and effective.

- We set up a corner of the library as a parent information center on child-rearing and education. We added a coffee pot and room for strollers. It became a busy center for parents waiting to pick up children or a place where lonely parents could make new friends.

- We designed a summary report of the week's work for children, initialled it and asked parents to return it with questions or comments.

- We opened the school in the evenings for families to access the gym for sports games and the library, with staff members taking turns hosting the evenings to ensure safety and facility issues. These events were a great success.

- Our district mandated three reports a year: We met that criteria, but staff members agreed to report on three children a week, in writing and in person if necessary. I highly recommend this process: It resulted in less stress for teachers who didn't have to write 25 report cards all at the same time; they could choose the children they felt were most in need of a report at that time; they were able to balance challenging student reports with more positive feedback.

Celebrating Parents

- We celebrated parents at every opportunity. We gave volunteers roses unexpectedly; we nominated them for media acknowledgements; we wrote letters to the newspaper and arranged for reporters to feature their contributions; we left child-created art gifts anonymously on their doorstops; we set up messages of thanks by raising spotlit signs on the school roof at Christmas.

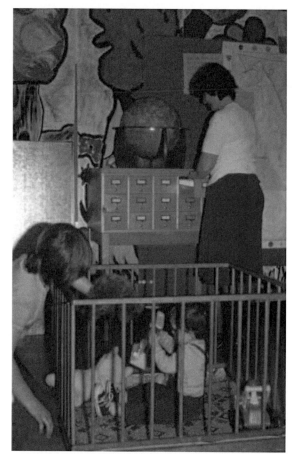

Parents were welcome to bring babies to school.

What is the point I really want to make in this chapter? Parents of vulnerable children, or vulnerable parents of children, need our compassion and patience. We have the skills and experience. Our ultimate goal is a successful education for their children, and we know how to achieve it. We will go farther and faster if we work with parents as a team, and we know that at times, we have to sit on our own feelings in order to hear and understand theirs.

Remember—It's all about relationships, relationships, relationships!

Janet

Research and Recommended Books

Reading Essentials

(Routman, 2003)

Communicate with parents before problems arise. Make phone calls early in the school year with a compliment about each student, explain the use of invented spelling by young writers before papers go home, share required rubrics and grading guidelines, and so on. Establish a relationship with parents prior to school-mandated conferences so they are comfortable talking with you about their child. If concerns later arise, the parent will be more likely to listen without becoming defensive (p. 42).

When Readers Struggle: Teaching that Works

(Pinnell & Fountas, 2009)

Connections to students' homes are very important in supporting struggling readers. The intervention lessons include activities children can take home to do with their family members. Often, the activity is the same one children have done in the classroom. And children should always take home a book they have previously read with success. Home activities should:

- Allow the child to demonstrate success.
- Be very clear to families in terms of the routines and tasks (send a short letter home with each task).
- Demonstrate the child's ability to use phonics, write, and read continuous text (p. 513).

Summer Reading:
Closing the Rich/Poor Reading Achievement Gap

(Allington & McGill-Franzen, 2013)

Janet's Comment

This is a very important book about an issue that few schools have successfully met. If we understand the following quote from Allington and McGill-Franzen, why would we work so hard to raise reading levels for ten months a year and then ignore reading levels in the summer months?

"…summer reading loss accounts for roughly 80% of the reading achievement gap between more and less economically advantaged children."

According to these authors, "It seems now that the lack of reading activity during the summer months that some children experience is the primary basis for explaining what has been observed repeatedly. Poor children typically lose reading proficiency during the summers and more advantaged children show modest reading growth during the same period." This is largely due to lack of access to books.

In Chapter Two, a guest author explores experimental studies demonstrating that increasing access to books, both during the school year and during the summer months, has more positive effects on reading achievement than most other educational interventions. In Chapter Three the authors summarize studies that feature a variety of creative and affordable ways schools have enhanced access to books for disadvantaged children. These strategies focus on self-selected, voluntary reading organized through a carefully designed spring book fair program. Reading achievement increased by up to six months rather than two to three months of reading loss. Chapter Four emphasizes the importance of self-selection of books that reflect a "kid's culture."

The book introduces case studies of a variety of successful summer reading loss projects that demonstrate can-do creative approaches to supporting children through the summer:

- Book fair interventions,
- A mobile RV (recreational vehicle) making neighbourhood stops with teacher tutors on board,
- A phone-in reading program on the school answering machine,
- School library openings during the summer,
- Creative school partnerships with public libraries,
- Community businesses offering rewards and incentives for families to read,
- Mid-summer reading reunions with volunteer teachers,
- A post card to teacher project as each book is read and logged, and
- A first-grade teacher who created her own *Summer Books* truck-mobile to visit her students at their own homes.

In my opinion, every school staff in the country should conduct a compulsory book-club review of *Summer Reading Loss*. It is a compelling read; educators will feel a moral responsibility to act.

Janet

Early Literacy in Preschool and Kindergarten

(Beaty & Pratt, 2011, pp. 262, 263)

Family Literacy Workshops

Some programs help parents become involved with their children's reading at home or through workshops held in the preschool or kindergarten. Mothers are often the primary participants, but some fathers and grandparents attend. Meier (2000) discusses a series of family literacy workshops he has conducted. His goals include the following:

5. To increase dialogue about literacy among families,
6. To introduce ways of reading with and to preschool-age children,
7. To introduce a variety of high-quality multicultural children's literature, and
8. To discuss children's literacy development and cultural and linguistic diversity.

Parents contribute questions about reading and writing with their children, such as how often to read or the appropriate content of books. Meier also asks participants to share things that work for them in their home reading. Book reading is demonstrated, showing enjoyable and effective ways to read out loud.

Burningham and Deer (2000) tell of research suggesting that parents with lower literacy levels place more importance on providing their children with tools such as flash cards, coloring books and posters, whereas those with high levels of literacy place more importance on modeling literate behaviors through reading to and with their children. Both may be important in setting up workshops, just as combining family literacy bags with in-school workshops seems to be important.

Dever and Burts's (2002) workshops used literacy bags containing three high quality children's books on a common theme along with some activities and a parent guidebook that included information on how to read and discuss the books with the children. It reminded parents to be seated comfortably so that the children could see the text and pictures and encouraged them to re-read the books at the children's request. Questions to guide discussions about the books were also included. Four two-hour workshops were held in the evening in children's classrooms and a library/media center. During the first hour, teachers worked with parents on how to use the literacy bags and free materials such as store ads, coupons, sales flyers, and junk mail. During the second hour, the children joined them, and the parents engaged their children in the literacy activities they had just learned. Translators were available for Spanish-speaking parents. Free books were given to the parents at the end of each session.

Building Oral Language Skills in Pre-K and K

(Middendorf, 2009)

Janet's Comment

I highly recommend this book. It is research-based and, at the same time, rich with practical ideas for whole, group activities and strategies and oral language in centers. I particularly like how she emphasizes the connections between oral language, phonemic awareness, writing, conceptual knowledge, comprehension and emotional relationships.

Janet

"My goal in this book is to help you effortlessly weave focused oral language activities into your busy day … and this book will provide you with a plan, a focus, and a resource for making the most of those opportunities" (p. 6).

Particularly impressive is a 40-page chapter on how to engage families in oral language activities in concert with home where the author proposes the following creative and practical strategies:

- Designing Home Talk topics to address academic standards and promote oral language,
- Writing class newsletters that help parents respond to the "nothing" response to inquiries about school activities,
- Encouraging parents to do parallel thinking on a Family Comment page,
- Assembling a Class Family Album that connects school family to home family,
- Promoting language and literacy through Book Talks,
- Creating take-home bags for learning fun, and
- A Home-Talk strategy that reinforces to families the power of conversation, acknowledges the family's role as the best teacher for their child, and asks families to share stories from their childhood memories (p. 87).

Teachers' Stories

Introducing Teacher
Ann George

Janet's Comment

Ann, a primary teacher for her entire career, has been a regular speaker at our Summits for Vulnerable Children. Children excel in the dynamic learning environment she creates and parents love her. In my visits to her classroom, I witnessed the excitement her children have for becoming readers. We called her sessions at the Summits *Operation Alphabet*. Her students are so motivated by the alphabet that they even spend snack and lunchtime celebrating the many ways they can arrange their apple pieces to create letters. The playful, competitive challenge becomes infectious; it isn't long before letters are transformed into words, and parents are pulled into the classroom celebration to read, select books and admire progress as they pick up and drop off their children.

Ann is a joy: I invited her, as a contribution to this book, to describe how she engages parents. The following seven stories are written by Ann and describe:

- Heart-warming stories about connections between children, teachers and parents,
- Appreciation parents show when children make progress,
- How parental fears and anxieties can express themselves negatively and how teachers can facilitate cooperation,
- Interesting, practical ways to build relationships with parents and literacy support for children,
- Ideas for *Home Reading Programs,*
- Strategies for matching books with abilities, and
- A heightened consciousness about the need for parent-school partnerships.

Janet

1. Celebratory Tales

- One of my favourite memories from my teaching career comes out of the home reading program. A little girl registered in my class was the first member of her family to attend school in Canada. Circumstances had led her family to move to four nations over the years and when she began Kindergarten, they were living in a predominantly English speaking part of the country. Her parents were already fluent speakers of five or six different languages, but were English Language Learners. Each day, the family would read the simple home reading texts together, and as the child learned extremely quickly, she was soon reading with beautiful expression and strong comprehension.

- When the school year ended, the mother returned the final home reading title to me and thanked me profusely for my role in helping her learn to read English. She had learned English grammatical structures and the rhythm and pronunciation of the spoken language along with her child through daily practice with simple children's stories. This mother's competence in the English language grew until she was able to enter university and then qualify to practise dentistry in Canada, as she had done in her native country.

- When their first child entered school, one set of young parents had poor skills in interacting and communicating with their son and appeared unsure of their role as parents, despite an obvious love for their child and a genuine effort on their part to engage with him. They were very fortunate to be in a class with a highly nurturing group of parents who subtly modeled conversing and interacting with young children and made sure to include this family in birthday parties and outings to the park.

During Family Reading Time each school morning, various parents included the boy in their story groups and encouraged his parents to join them. Over time, this family learned to look at books and read together, and enjoyed a physical closeness that they hadn't known before. By the time the home reading program began later in the school year, the parents had

Volunteer parents include students in Family Reading Time.

become much more patient with their child and were able to incorporate my suggestions for supporting and developing the boy's early reading skills.

Children who are taught the importance of expression and fluency as they learn to read are generally excited about their reading as it flows naturally, sounds interesting and draws others in. They like to read humorous excerpts to their friends and receive many accolades from their parents and teachers about their reading proficiency. To develop these highly important reading skills in children, I introduce them to simple but humorous children's stories such as Mo Willem's *Elephant and Piggie* tales. I think adults enjoy them as much as children do, as parents and children can assume different roles and read the characters' funny conversations aloud using a variety of facial expressions and voices.

- After school one day, a parent dropped by the classroom to share her enjoyment of these stories with me and to exclaim about how surprised and pleased she was with her child's oral reading skill. The conversation lasted several minutes and as that parent was leaving, another parent came to see me to deliver exactly the same message. There was much laughter and shared delight as these two parents formed a bond over children's literature. They understood the value of fluent and expressive reading at an early age and made it a point throughout that school year to help other parents come to the same understanding.

Learning to enjoy reading with a big sister.

- Parents are encouraged to bring their pre-school children into the classroom for Family Reading Time each day. The younger siblings enjoy listening to stories and looking at books and learn to emulate their kindergarten age brothers and sisters, choosing books from the shelves and lying on the floor or sitting at a table to enjoy a book. Some pre-schoolers join informal story groups while others prefer to engage with books independently. What is common to both groups of pre-schoolers is a reluctance to end book time and leave the classroom as their older siblings gather with the teacher to begin whole group work. Parents occasionally have to carry a noisily protesting pre-schooler out of the classroom.

When these children begin their kindergarten year, they already know the classroom expectations and have established a love of books and reading.

2. Cautionary Tales

- With good intentions, one family had engaged someone to teach their child to read before he started school. Unfortunately, this person was not a trained reading teacher and the child developed some undesirable reading behaviors as he learned to read. The aim of the parents was to have the child reading at an advanced level so he could develop his knowledge base and satisfy his curiosity about the world in general. When he entered kindergarten, the child was being provided with texts well beyond his reading ability and maturity level. Reading for this child was a slow and laborious process where meaning was lost, fluency did not exist and he was reduced to sounding out isolated words.

- I started this child's home reading program with high interest stories containing a reduced amount of print. He needed to develop strong basic reading skills and understand that books convey meaningful information and interesting stories and do not contain just a series of word deciphering activities. The parents were highly resistant to what they saw as a demotion for their child and a less than challenging approach to instruction on my part. Initially, I focused on the child reading phrases and sentences as a fluent unit, rather than the word-by-word monotonous approach he was accustomed to using. He also needed to focus on reading for meaning, as he was in the habit of substituting random words with the same initial letter (table for together, coming for cat, puppet for playground). In time, the child became a more fluent and independent reader. However, I never really convinced the parents of the importance of consistently providing their son with texts appropriate to his age and reading ability.

- As children complete their individual reading sessions each day, a sticker is attached to their reading bags as a reward and an incentive to bring their books to school. For nearly all children, it is seen as a celebration of their growth and accomplishment in learning to read and a visual reminder of the number of books they have read. At the end of the school year, the sticker covered reading bag is a memento of the home reading program. However, for the occasional student, the focus becomes the sticker collection and not the reading success. One child in particular was absent from school for several days and she and her parents both demanded that I put a sticker on her reading bag for each day she had missed. I worked closely with that family over a period of time to help them come to the understanding that the goal for the child was to become a reader and not a sticker collector.

- Another child and his family were extremely competitive and their goal for him was to be the first child in the class to read all books in a home reading series or to reach milestones such as twenty books read. (Years ago, I gave children a certificate for every ten books read, but discontinued that practice as it was time consuming and the pieces of paper were not particularly valued by young students.) This particular family would ask to take home several books per day, instead of one as the other children did, in order to read a greater number than the child's classmates. For the first few days, my impression was that they were highly interested and motivated in the child learning to read, but when I realized their true intention, I restricted them to one book per day. The family's focus had been on the child reading a volume of words, with little attention paid to meaning or expressive reading. Again, my task was to educate the family on the purpose of the home reading program and to help the parents develop the skills necessary to nurture their child's reading development.

3. Practical Ideas

- Make home reading a family activity so parents do not have to occupy their other children while they read with only one child.

- Establish a home reading routine where children place their reading bags in the same place every day so they are easy to access and don't get misplaced. Once the home reading has been finished, place the reading bag in the child's backpack so it is ready to be returned to school.

- Read in assorted places in the home to keep the activity fresh. Read in a dry bathtub full of comfortable cushions, fill a picnic basket with books and set up a picnic blanket on the living room floor, or drape a blanket over a low table to make a fort. Crawl under the table with a flashlight and pillow and start reading.

A comfy, fun place to read together.

- Create multiple opportunities to practice reading the same book by widening the audience and reading to the family pet or favorite dolls or stuffed animals.

- Read outside under a shady tree. Better yet, climb the tree and read in its branches.

- Attend free story times for pre-schoolers at local bookstores and libraries.

- Borrow materials from public libraries frequently. Libraries have items such as felt board story sets, book and CD sets and magazines available for children, as well as books.

- Public libraries allow for free access to Tumble books, animated children's stories available to view on computers.

- Join the Summer Reading Club at the local library. Many reading incentives, as well as reading buddies, are available to keep children reading throughout the summer.

- Participate in Family Literacy events at the school. Children are inspired to read when they can do it in their pyjamas in the school gym.

- Treat children to a new book each month and build a home library. Book club flyers sent home from schools offer books for as little as $1.99 each. Online book sellers are also good sources for very inexpensive children's books.

- Access pre-school programs such as Strong Start which distribute bags of books for families to keep each month. Ideally, children will have had experience with 1000 books by the age of five.

- Create a notebook of your own stories, poems and sentences for children to read. Have the children illustrate the writing with drawings or magazine pictures.

- Write funny sentences and poems for children to read outside using sidewalk chalk.

- Many computer apps such as *Book Creator* are available allowing families to create their own captioned digital stories using photographs of their children and events and places in their lives.

- Make literacy an ongoing family habit—write in the sand at the beach, read license plates, point out words in the neighbourhood when out for a walk, play word games such as stating one word for each letter of the alphabet.

4. Home Reading Programs

Building anticipation in children is one of the key elements in running a successful home reading program. Throughout the school year, when the children hear a story they particularly enjoy and connect with, I casually mention that one day they will be taking classroom books home to read with their families. Over time, I share this idea with the children with a growing sense of excitement in my voice and demeanor, until at last I count down to a specific date for the home reading program to begin—in ten days, next week, tomorrow. I also build anticipation and awareness of home reading with the parents by mentioning it in the monthly calendar newsletters and in casual conversations.

Parent involvement and participation is essential to the success of a home reading program. Many parents are as excited as their children to begin this new phase of academic growth and development, yet others will need encouragement and nurturing from the teacher to be able to support their children fully. I begin developing a relationship of trust and understanding with the parents of my students from the first time we meet. I ask the adults to call me by my first name and explain that we will be partners working together to help their children grow and learn and achieve all they can. During the school year, I get to know the members of their families including grandparents and caregivers and I share details of my family, too.

Each school day begins with Family Reading Time when parents come into the classroom and read with the children for a few minutes. This ensures that students are engaged in a literacy activity as soon as they arrive in the classroom, and it allows me time to circulate and greet children and parents, collect notes from home, help fit items into lockers and so forth. During this time, I can soothe children anxious because they are leaving their parents, have private conversations with adults, introduce parents to each other to help facilitate new friendships amongst both children and adults, and ensure that all children are included in one of the informal story groups. Pre-schoolers, too, are welcome and encouraged to participate in Family Reading Time. Parents get to know their child's classmates and younger siblings, as well as the other parents. A strong sense of community develops through the shared enjoyment of children's literature.

Volunteer parents encourage the home reading program.

As our relationships develop, I come to know which parents have issues such as unhappy memories of their own schooling, or struggle with reading and writing, or don't have a strong and healthy bond with their child. These unfortunate circumstances all have an effect on the literacy development of my students and are a detriment to their participation in the home reading program. Therefore, it is my responsibility as a classroom teacher to empower parents to support and engage with their children through reading. This could involve modeling how to share a book with a child, complimenting a parent on her expressive reading which draws other students to the story, or simply making a joke about how the parent should be the one getting a sticker for returning the home reading bags regularly.

The timing of my kindergarten home reading program changes slightly from year-to-year. I usually begin sending books home with my students in late April, but I have occasionally started the program as early as March, depending on various factors such as the reading ability of the class, their interest level and enthusiasm for literacy and the maturity of the children. At this point in the school year, after seven or eight months of being read to daily by many adults and older students, my Kindergarten students are ready to begin reading simple texts independently to others.

The first week of the home reading program changes from year-to-year as well. If the class is highly motivated and interested in learning to read and has shown a pattern during the school year of returning library books, permission slips and other paper work promptly, I will begin all students' programs on the same day. However, if a portion of the class is reluctant about reading or has been unreliable about returning items to school, I will start a select group on the first day of those that I expect will return their home reading bags the following day and will create a buzz of excitement about this new venture. The second day will see a few more students added to the home reading roster and so forth, until by the end of the first week, all students in the class are taking books home to read with their families. Another benefit of starting a home reading program in stages is that it allows the teacher and students a few extra days to become accustomed to this change in classroom routine and activity.

5. Home Reading Books

Having a wide variety of books available for use as home reading texts is a necessity, as a class of children will encompass a wide range of reading abilities, as well as have myriad interests in early literature. To that end, I have amassed hundreds of books specifically for use in home reading. Garage sales and second hand stores are useful sources for books suitable for home reading selections, as are sales held when libraries cull their collections. School district resource centers occasionally distribute books for permanent use in classrooms, and have "give away" tables, as do school libraries.

Opportunities to participate in action research projects or professional development activities occur regularly. Such opportunities are often funded by grants supplied by school districts or professional teacher organizations. Home reading materials could be purchased with these funds to further the research or professional development.

Parents generously donate books to classrooms as their children outgrow them and service clubs such as Kiwanis or Rotary can be approached for donations to specific literacy initiatives such as home reading programs. Parent Advisory Councils often allocate funds to classrooms for book purchases, as do individual schools. Book publishers occasionally provide schools with new series of books to pilot, and regularly provide teachers with dividends for holding book fairs in schools or making book club flyers available to families.

Online booksellers have become an extremely useful source of very inexpensive children's books, both for newer publications and older favourite titles that can be difficult to obtain. I have been able to purchase many books for as little as one cent, thereby stretching limited school book budgets to the maximum.

6. Pairing Children with Books

Throughout the school year, I continually assess and document each kindergarten student's developing reading ability so that when it is time to introduce the home reading program, I know which books are appropriate for each child. Pairing suitable books with children requires knowledge not only of the child's reading level, but also consideration of individual interests such as a preference for non-fiction books or enjoyment of a certain literary character. Ensuring that children are exposed to "just right" books from the beginning of the home reading experience heightens their enjoyment and strengthens their commitment to daily reading.

Enjoying the story together.

Teachers must be very familiar with all books being used in their home reading programs in order to avoid giving children texts that are too difficult and cause frustration, or ones that are too easy and don't provide an adequate academic challenge or sustain the reader's interest. Both situations will interfere with children steadily building on their early and emergent reading skills and developing positive self-images as readers.

For kindergarten children who are beginning to read somewhat independently, I like to begin their home reading programs with the *Elephant and Piggie* stories by Mo Willems, whom I consider to be the Dr. Seuss for the current generation of beginning readers. These humorous stories are told through conversations between the two main characters, with minimal text presented in word balloons. The conversations flow naturally and are filled with opportunities for beginning readers to become familiar with punctuation and expression. My aim in using these stories at the outset of home reading is to make sure that children learn to read with fluency and expression at the earliest opportunity, skills they must have to be considered capable and independent readers.

For the earliest readers, series of simple photographic texts captioned with sentence stems such as *"Here is a ...."* or *"I see a ..."* are not intimidating and make good selections to begin their home reading programs. Children who are further along the reading continuum might enjoy the challenge of a book series with more complex sentences such as *"The dog is playing with a ball."*

As the children progress through the home reading program, I monitor their progress closely and continually adjust the book choices to match their ability levels and interests. Occasionally, children request specific but unsuitable titles because their friends have read the stories. I might provide the child with the requested story, explaining that it is a book her parents will read to her because it is beyond her ability level, or I might hold it back for a while as an incentive for the child to improve his reading level so that he can read it independently.

7. Administration of the Home Reading Program

Books are sent home in large Ziploc® freezer bags labelled with the child's name and division. On the first day of the program, I include a letter to parents explaining how the program works. The language is conversational and avoids educational jargon which might be intimidating to readers. Adults are encouraged to make this daily reading and sharing of books with children an enjoyable experience rather than turning it into a formal or stressful reading lesson and are asked to include a variety of women and men in the home reading sessions. As the children's excitement about becoming readers often leads to them wanting to read the books multiple times, I suggest that children could read to the family pets or their dolls or stuffed animals so the home reading task doesn't become onerous for busy parents.

During the school week, I send home one book per day with each child and occasionally, on weekends or school holidays, will send home two or three books. I do accommodate specific requests from parents for more books if a child will be absent due to illness or other special circumstances. In years past, I sent home a week's selection of books each Monday. I found that the bag of books was often neglected and returned to school unread or with only one or two titles looked at. That volume of books was daunting for some families and discouraged them from reading with their children at all. The expectation to read one book per day is manageable and families are able to schedule a few minutes to read the simple texts together. Also, the daily routine ensures that books are rarely misplaced and helps families to make reading a habitual activity.

Families are expected to return home reading bags daily, in exchange for the next book in a series or a slightly more difficult or challenging book. The anticipation and excitement about what they will receive next ensures that books are returned to school regularly. Children also like to see what their classmates are reading and compare whether they, too, have read a certain title. If a reading bag is not returned to school for two or three days, I contact the parents to ensure the bag has not been misplaced or forgotten, and to help the family get back into a regular reading routine. I find a gentle, understanding and encouraging approach yields the best results. Families genuinely try to follow the routine and care for the books but unexpected events do occur, causing a disruption to the home reading schedule. In my several decades long teaching career, I have had no more than a dozen home reading books lost or not returned, and of those, several were replaced with another title from the family's book collection.

All books in my home reading collection are grouped by series, character, author, reading level, publisher or some other easily identifiable feature and stored in plastic bins with clearly marked dividers between each set of books. Every group of books is recorded on a separate grid with individual titles across the top of the grid and the children's names down the left side. When a child takes a book home the corresponding space on the grid is marked with a forward slash and when it is returned, the slash is crossed to form an **X**. It is easy to see at a glance which boxes on the grids are crossed off, indicating which titles each child has read.

During Family Reading Time each morning, the children deposit their home reading bags in a labelled plastic bin and once everyone is settled into an informal reading group, I have individual children read the previous day's selection to me. Throughout the school day, each child has the opportunity to read to me, allowing me to check that books have been read, assess progress and provide individualized reading instruction. As each child's needs differ, the focus could be on checking the picture for cues, or reviewing sight words, or attending to the meaning of a story, or reading with fluency and so on.

Children and families are accountable to read and return books daily and as children eagerly await their individual reading turns, with many requests to be one of the first readers of the day, books are rarely left at home. A sticker attached to the reading bag at the end of each individual reading session is an added incentive to bring books to school. If it is evident that a book has been returned to school but not read at home, I might send the book home again or have the child practice reading it at school with an older student.

Occasionally, a family's circumstances make it difficult for them to participate fully in the home reading program. Rather than limit children due to situations beyond their control, I arrange for someone to provide them with daily reading support so they don't fall behind their peers. A classroom assistant, or a "reading buddy" from an older class, or another child's parent could provide this support.

Janet's Comment

The Alphabet Binder is a "home support" program to help those families who are able/interested in supporting their children's learning at home. Wendy set it up in a large fabric-covered zippered binder. She provided it only to parents who showed interest in supporting their children at home; in that way the binder actually became a highly desired activity for children who persuaded parents to ask for it and for parents who then requested to have it next. Parents were given a limited time to have it at home before returning it for the next family.

Janet

"Alphabet Fun!" Binder

(Wendy de Groot)

Materials in the Binder *(In Binder Pencil Case)*:

* 1 set uppercase alphabet cards,
* 1 set lowercase alphabet cards, and
* 1 picture set of alphabet cards.

Letter in the Binder:

Dear [Parent]

The most recent assessment of _____ showed that he/she is not confident in identifying the following letters. (Highlighted) This may have changed by the time you are going through these cards but, this will still give you a good starting point. Feel free to use the blank letter list below to track your child's progress as you practice during the next few weeks.

Have fun!

Mrs. De Groot

Two Pages of Letters in the Binder:

Letters were equally spaced and the teacher highlighted the letters the child still did not know.

I'm learning my letters!

Date:_____

A	B	C	D	E	F	G	H	I	J	K	L	M
N	O	P	Q	R	S	T	U	V	W	X	Y	Z

a	b	c	d	e	f	g	h	i	j	k	l	m
n	o	p	q	r	s	t	u	v	w	x	y	z

Alphabet Fun Instructions in the Binder:

Alphabet Fun!

1. *Identifying the letters of the Alphabet is a key stepping-stone to beginning reading. Start with Uppercase Letter identification and then move to lowercase letter identification.*

2. *Go through the Uppercase Cards and see how many your child already knows. Chances are, they already know quite a few. Put the letters they don't know into a separate pile—those are the ones you want to focus on. Next, pull out three or four of the cards they can identify, then take two cards from your "need to work on" pile and add them to your stack. You should have five to six cards. Go through those cards with your child and help them identify the ones "they forget."*

3. *Next, find the matching lowercase cards. See how many cards your child can match with the Uppercase letters and help them make the matches if necessary. The key is to do only a few at a time and record the letters your child still needs to practice.*

Alphabet Fun, continued…

Keep doing this until you have gone through the entire "need to work on" pile. Gradually add more of the "know" cards to your pile. Remember, it is important to keep reviewing letters often, especially if your child is struggling with letter learning. Cereal boxes, store signage, flyers, toy packages all provide great letter reviewing opportunities. Just make it part of your family routine and include other family members whenever possible.

Other Ideas:

Go on a "letter hunt" while you are reading to your child. Look for one of the letters that your child has still not mastered. Remember that it is important not to turn your reading time into a reading lesson or you run the risk of turning your child off learning. Everything should be organized around games like "I Spy". As you begin your reading time, ask your child which letter they would like to search for from their "need to work on pile." Each time you come across this letter, keep track by counting or jot it down. At the end, talk about how many you found.

You may also want to use the Picture Cards. Find the matching Picture Cards that go with your "need to work on" cards and set up a Memory Game. Lay them out in mixed order, face down and see how many pairs your child can find by remembering where they were placed. Take turns and include other family members to make it more energized.

Wendy reviews the Binder at a sit-down meeting with parents so that they have a real understanding of how best to implement it. It is signed out and she sets up an appointment for them to meet again in six weeks to go over progress. Students from families who have used it always showed improvement.

Janet's Comment

My university classes were focused on how to enhance our support for vulnerable children. As a class, we reviewed all of the relevant research and practiced implementing strategies that would demonstrate what the research would look like in action. One of the last assignments I gave my university class was to consider how they would explain the importance of the latest theories to parents. One of my students, Teresa Fayant, created the following PowerPoint for her first parent meeting of the year and gave me permission to share it with you. Enjoy, and feel free to adapt it to suit your own classroom and parent group.

Janet

Parent Information Powerpoint

(Teresa Fayant)

Welcome to Kindergarten
Stz'uminus Bambi School

Why Bambi?

Stz'uminus Bambi school offers:
- A play-based, student centred program
- Small class sizes for more one-on-support
- A safe & supportive learning environment
- Instruction is dynamic, varied, & meaningful for students
- A strong focus on literacy
- Hulq'umin'um language
- High expectations

Learning Through Play

- Research proves that students learn best through play
- Play nurtures intellectual, social, physical, and emotional skills for life
- Play should be both child driven and teacher intentional
- Play fosters a natural love of learning

An Active Process

- Students have an active role in their learning, asking questions, being responsible, etc.
- Skills and concepts are taught, modelled, and repeatedly practiced
- Practice and play, the terms can be synonymous
- Students take ownership, and are held accountable for their learning.

A Balanced Approach

- No one program used; dynamic teaching allows us to truly meet the needs of all learners
- Teaching through whole class, small group, and one-on-one instruction
- Activities are open ended and differentiated for individual focus
- Interventions / extra doses ensure no child is left behind

Meaning Makers

Learning is fostered when:
- Students are able to connect to their own lives and experiences
- When the concepts are built on what is already known
- Given time to practice and apply skills

A Supportive Environment

Social Emotional Development is nurtured as students learn to:

- *Self-regulate*
- *Problem solve*
- *Support one another*
- *Take risks*
- *Develop empathy*
- *Accept learning challenges*

A Day in Kindergarten

8:45 Breakfast	Breakfast	Students eat, brush their teeth, sign in, and read a book
9:00	Free Centres	Small group instruction/ intervention
10:00	Protocol	Prayer/Song, Helper chosen, Calendar, ABC's
10:30	Math	Whole group/ small group
10:45	Recess	
11:00	Literacy	Morning Message - shared reading, shared writing, read aloud, literacy group work
12:00	Lunch	Recess
1:00	Literacy	Read to Self – work stations
1:45	Theme	Read Aloud – Science, Socials, Journals
2:25	Snack	
2:30	Hauqueralum	Songs, stories, theme vocabulary
3:00	Home	Ticket out the door to check for understanding

Literacy: Not Just Reading

Literacy encompasses so many skills and is the foundation for all other learning

- *Oral language development*
- *Phonological awareness* (rhyme, letters, sounds, etc.)
- *Concepts of print*
- *Comprehension*
- *Inquiry & Critical thinking*
- *Problem solving/ decoding*

Why Shared Activities?

- *Allow students to have a role in the learning process, asking questions, making their ideas visible, etc.*
- *Provide a opportunity for exploring language, constructing and organizing ideas*
- *Becomes a foundation for thinking, talking, reading, writing, listening, and understanding*

Shared Reading

Literacy encompasses so many skills and is the foundation for all other learning, including:

- *Oral language development*
- *Phonological awareness (rhyme, letters, sounds, etc.)*
- *Concepts of print*
- *Critical thinking*
- *Expression & Fluency*

Shared Writing

- *Is proven to teach both reading and writing*
- *Allows students to understand the connection between oral & written language*
- *Bridges the gap to independent writing*
- *Allows students to observe concepts of print in action, explore language, and build understanding*

Assessment

- Assessment, when done effectively, is necessary for learning
- Formative – to guide learning
- Summative – to show a concept has been attained
- As students learn through engaging activities we can assess in the same way

(rubrics, checklists, discussions, games, etc.)

 ## Hulq'umin'um

- Themes are planned based on the Hulq'umin'um cultural calendar
- Students participate in daily protocol, songs, and prayers
- Students are given explicit language instruction
- Hulq'umin'um is used throughout the day (questions, general instructions, basic commands)

It's not just about the Curriculum

We teach the foundational skills needed for while nurturing the social and emotional development of the child for true success.

As evident in our kindergarten classroom mantra

"We use our hearts, we use or mind, we follow the rules, and we are kind."

Ways to Support Learning

- Talk with your child often, think aloud, whenever possible (cooking, shopping, etc.)
- Sing nursery rhymes, read books, make grocery lists together, etc.
- Play with the alphabet – pointing out the letters and sounds in family members names, favorite video games, etc.
- Celebrate their learning – draw pictures, make a letter out of food, identify a sound, etc.
- Ensure consistent attendance – we learn a lot!

Huy' ce:ep qa!

We are proud of our dynamic program, and strive to foster a life long love of learning, a positive self concept and Stz'uminus pride

Janet's Summary

You did your best but...

It didn't work! You did your best but their parents wouldn't cooperate. They didn't have time; they were angry; maybe they were even rude. Regardless, we all have to carry on—without judgment.

It is wonderful when we can work in partnership with parents but, in reality, it is our responsibility to serve the needs of our children with or without the support of their parents. We have no idea the circumstances children live with behind closed doors. Perhaps their time at school is actually a respite for some children—a break from fear, loneliness, hunger or anxiety.

If we are rebuffed by unavailable parents we must turn our attention to finding other supports for our vulnerable children—finding ways to comfort, nurture and demonstrate tangibly that the world can be a loving and caring place for them, too. This can take the form of adoptive grandparents who volunteer in the classroom, grade seven peers who spend time with them weekly who don't just coach them but play with them outside or accompany them on local field trips. It can be special time spent with the principal or the secretary or the janitor—someone who will build safe bonds with them and build their confidence and trust.

It is only when children are emotionally safe that they can readily learn. If their families can't provide it right now, we can and will find other ways—we'll create a safe place for them. By doing so we are providing their families with support—just in a different way. We are creating the proverbial "village" for our most vulnerable children.

They're worth it! All the best...

Janet

Learning to cooperate and plan together in a vibrant classroom environment.

Implement *The Ideal Classroom* Checklist

Critical Criteria for the Effective Early Learning Classroom

 ## Janet's Introduction

Prior to writing this book I spent several months conducting a complete literature review of the research on Early Learning once I became aware of significant new research available post-2009. My intention was to write a publishable document that would be a resource for educators to guide their practice and to reflect on research-based practices endorsed by leading researchers and authors. (The books and articles in the reference list at the end of this book were included in the search.)

Since I began teaching at the university, I have worked with new university graduates as well as very experienced primary teachers. These were all wonderfully committed teachers who shared my passion for providing more vulnerable children with greater opportunities for success. I quickly became aware that the new graduates were ill informed about the most recent literacy research; in particular I was shocked that they could name few of the 50 essential literacy skills. The experienced teachers knew considerably more but were eager for advanced professional development and guidance from the research; many districts do not provide the 60 hours a year that Allington (2014) recommends.

I have also always been concerned that although many administrators do not have primary training they are responsible for making many important decisions: purchasing resources for primary classrooms, making organizational decisions and scheduling classes, assigning human resources as support services, mediating with parents, supervising teachers and sometimes evaluating them. Many primary teachers complain that they rarely see administrators in their classrooms; my theory is that many feel uncomfortable in primary classrooms because they simply don't understand the environment and the theory underlying it. I believe they want to be supportive of all staff: How can administrators confidently make intelligent decisions in a collaborative way with primary teachers or provide helpful suggestions when they lack the theoretical background?

I created this document to support sincere and caring educators, teachers and administrators who want to respond to the research. They want to transform classroom practices as an investment in, not just vulnerable children but every child. All children will benefit from implementation of the criteria in this document.

I wanted the document to be readily usable to provide the reader with a variety of features. Each chapter is organized into six categories:

1. Creating a Dynamic Learning Environment
2. Teaching Research-based Essential Literacy Skills
3. Learning Through Child-initiated Play
4. Learning Through Inquiry, Self-regulation and Projects
5. Assessing and Tracking Children's Learning and Development
6. Developing Relationships with and Supporting Families

Each section is organized with a series of Desired Outcome statements based on the research, followed by a number of criteria providing more specific statements that elaborate on the outcome statement. The criteria statements are followed by a list of indicators that describe what observers would see as evidence of implemented criteria if they visited the classroom.

I suggest that as you peruse this chapter you use two coloured "sticky-note" pads: Use one colour to mark the sections where you think you need or want to improve; use the other colour to mark the sections where you believe you excel or at least are making progress. It's important to give yourself a pat on the back every single day. You work in the most important profession on the planet! All the best in your contemplation…

Janet

An Ideal Primary Classroom Environment

CRITICAL CRITERIA for the EFFECTIVE EARLY LEARNING CLASSROOM

Janet Nadine Mort PhD

A First Class Beginning:
Early Learning INC.

Section 1: Create a Dynamic Learning Environment

Create a Child-friendly Active Learning Environment

The children help to create the physical environment so that it connects to their interests and allows them to engage in learning through a variety of interesting, playful activities.

1.1   Criteria

The environment shows respect for individuals and their differences. It provides places to play alone, collaboratively, quietly or noisily.

Observable indicators
- Spaces separated by shelves or other dividers
- Space for quiet activity
- Space for collaborative work
- Space for resting
- Space for communicating and sharing

1.2   Criteria

The displays, activities and behaviours reflect and respect the cultures of the families who attend.

Observable indicators
- Photographs of families
- Art that reflects the many cultures of the families represented in the classroom
- Visitors and field trips which reflect the multicultural families represented in the classroom
- Displays that reflect the values and history of multicultural families represented in the classroom

1.3   Criteria

The displays honour children's work, provide documentation for families and model possibilities for others.

Observable indicators
Documentation through:
- Learning stories
- Photographs
- Portfolios
- Communication with home
- A focus on process

1.4   Criteria

The classroom demonstrates that it values literacy through environmental print.

Observable indicators
- Calendars
- Schedules
- Signs
- Directions
- Evidence of student literacy activity

1.5   Criteria

The atmosphere is comfortable and helps the children feel that they belong.

Observable indicators
- Elements that encourage connections between classroom and community
- Contributions from families and homes
- Elements that focus on family connections
- Elements that minimize the institutional nature of schools
- Child-friendly objects in the room
- Multilevel floor spaces

Create a Flexible Learning Environment

The learning environment should be flexible, with the teacher recognizing that children learn holisically and that learners have individual needs. Teachers should plan for an environment that engages chidren with a wide variety of abilities, learning styles and preferences, and while also accommodating thoe children with special needs.

1.6   Criteria

The layout of the space encourages collaboration and communication.

Observable indicators
Design of a classroom that encourages:
- Individual and small group work
- Collaboration
- Various levels of stimulation
- Similar areas and materials grouped together
- Appropriate behavior

1.7   Criteria

The organization of classroom space accommodates multiple types of learning activities.

Observable indicators
Space for:
- Multiple learning centres
- Circle time
- Wet areas
- Large-muscle floor activities
- Organized storage for diverse learning activities220

1.8   Criteria

The arrangement of structures, objects and activities encourage active learning.

Observable indicators

Arrangements that encourage:
- Choices
- Problem solving
- Experimentation
- Discoveries
- Hands-on materials

1.9   Criteria

Teachers can observe children across the classroom despite barriers and separate activity areas.

Observable indicators
- Creative dividers on the floor
- Creative dividers from the ceiling
- Activity areas clearly and physically delineated
- Activity areas at different heights
- Visual separation for children but transparency for the teacher

1.10 Criteria

Storage options invite children to take responsibility for cleaning up and putting away.
learning resources.

Observable indicators

Storage units that are:
- Labeled or make contents visible
- Attract children to engage in activities
- Make it easy for children to clean up and put away

1.11 Criteria

The child-oriented and aesthetically pleasing environment pays attention to detail, it appeals to the sense in colours, shapes and arrangements.

Observable indicators

Design details may include:
- Attractive colours combined with unusual items and lights and mirrors
- Unusual, intriguing objects or equipment that encourage exploration
- Treasures that encourage extended thinking
- Collections that challenge all the senses

1.12 Criteria

The classroom is visually inviting, child-oriented and magical. Children respond with enthusiasm to visible invitations to learn and explore.

Observable indicators

Children are invited to engage through:
- Structures that attract them such as lofts, tents, places to hide
- Ceiling hangings like parachutes, umbrellas, colourful fabric, and glass beads
- Light tables that encourage experiments with colour and shapes
- Water-play devices
- Collections of props that encourage inventions

1.13 Criteria

Classroom activities are linked to outdoor activities as an extension of learning.

Observable indicators

Activities in the centres that:
- Prepare for an outdoor exploration
- Study the natural environment
- Provide collections that stimulate discovery and research
- Use natural objects for sorting, classifying, creating patterns and developing numeracy skills
- Provide sensory experiences with natural objects

1.14 Criteria

Program spaces are designed with flexible options so that things can be moved and rearranged.

Observable indicators

Children are encouraged to:
- To take items from one centre to another
- To use resources in unique ways

Centre(s):
- Are easily adjusted or moved as interests change
- Are changed regularly and/or activities are changed regularly
- Can accommodate different numbers of children based on interests and priorities

1.15 Criteria

Multilevel spaces are provided so children can explore spatial relationships.

Observable indicators

Multilevel spaces created through:
- Lofts
- Risers or elevated platforms
- Display stands
- Large blocks combined with other resources
- Step stools and ladders

Create Dynamic Learning Centres

Learning centres are designated areas where materials are arranged to guide children's learning. Play at learning centres can be exploratory, with hands-on learning. Interactive play at learning centres is encuraged. Centres are arranged to accommodate individuals or groups. Explorations are designed to meet thneeds of all students recognizing their diverse learning styles, including kinaesthetic, auditory, and visual learning.

1.16 Criteria

Centres are print-rich but also offer multiple opportunities for children to participate in and witness processes of reading and writing for pleasure as well as for function.

Observable indicators

Centres include:
- A wide variety of types and levels of books and other written material
- A wide variety of writing tools
- Games and activities include Essential Literacy Skills
- A wide variety of strategies to use and play with words
- Auditory and kinaesthetic opportunities to experience print
- Displays of children's successes with reading and writing

1.17 Criteria

Numeracy concepts are addressed through play with games and found objects and integrated in multiple centres.

Observable indicators

Centres include:
- Numeracy games
- Use of found objects to explore numeracy
- Activities that encourage real-life use of numeracy concepts
- A variety of tools for measuring, weighing and calculating
- Activities that integrate numeracy with other curricular areas

1.18 Criteria

Materials invite children to make representations through creative arts.

Observable indicators

Materials encourage:
- Exploration of new tools to make creations (glue gun, screwdriver, Velcro)
- Building of sculptures
- Three dimensional structures
- Use of recycled materials in novel ways
- Display and documentation of creations

1.19 Criteria

Activities invite children to see things from different perspective through dramatic play.

Observable indicators

Centres include:
- Collections of costumes
- Adult career-related props (cash registers, tool belts)
- Props that encourage imagination (crowns, fairy tale objects, historical items)
- Props connected to stories recently read
- Toys that encourage collaborative play (puppets)

1.20 Criteria

Traditional resources are used in creative new ways.

Observable indicators

Try:
- Sheer fabrics draped on dowels from the ceiling
- Cultural tapestries on the walls
- Bargains found at yard sales, flea markets, recycle centres
- Creative displays (clotheslines or patio umbrellas)
- Outside structures brought inside (a gazebo or trellis)

Section 2: Teach Research-based Essential Literacy Skills – NELP
(National Early Literacy Panel, 2009)

Ensuring Assessment, Teaching and Tracking of Each Child's Skill Development

Vulnerable children enter kindergarten with many gaps in their literacy development for a variety of reasons. Research consistently asserts that interventions for these children must begin in kindergarten in order to ensure that over 90% of all children are achieving at grade level by the end of grade two. Interventions are best implemented in a play-based classroom environment. Kindergarten children will be assessed at the beginning of the school year (or earlier if possible) to determine essential literacy skill gaps. These are informal assessments conducted by the classroom teacher in order to structure flexible small group instruction until skill mastery is achieved.

Essential Skills List

2.1 Letter and Sound Association. Ability to identify: • Names • Sounds • Finding and proposing words with the sounds	
2.2 Phonological/Phonemic Awareness. (Phonemic Awareness is a subset of Phonological Awareness). Ability to identify: • Rhyming discrimination • Rhyming production • Isolation (initial, medial and final letters) • Blending phonemes and letters • Blending syllables (parts of words) • Segmentation (words in sentences) • Segmentation (compound words) • Segmentation (phonemes) • Deletion (compound words)	
2.3 Print Concepts. Ability to identify: • Books – including front and back, title, author, illustrator • Directionality • Voice to print • Word and letter concept • First and last word in sentences • Punctuation (period, question mark, exclamation)	
2.4 Oral language and Comprehension: Expressive (Speaking) and Receptive (Listening). Ability to: • Demonstrate vocabulary and concept development • Retell simple narrative and nonfiction text • Read the illustrations/pictures • Question and use language for problem solving and inquiring • Use language to explain, explore and compare • Predict • Enjoy being read to and listening to storytelling, stories being told • Use language to interact with others including extending conversations • Speak in a manner that is readily understood by others, adults and peers	

2.5 **Word Reading.** Ability to identify: • Names, environmental print	
2.6 **Word Work and Phonics.** Ability to: • Develop skill in letter/sound correspondence • Match initial letter sounds and key words/pictures • Identify high frequency words • Recognize word families • Use cueing systems • Recognize and read punctuation	
2.7 **Word Writing.** Ability to: • Name and copy environmental print	
2.8 **Reading.** Ability to read: • From memory • From own writing and shared writings • From shared readings and environmental print • From leveled and other simple texts	
2.9 **Writing.** Ability to: • Draw and write letter-like forms • Copy letters • Write his/her name • Write words including invented or temporary spelling • Write sentence(s) • Leave spaces between words • Copy and write text such as lists, labels, notes and personal stories • Illustrate stories	

Section 3: Provide Opportunities for Child-initiated Play

3.1 **Criteria** Activities offer opportunities for logical and mathematical thinking. **Observable indicators** Offerings include: • Board and floor games that use numerals • Centres that use real-life counting experiences with money • Measurement experiences • Sorting and classifying activities that compare quantities • Oral group activities that use numbers (calendars, grouping of children)	
3.2 **Criteria** Activities offer opportunities for scientific reasoning. **Observable indicators** Offerings include: • Collections of natural materials and related resources • Materials that encourage simple science experiments • Live creatures and related resources • Field trips that encourage studies of local flora, fauna and creatures • Growing plants and miniature greenhouses in the classroom	

3.3   Criteria

Aesthetic and artistic development activities are encouraged.

Observable indicators

Offerings:
- Musical instruments are available to create compositions
- Found materials and art tools provide open-ended possibilities for creations
- Art displays honour children's work and culture
- Space is available for creative movement
- Dramatic play is encouraged through props

3.4   Criteria

Activities offer opportunities for cognitive problem solving.

Observable indicators

Examples:
- Provide unusual material that, combined, create new possibilities
- Create centre activities that are focused around the 'why' question
- Teach simple problem solving models
- Encourage collaborative solution-finding activities
- Provide unusual equipment like pulleys, tubes, building tools that encourage building creative structures in response to teacher-proposed challenges

3.5   Criteria

Active play is encouraged.

Observable indicators

For instance:
- All centres offer hands-on activities with creative resources
- Combinations of material are offered for sensory exploration
- Opportunities are offered for creating constructions
- Dramatic play is encouraged
- Play is encouraged through games

3.6   Criteria

Group play is encouraged.

Observable indicators

For instance:
- Teach and coach strategies of negotiation and social responsibility
- Provide guided experiences that encourage children to work through conflict
- Encourage small and large group projects by posing opportunities and seeking volunteers
- Celebrate examples of collaborative and cooperative experiences and outcomes daily while discussing negotiating skills and conflict resolution
- Ensure balance between individual, small group and large group activities

Section 4: Provide Opportunities for Learning through Self-regulation and Projects

Inquiry

Inquiry implies involvement that leads to understanding. Involvement in learning implies possessing skills and attitudes that permit you to seek a resolution to questions and issues while you construct new knowledge.

4.1 Criteria

There is balance between open-ended materials and single-purpose materials.

Observable indicators

Open-ended activities:
- To be creative
- To use familiar materials in new ways
- To extend their thinking

Single-purpose activities:
- To demonstrate they can achieve a teacher-organized learning outcome
- To master a skill
- To apply new learning

Instructions are clear as to whether the expectations are open-ended or single-purpose; there is balance in the opportunities provided

4.2 Criteria

Recycled materials are offered to children so they can create imaginative experiences.

Observable indicators

Recycled materials are available for:
- Creative art and representations
- Classifying, sorting and numeracy
- Experimentation and explorations
- Making community connections
- Socio-dramatic play

4.3 Criteria

Offerings inspire active learning, experimentation and discovery.

Observable indicators

Offerings include:
- Objects that move (pulley, wheels, balls, marbles, wind chimes)
- Construction opportunities
- Science experiments
- Living things (plants, insects, animals) to study
- Collections from the natural environment

4.4   Criteria

Simple technologies like projectors, fans or sources of light provide special learning experiences.

Observable indicators

Look for:

- Light sources (projectors, flashlights, light table) and resources that encourage exploration of big ideas such as light
- Objects that encourage exploration of motion (fans, pulleys, tunnels)
- Use of real tools such as air pump, hammers
- Combinations of unusual props (a wall mirror, mobiles, a fan)
- Teacher-guided play experiences with adult tools such as a vacuum cleaner, a hair dryer, a hand drill, a sander, cameras

4.5   Criteria

Intriguing objects and events stimulate inquiry.

Observation indicators

Look for experiences that promote inquiry:

- Collections of treasures and related resource materials
- Intriguing visitors come to the classroom
- Field trips to promote project work
- Organization of materials to highlight a learning domain (the alphabet)
- Real creatures, a magnifying glass and books about the creature

4.6   Criteria

Activities present questions that result in research and problem solving. They encourage children to construct new knowledge and drive the curiosity of the learner.

Observation indicators

Examples:

- The sandbox is filled with unusual materials to encourage creative use of sand.
- Painting activities stretch beyond the easel to unusual applications.
- Materials reflect an advanced view of children's capabilities yet they are offered with safety in mind (glue guns and real adult tools).
- Materials move away from cause and effect and challenge the child to apply them.
- Familiar materials like blocks, puzzles, and dress-up clothes are offered in different combinations or different settings to stimulate complex thinking (blocks and mirrors, clotheslines and pulleys, hospital uniforms in the dress-up centre).
- Aesthetic beauty is provided in articles that provide experiences with shapes, forms, lines, patterns, textures, lights, colours and shadows.
- Materials are open-ended and can be transformed; use recycled materials and special collections of treasure.

Encourage Self-regulation

This term refers to a person's ability to order thoughts, process information in a coherent way, hold relevan r details in the short-term memory and avoid distractions, a skill now considered by many to be t ng stro indicator of future success. Children have the opportunity to practice self-regulation.

4.7   Criteria

Children are engaged in the design of their learning experiences.

Observable indicators
- Activities encourage children to plan, monitor, revise and reflect on their learning, exchange points of view, represent their learning and form their own hypotheses.
- Activities offer choices and decisions but not always. Some decisions are not negotiable.

4.8   Criteria

Children are developing the ability to control their urges.

Observable indicators
- Children are calmly focused and engaged; optimal levels of arousal are maintained.
- Children change behaviours at prompts from the teacher.
- Children cooperatively perform tasks even if they didn't choose them.
- Children demonstrate the ability to set limits for themselves.
- The teacher is helping children through their inappropriate urges.
- Limits are set up so that children feel supported and valued, not judged and rejected.

4.9   Criteria

Children are beginning to show 'effortful control'.

Observable indicators
- Children demonstrate awareness that there are expectations that they are expected to meet – such as cleaning up tasks, lower voice levels, and cooperative behaviours.
- Children are aware of the 'dos' and the 'don'ts'. (Do's include things they may not want to do while don't include stopping themselves from doing something they want to do.)
- Children are beginning to internalize other people's expectations.
- Most children follow instructions.
- Teachers acknowledge the behaviours of children who are 'doing things right'.
- Children are learning that frustrations are part of day-to-day life and learning.

4.10   Criteria

Children are demonstrating traits of sympathy and conscience.

Observable indicators
- The teacher leads discussions during group time where children discuss story characters or classroom activities where these characteristics are applied.
- Children are beginning to coach each other in daily activities that apply these concepts.
- They model the concepts in their interactions.

4.9   Criteria

Social skills and interactions are taught, monitored and mediated by the teacher.

Observable indicators
- The teacher actively teaches and coaches children about appropriate social interactions on a daily basis – formally and informally.

4.10 Criteria

Planned teacher-led conversations with individuals and with groups build bridges between ideas, feelings and facts.

Observable indicators

- The teacher actively makes note of developing ideas and scaffolds children's understanding in a systematic way.
- Develop learning strategies from first-hand interactions with real-life objects and exchanging points of view.

Provide Opportunities for Project Work

Project-based learning is an individual or group activity that occurs over time and results in a product, presentation or performance. It has a timeline, milestones and is learner centered. Students have a significant voice in selecting the content areas, understanding why they are important and setting goals for assessment. Active engagement, collaboration, deeper learning and challenges are hallmarks of project work.

4.11 Criteria

Teachers explore children's theories at work and offer resources and opportunities to extend them to projects for deeper learning (as indicated in the examples in column 2).

Observable indicators

For example:
- Big ideas, aligned with children's interests, guide the project planning process; this is not a teacher pre-planned unit.
- As small groups of children become interested in one child's work, the teacher begins to organize small group activities and align PLO's with the possibilities, driven by children's interests.
- The teacher offers multiple mediums and resources so that children recognize different aspects of the ideas they are pursuing.
- Children are asked to explain, represent and disclose their theories.
- The teacher helps students revisit their ideas to spark further interest, bring up new questions and stimulate more action. Projects reach a natural closure as children lose interest and move on to new ideas.

Section 5: Assess Children's Learning and Development

5.1 Criteria Available Early Learning Assessments are included in assessment considerations to inform daily skill instruction and daily practice. **Observable indicators** A variety of Early Learning Assessments are available or many become available such as: • Preschool assessments • The EDI assessment • Assessments that include the Essential Literacy Skills Teachers consider all information available in making their own assessments.	
5.2 Criteria Assessment is on-going; strategies are varied. **Observable indicators** • No one strategy is used for assessments. Various strategies are used in inter-related, systematic way.	
5.3 Criteria Assessment is embedded in the context of daily activities. **Observable indicators** • Most assessment strategies are used in the context of daily activities, not out-of-context tests. • The teacher circulates during Learning Centre time, making notations about student learning. • The teacher engages small groups of children with similar needs during Learning Centre time for small-group instruction. • Displays of documentation of student work encourage children. • Documentation is frequently shared with families and engages families in the children's work.	
5.4 Criteria Assessment is based on authentic and reliable information. **Observable indicators** • Portfolio collections are used to gather collections of student work over time. • Anecdotal records are used to interpret developmental progress. • Teachers use a checklist or continuum to document the development of specific skills or concepts. • Children are offered many ways to represent their learning.	
5.5 Criteria Learning Stories comprise an important part of ongoing documentation. **Observable indicators** • Learning Stories document the children's thinking through their actions. • The teacher uses the documentation to analyse learning domains: language, literacy, social/emotional development, creative expression, symbolic thinking, critical thinking etc., as the basis of planning. • Teachers study the documentation of student work to determine "next steps" or new perspectives in planning new resources and possibilities to extend children's learning. • The child's family becomes engaged to reflect on connected activities at home, views from the home perspective, and how the activity fits with the family's beliefs, values and culture. • Videos, photographs and other media are used to supplement the child's "voice" in the Learning Stories.	

Section 6: Develop Relationships with and Support Families

6.1 Criteria Communication patterns with homes are well-established. **Observable indicators** For example: • Communication about how children learn is routinely sent home. • Communication offer parents opportunities to practice new child learning at home. • Communication identify school and classroom expectations. • Report procedures about progress are on-going.	
6.2 Criteria The environment welcomes and engages families. **Observable indicators** • Displays of photos or family artifacts • A place for families to sign in or drop off child belongings • An activity families engage in as they enter the classroom • A communication board or folder for announcements/articles • A comfortable space for families to wait or observe	
6.3 Criteria The environment helps children transition from the home to the school environment. **Observable indicators** • Home like-lights, plants, pictures and mirrors • Soft furnishings if appropriate • Displays of artifacts brought from home • Family photos • Colours, textures and living things consistent with cultures and homes	
6.4 Criteria Efforts are made to build connections and relationships with families. **Observable indicators** For example: • Routines are established that welcome and greet families as children arrive. • Classroom displays reflect the culture(s) of the children attending. • Projects examine the traditions, cultures and diversity of the community. • Family and community members are a regular part of program offerings. • Staff from Early Learning Agencies in the community regularly participate in classroom activities. • Families are encouraged to participate in classroom related activities.	

Janet's Summary

The purpose of the *Ideal Classroom* Checklist is to provide educators with a reflective document that can be used to create classroom environments aligned with prevailing research. As you peruse the checklist and the ideas and strategies proposed therein, please trust that you are considering research-based theories that have become action possibilities as interpreted by me and other authors listed in the References. As I created the checklist, numerous possibilities for its use came to mind.

Professional Learning Communities: Prime among my intentions was its use in professional learning communities. It would be a wonderful tool for a group of enthusiastic professionals to select a topic, discuss its ramifications for classroom practice, research it further, apply it in classrooms and return to the next meeting with photos and artefacts, to discuss the impact it had in classroom practice to share ideas.

District, School or Individual Improvement Plans: A school staff (or individual) could identify the criteria that they believe to be the highest priority for improvement; decide to create a long-term timeline placing the key criteria in an implementation plan; and use the plan as the basis for systemic improvement.

Professional Development: A district committee could use the checklist as a prompt for discussion of long term planning; the checklist could be adapted to be a survey and circulated to participants as a needs assessment.

Supervision of Instruction: Administrators could use the checklist as a tool for engaging primary teachers in discussion about their classroom practices. I would recommend a bi-monthly meeting to discuss selected criteria so that the administrators could engage in meaningful dialogue about research-based concepts.

It is important to view the checklist as a proactive tool intended for the benefit of children. I expect teachers to implement parts of it or variations of it that are consistent with their own teaching styles. It was never intended that the entire checklist be implemented as described. Rather, I wanted to interpret credible research as a vision of what might be possible if we could see the research in action.

Have fun with it: Stretch my proposed ideas to create your own and document them in photos to share with your colleagues. Celebrate your successes!

Janet

Getting the alphabet in the right order (Quesnel School District No. 28)

CHAPTER NINE

Stepping Stone **9**

Make Systemic Change *(PLC's and Case Studies)*

Case Studies: Implementing Stepping Stones with SUCCESS

Case Study 1: School District 28 (Quesnel)
Teacher Shauna Lothrop

Case Study 2: School District 59 (Peace River South)
A School District: 55 Teachers

Case Study 3: School District 23 (Central Okanagan)
A School District: 60 Primary Teachers

 Janet's Introduction

While drawing the significance of explicit skill instruction to our attention, the NELP (*National Early Literacy Panel Report*) also featured the instructional strategies, programs and practices that would best impart conventional literacy skills to young children.

Code-focused Interventions

Code focused interventions reported statistically significant and moderate-to-large effects across a broad spectrum of early literacy outcomes. Code-focused interventions consistently demonstrated positive effects directly on children's conventional literacy skills.

Small-group Interventions

The interventions that produced large and positive effects on children's code-related skills and conventional literacy skills were usually conducted as small group instructional activities in the classroom. These activities tended to be teacher-directed and focused on helping children learn skills by engaging in the use of and practice of those skills in small groups. Almost all of the code-focused interventions included some form of Phonological Awareness (PA) interventions. These PA activities generally required children to detect or manipulate (e.g., delete or blend) small units of sounds in words. Teaching children about the alphabet (e.g., letter names and letter sounds) or simple phonics tasks (e.g., blending letter sounds to make words) enhanced the effects of PA training.

These variables have been shown in research to be causally connected to literacy achievement. If those skills are taught, children attain higher levels of literacy. The NELP Report, however, noted that most of the high-impact instructional strategies involved activities and procedures implemented by researchers and were not typically found in early learning classrooms.

I began to imagine K to 2 classrooms where the focus would be, not only on code-focused interventions, but also on the other major interventions identified in the NELP research – namely shared-reading interventions, home and parent programs, preschool and kindergarten programs and language-enhancement interventions.

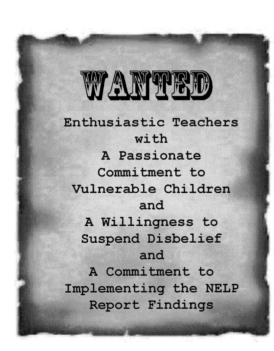

The **WANTED** poster for my research study might have read like this.

My personal mission became finding real classroom teachers who were willing to work with me to prove that if we implemented the findings in the NELP Report we could significantly raise the literacy achievement of vulnerable children.

I had spent four years earning a PhD in Language and Literacy (Early Learning). For seven years I conducted research projects in school districts studying what some districts were doing to raise literacy levels.

Once I had examined and analyzed the findings in the 230-page NELP Report, I had reached the stage where I believed deeply that I knew what the implementation package would look like if we wanted literacy early intervention strategies to change the life trajectories of vulnerable children. It was not an overnight stroke of brilliance. It was the result of a longitudinal study of the work of many of my administrative colleagues, the impressive authors quoted in this book and brilliant researchers along with my experience as a principal and superintendent. It was like putting a giant jigsaw puzzle together with the help of my friends.

I subtly (and not so subtly) put the word out in BC's educational network that I was available to conduct a pilot in interested school districts to prove that over 90% of all children could be reading by grade level by the end of grade two. It was a humbling experience. I made presentations to committees in at least six school districts who were intrigued and respectful but didn't call back. After a lifetime of career success and now proposing an urgently needed solution for thousands of vulnerable children, I couldn't comprehend why districts didn't jump at the opportunity.

I know why now. The fact that I was proposing a solution to a decades-old issue was taken as a criticism by in-district literacy coordinators who had not been able to make a significant change in the data. If I was right, then how could they explain they weren't doing the right things? This was complicated by the fact that I was openly critical about the fact that our provincial jurisdiction had gone too far into the "play works best!" mentality promoted by government bureaucrats. Now we were into politics as well as territorial and ego-driven prerogatives!

Solving the puzzle with a little help from friends.

Subsequently, I began speaking about my findings at the *Summits: When Vulnerable Children Thrive Dreams Come True.*

One special day, when I was feeling despondent and somewhat rejected, Director of Instruction Leslie Lambie of School District 59 (Peace River South) called to discuss possibilities in her district. Our pilot began almost immediately and was followed several months later by requests from two other school districts to participate (School District 84, Vancouver Island West and School District 28, Quesnel). Of these three school districts, this chapter documents the progress of only one of the districts and one of the teachers in a second district.

There are two explanations for this:

1. Two of the school districts began the implementation process four months later than Leslie's school district so they have not yet completed a full-year cycle for data-collection purposes; and

2. By late May 2014, the teachers' union and government had reached a stalemate in contract negotiations and our pilot projects had to be set aside temporarily. Data collection ground to a halt and some planned visits were cancelled. We had enough data already to know we are achieving significant success and since this is a three-year project (with an attempt to have over 90% reading fluently at grade level by the end of grade two) this data was intended to help us plan the next year, not as a measure of project success. We were still able to collect enough to draw preliminary conclusions. The remainder of the project data for year one will be collected in the fall of 2014.

Why are pilot sites so important in the making of systemic change?

Pilot sites are laboratories where we can pre- and post-test each child's progress and draw conclusions about implementation success. We can apply theories and measure their success. We can celebrate victories that nourish faith in the change process. We can provide a snapshot of what the change would look like. We can reward those who are ready for change by acknowledging their efforts on behalf of the system. We can provide evidence that will keep the critics at bay. We can grow momentum for those who are ready to implement in the second stage and we can achieve "quick wins."

Quick Wins: What are they and how do we achieve them?

Quick Wins are achievements that are aligned with the overall goals of the project and are immediate evidence that progress is being made. For example, a school population may have been historically low achievers on a data-measure. After a blitz of new resources and instructional processes the school could document, in a six-month period, that 70% of the kindergarten children had learned the alphabet. In a further two-month period, after realigning human resources as support teams to target struggling learners, the school was able to announce that 92% of the same children knew and could apply the alphabet in daily tasks. This is a true story from our case studies. It heartened other staff to adopt a "we can do it" attitude and gave them proven strategies they could try.

We can achieve quick wins by: (a) planning for visible improvements in performance, (b) achieving the wins, (c) communicating the wins visibly and convincingly, and (d) embedding the learning into long-term results. We can achieve visible improvements and quick wins by ensuring they are:

- Measurable,

- Visible, and

- Relevant to stakeholders, objectives, the existing situation and the people.

To achieve quick wins in our pilots we must:
- Build a project plan,
- Identify early implementers for pilots or demonstration,
- Identify short-term wins,
- Build specific tasks and goals into the project plan and budget,
- Give clear accountability for achieving quick wins,
- Assign responsibilities within the guiding teams for monitoring efforts, and
- Ensure there are measurement systems to track data and demonstrate improvements.

To keep the momentum moving year after year we have to communicate the wins visibly and convincingly by setting objectives, targeting audiences, and delivering key and truthful messages using effective mechanisms.

Most importantly, we need to embed the learning into long-term results. Quick results (positive or negative) will provide useful information about the validity of the vision and the feasibility of the change effort. The results will:

- Give you confidence that you have a change plan built on concrete evidence of feasibility and vision,
- Generate support from people in power and with influence,
- Provide momentum for the change effort with more people becoming active supporters and helpers,
- Inspire catalyst teams with renewed motivation for the task of inspiring others to join, and
- Build a sense of excitement as people *see* change happening, *feel* the momentum and want to *act*.

As implementation proceeds, attention will turn, after the first year, into establishing long-term goals that embed the short-term quick wins.

What do change leaders need to consider when establishing pilot sites?

- The degree of need at the site,
- Accessibility issues, facility and resource issues,
- Staff attitudes and capability,
- Curriculum and pedagogy, variety in program models,
- Parent participation,
- Evidence-based practices,
- A staged implementation plan,
- Funding sources, staffing, renovations and resources,
- Quality selection of toys, equipment and resources,
- Multiple levels of leadership,
- Training – timing, content and flexibility, and
- An ongoing supervision plan.

An evaluation plan is critical to implementing systemic change.

Consider:

- The purpose,
- The evaluation principles,
- Input, output and outcome indicators,
- Capacity building,
- Social mobilization,
- A research and documentation agenda,
- Monitoring and measurement plans and, of course
- Regular celebrations.

I highly recommend *The Heart of Change Field Guide: Tools and Tactics for Leading Change in Your Organization* by Dan S. Cohen (Harvard Business School, 2005). It provides very helpful insights into the implementation of pilot projects.

Where and when did we implement Pilot Projects?

Pilot Project #	Place and Grades	Year	Status	Final Report
1.	Bella Bella Community School Kindergarten and Grade Two	2009	One-year project completed	N/A – no written report filed
2.	Vancouver Island University	2012 to 2014	Kindergarten Intervention classes implemented chunks of pilot innovation as a result of assignments	Some Stepping Stones results are reported in Teachers' Stories throughout this book (with the permission of individual students)
3.	School District 59 (Peace River South)	June 2013 to September 2014	Data-collection to be completed in the fall of 2014	Progress Report presented in this chapter
4.	School District 28 (Quesnel)	November 2013 to 2014	Cycle not yet complete	TBA
5.	School District 84 (Vancouver Island West)	December 2013 to 2014	Cycle not yet complete	TBA
6.	Lau'wel nau Tribal School Saanich	June 2014 to 2015	Underway	TBA

Note: It was anticipated that Project # 3 would be fully reported in this book chapter; however, due to provincial job action, the final and detailed data from 55 individual teachers could not be collected in June 2014; rather will be collected in the fall of 2014 and the final report completed at that time.

The following Case Studies with real stories from real teachers will provide you with inspiration I feel sure. Enjoy Stepping Stones in action!

Janet

Research and Recommended Books

Read, Write, Lead

(Routman, 2014)

My dear colleague and friend, Regie Routman, recently sent me a copy of her latest book: *Read, Write, Lead* (2014). This is an important book because it invites—perhaps insists—that the presence of leaders at all levels in the literacy process is essential. This is exactly what became so apparent in the case studies in this chapter. I couldn't have said it better than she did in her introduction. In Regie's words:

Why This Book and Who Is It For?

This is a book about literacy and leadership. Through a lifetime of working in schools, one of my most powerful insights and core beliefs is that teachers must be leaders and principals must know literacy. Without a synergy between literacy and leadership and a committed, joint effort by teachers and principals, fragile achievement gains do not hold. Although much has been written about leadership and learning as well as literacy and learning, little has been written about the crucial interconnection between literacy and leadership for ensuring that all students become effective readers and writers. That partnership is at the heart of successful school-wide literacy and at the heart of this book (page 1).

Brainstorming ideas for our story on the carpet.

I highly recommend this book for school leaders at all levels. Its emphasis on increased achievement through a high-trust school culture of professional commitment, learning, enjoyment and literacy success reflects and references the work of some of my favorite leadership experts such as Michael Fullan and Andy Hargreaves.

Case Study 1: School District 28 (Quesnel)

Teacher Shauna Lothrop

Background

In August my principal invited me to be a part of an Early Literacy Team for our school; we would be attending workshops and training sessions with Dr. Janet Mort. The invitation was exciting because the topic was an area of personal interest for me and I felt it would provide me with an opportunity for professional growth: my students could only benefit from me taking part in this experience.

As well, I was pleased that the district was committing to early literacy since I so strongly believed in it; however, I often felt that I was the last classroom to get support in the school. With the district committing to the project, I hoped early literacy awareness would be raised in our schools. I also liked the idea of a school team being involved in the workshops and training. More people would become aware of the need, and I would have in-school support when I advocated for assistance. Discussing the workshop topics with colleagues would be another benefit.

Initially my principal said that, as a team, we would commit to attending a meeting in September and likely a few more sessions during the school year. Although I anticipated attending a few meetings and walking away with some new ideas to try in class, I never anticipated learning about and understanding the research base so clearly. I felt challenged and excited about re-examining my literacy program. Exploring the variety of ideas gathered through Janet's visits, school district workshops, the *Summits*, and other opportunities (assessment focus groups, phonemic awareness workshop planning, presenting at Pro-D events) was an affirmation that my current practices were right on track.

Janet Mort's Visits

Being introduced to the research base for effective early instruction was most valuable. Previously, I had found literacy instruction to be a series of hit or miss attempts. I might read about an instructional approach or framework but the challenge remained how to determine what was most important for kindergarten students to learn. How could I fit those skills into the new approach or framework? Some ideas succeeded, but others didn't. Now that I know what have been proven essentials for young literacy learners, I can build my instruction on this knowledge.

Janet's encouragement for us to work together as a team and to think "outside the box" led me and the grade 1 teacher to platoon with our students. We met together for 45 minutes of literacy instruction three times a week. I felt I was not meeting the needs of two kindergarten students who were quite good readers. The grade 1 teacher was struggling with students who had not yet mastered some basic phonemic awareness skills. Together with our resource teacher, we split the students into small groups for instruction and practice. With each of us responsible for a number of smaller groups, we would decide how to organize our instruction during those 45-minute periods.

Using a Team Approach

I sent my stronger students to the grade one room to participate with similarly skilled students on appropriate concepts. Five grade-one students who required extra instruction and practice joined my class three times a week. After assessing those children, I split all of the students into groups based on the skills and concepts they needed to practice; the resource teacher and I then worked with different small groups. When not working with one of the teachers, the children were engaged in literacy station activities with the support of an EA (Educational Assistant).

Fabric letters in alphabetical order on the carpet – feel and manipulate the letters with practice singing the ABC song or looking at alphabetical charts to see which letters come next.

Having that time to work with small groups, even for just three days a week, made a significant impact on my students' progress. During these sessions, I assessed the students using the *Circle Charts* and then planned the appropriate instructional activities. With the charts updated, I had a clear picture of each child's standing and what he or she would require in order to move forward. I loved that the small groups were so fluid, with students entering and leaving groups as their skills changed.

Throughout the year, the resource teacher and I switched with the small group instruction sessions so that I could interact with all my students. She would work with students who were right on track or with those who needed more practice in certain skill areas. For example, I might work with a small group of students on initial sounds. Once they began to demonstrate mastery, I could exchange groups with the resource teacher, freeing me to work with a new group. She would continue practicing the skill, yet could also begin instruction in a different skill or concept. Such flexibility was fundamental in providing each student's needs when appropriate.

"Tweaking" My Practices

I was happy to see that many of my literacy practices were affirmed as effective classroom practices. All I needed to do was tweak my current strategies, reintroduce some of my past ideas and experiment with some new literacy practices. My best example of this was re-introducing the Morning Message. Janet talked about the power of shared reading and writing experiences, and that reminded me of my past habit of writing a morning message to my students and then working with them to complete and read it.

I reinstated it, turning it into probably one of the most effective, easily differentiated and useful literacy activities I did with my students this year. We began the year simply looking for target letters in the message, an exercise which soon turned into identifying and reading common sight words such as *we, a, the, is*. They appeared often and so became the first sight words we learned to identify and read.

Integrating Skills Naturally

As we continued, more words, not always just sight words, became familiar and easily read in context. The Morning Message was a perfect place to talk about words, look for letter patterns in words, practice rhyming skills, and discuss punctuation and capitalization. Other reading and writing skills and concepts that we studied were rhyming words, *ee* (screaming *e*'s), *ing* endings, magic *e* words, plurals, contractions, word families, sentence comprehension, punctuation, capitalization and little words inside big words. I realized I had never discussed some of these concepts with my previous kindergarten classes.

The Morning Message provided me with an opportunity to differentiate instruction. Asking the children to help me fill in the blanks allowed me to target certain students for certain concepts thus creating opportunities for all students to participate successfully.

Playing teacher and using a fancy pointer to re-read the Morning Message was a favorite free play activity all year long.

Through investigation of the research base for effective early literacy instruction, I learned that k students were capable of becoming proficient in more than just letter names and sounds. Kindergarten was, in fact, an excellent time to teach fundamental skills. In some way, I felt as if I had finally been given permission to teach what had previously been considered grade one concepts. In the past, I had worried that my classroom would be looked upon as too skill-oriented if I pushed too far forward with literacy skills.

A New Understanding of "Play"

I walked away with a new comprehension of play-based learning. My previous understanding had been that by providing organized, open-ended play opportunities, students would absorb new skills and concepts when they were ready. I had always struggled with not feeling permitted to directly teach to those concepts. The premise had been that children would attain skill competency through play. In the work with Janet, I realized that it was not only relevant and right to plan, organize, and create playful activities and games, but also appropriate to address certain skills and concepts. This permission to organize and to be thoughtfully specific about play activities lifted a weight off my shoulders. Once that was gone, I found it easy to differentiate instruction for my students. Yes, it is work to create the games and learning opportunities for a wide range of students' needs, but hopefully the preparation, in time, will become less because I will have materials created and ready.

These boys decided to use the "Letter Construction' kit to build one of their favorite words – Spiderman. They used their letter-sound knowledge to start spelling the word then realized that 2 of them had the word right on their shirts.

The Value of the Circle Charts

With the *Circle Charts* promoting continuous assessment, my teaching became more responsive and targeted. I used the charts during small group instruction time and also as an indicator for the focus issues for me and the EA (Education Assistant). Short, frequent assessment checks to update the charts were not arduous. Because a student could perform a skill once didn't necessarily mean a filled-in circle. I wanted to see repeated correct use of that skill or concept before I would fill it in.

I used the *Circle Charts* as a working document and at the end of the year transferred the information to a single page record that displayed results clearly showing where students were at the beginning of the year and where they were at the end. In future, I will likely change the alphabet recognition charts to include vowels since I teach them concurrently with consonants. I liked using different colors for different times of the year. When I look over the charts now, I readily see when certain skills and concepts blossomed for certain students. Noting trends in the charts enables me to fine-tune my teaching and be better prepared with certain activities in the coming years.

Following our first session with Janet, I included more daily shared reading. Whenever possible, and in any subject area, I asked students to help me read, pointing out things we already knew and using that text as a teaching moment. Soon, students began to automatically notice things in text and draw my attention to them. Other teachers began to notice when a kindergarten student would point out *ing* in a word during library time, or correctly identify a question mark and why it was used.

The Importance of Explicit Skill Instruction

My appreciation and understanding of phonological awareness and its importance in early literacy definitely increased. Until this point I had been guilty of lumping phonological awareness together with phonics and using the terms interchangeably. Although I included many PA (Phonological Awareness) activities in my teaching, I didn't understand the scope of PA and the progression of skills. I am much more aware of those skills and more mindful of including them, teaching them, being aware of the level of individual students, and therefore, I've become more responsive in my teaching.

This student was practicing sight words with a "Read, Write, Smell' activity. She reads the first word in the column, writes it in the middle, then again in the third column with a smelly marker. The students LOVED using the smelly markers!

The Importance of Joy

"Literacy in a joyful environment" was a key quote for me. It became my mantra! I began to look at which items and activities engaged students most to help me with the planning and use of them. As much as possible, I tried to include novelty items such as smelly markers, magnifying glasses, dice, digital picture frames, beads, foam letters, bingo dobbers, and Play-Doh. I created a variety of resources so that students could practice the same skill but in numerous ways. Providing a range of activities for each skill or concept helped sustain their attention, keep them interested and furnish engaging, meaningful practice.

Professional Learning Communities Between Visits

I found the district's offering of sessions on make-and-take literacy centers, phonemic awareness and assessment between Janet's visits to be most valuable. Another helpful aspect was the direct link from the district's sessions to the visits because it fostered a common language for those of us in the program. We had opportunities to talk with other teachers and we all felt a sense of accountability to each other between the visits. In addition, we collected many new ideas and resources at each session.

Project Enhancements

Different teachers were at different places in their learning and acceptance of some of the ideas. Although I appreciated the school district's encouraging efforts, I found it challenging at times to move ahead slowly when I wanted to plow forward with all the new ideas and practices. I wondered about ways to encourage those who are more eager.

Our requirement next year will be to continue with focused Pro-D sessions, continued K teacher meetings, PLCs, and workshop events. *Question*: How will we share our learning from this year with teachers who will be new next year to the kindergarten and grade one classrooms next year? I thought highly of the February visit with Kamloops staff [another school district] where they shared with us some of their plans like setting up a mentorship program or series of sessions to share learning and help new teachers plan for effective literacy instruction. Teachers should be encouraged to attend out-of-district Pro-D events and then share the knowledge gained; however, funding for such events is limited. [We must be open to new possibilities.]

Question: How do you move teachers forward in their practice without squashing their individual autonomy? This question kept coming back to me because I would become personally frustrated when other teachers appeared to be resistant to change. We need support in our kindergarten classrooms in order to provide the best literacy instruction possible.

Having dedicated resource teacher time was invaluable. My students had access to our resource teacher for 30- to 45-minutes sessions four days a week from October until June. Together, she and I created programs to meet individual and small group needs. Having a strong, hard-working Education Assistant in my room was so important and we worked as a team in every way. I would share information with her after our workshops and explain new things I'd like to try. She would work one-on-one or with small groups on new initiatives. We communicated effectively about student progress, problem-solving when necessary, and I valued and trusted her opinions.

I truly believe that the students in my class this year had the best circumstances for learning: an enthusiastic teacher involved in the first year of the Early Learning project, a dedicated resource teacher, and a capable Education Assistant available in class on a consistent basis.

Class Schedule

Beginning the Day

The first part of the morning was a relaxed introduction to the day. We worked hard at creating routines around our yellow duo-tang work: alphabet and sight word practice, literacy games and reading books. In this way, as they entered the room, students would recognize which activity they would do to start their day. I began the year by introducing one letter of the alphabet each day during our literacy time. In their yellow duo-tangs, the students would complete a page that was a review of the previous day's work. The format of the yellow duo-tang activity stayed the same so that over time, the students could complete it individually.

Kindergarten Schedule 2013-2014

Time					
8:25	Students enter – coats, backpacks put away / Yellow duotang work or Alphabet/Sight Word Practice, Play Literacy Games, or Read Books				
8:45	Literacy Groups K, Gr 1, and RT	Morning Group Time	Literacy Groups K, Gr 1, and RT	Morning Group Time	
9:30	Morning Group Time	Morning Group Time	Journals	Morning Group Time	Journals
10:15	CENTERS				
10:30	RECESS				
10:50	SNACK				
	Literacy – Alphabet or Word Work				
11:20	CALENDAR MATH				
12:00 / 1:00	LUNCH				
	Socials/ Science	Roots of Empathy	Socials/ Science	Socials/ Science	PREP Library
1:45	P.E.	PREP Music	P.E.		
2:30					

An Alphabet PowerPoint

Later in the year when all students were familiar with all letters in the alphabet, I created a PowerPoint presentation for alphabet and sight word practice: it consisted of one letter (upper or lowercase) on each slide. The students would enter the classroom, see the PowerPoint on the Smart board and then move to sit in front of it, ready for the lesson. When I began the slide presentation, they would repeat the name and sound of the letter, and write it on their whiteboard. Once the presentation of 12-15 slides was complete, the students would check a friend's whiteboard for backward or missing letters. I also created a PowerPoint presentation using sight words.

Several mornings a week the students would grab whiteboards, pens and socks (for erasing) and gather in front of the Smartboard. I created a PowerPoint of 10-15 slides with individual letters or sight words. The students would read them and copy on their whiteboards. When done they would check their whiteboard with a friend.

Literacy Games and Practice

I have created and collected many simple literacy games. At times, I would put a variety of free-choice, simple games out on the rainbow table, giving me and me and my Education Assistant an opportunity to interact with the students through their play. We could easily introduce new games or practice old ones to address areas of need with particular students. Teaching new skills was not important during this time. The focus was on practice, practice and practice within a congenial environment.

Reading, Reading, Reading

If students didn't see other obvious activities, they knew this presented an opportunity to go to the classroom library and look at the books. I had organized many buckets, some by topic or author and others by guided reading levels. Students were free to choose any book during this time. Some of the conversations I overheard were just amazing! Good readers enjoyed reading books to students who were still learning letter names. Books I had used for read-alouds were reread in the student's own words, while others created their own stories for the illustrations. I purposefully changed my seasonal or thematic books every few weeks so that there was always something new to look at.

On the day the two-day old baby chicks arrived this student decided they needed to be read a story. He read each page aloud and then leaned over and showed the chicks the pictures.

Learning Independence

From September to January we did not use formal literacy groups or journals. There are many essential independent work skills, foundational skills and concepts that need to be taught in the beginning of the year and establishing these skills early gave the students from January to June the knowledge, skills and concepts to work somewhat independently.

A Letter-a-Day Focus

I started the second week of school introducing activities focused on one letter a day with the whole class using a series of Scholastic alphabet readers to introduce each letter. The books began with a child whose name started with the target letter; then there were four pages of items that started with that letter. They ended with a simple sentence including the child's name and some items mentioned in the book.

After reading the story, we all moved to the tables, and together, re-created the lower and uppercase target letter using Play-Doh. The students LOVED using this medium, since it provides a wonderful opportunity to build and strengthen important fine-motor skills. It's also a great kinesthetic activity for learning the shapes of each letter. We built in a lot of language skills by talking about straight lines, curved lines, diagonal lines, tall and short letters.

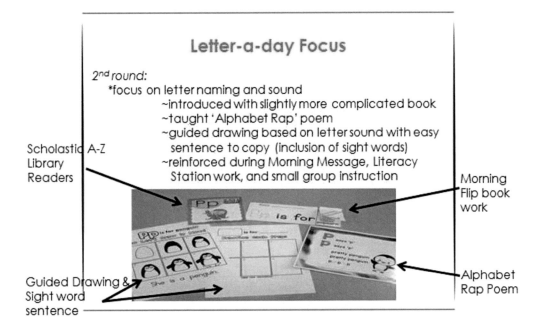

I drew each segment of the target letter on the Smart Board while students replicated it with Play-Doh. We worked together until we had built the upper and lowercase target letter, and I was easily able to move about the room and help students who were having difficulty.

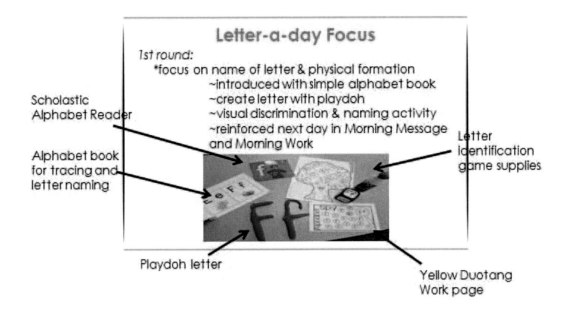

Once finished, I then challenged the students to squish their play-dough back together and rebuild the letter on their own. Some children really struggled to reproduce the letter from the Smart board onto their table. My EA worked with them separately at the rainbow table, using a small whiteboard placed right beside the student and drawing the lines on it for them. One particular child required even more support, and for him we provided large cardstock papers with upper and lowercase letters displayed with felt. He would roll a play-dough snake and then align it on top of the felt to reproduce each letter.

Linking Letters with Games

First Visit to the Alphabet: On the first visit we focused on letter name, recognition and physical formation (with some discussion about letter sound for those students who were ready).

Second Visit to the Alphabet: The second visit was focused on letter/sound association and thus a different set of activities was used to help build this association.

After learning several letters, we played a letter-identification game. I displayed a die, pre-programmed with familiar letters on the Smart Board and gave each child a thematic page and a bingo dobber. For example, if we had been discussing apples the page illustrated an apple tree or if we had read *Chicka Chicka Boom Boom*, the drawing would be a palm tree. Next, one of us touched the Smart Board to start the die rolling. When it stopped, the students all called out the letter name and then searched for it on their paper. Once they found it they covered it with a bingo dob. This was a

great activity for all student levels. Those who were confident called out the names and those still struggling saw and heard the letters repeatedly. As the students entered the classroom the next morning, they used their yellow duo-tangs to look for the previous day's letter. They covered the uppercase letter with one color and the lowercase letter with another. Again, the students saw and heard the names of the letters over and over again, and the coloring gave them some much-needed fine motor practice.

If students are not working with one of the teachers they are assigned an activity in one of four topics. This photo shows the 'Phonemic Awareness' and 'Sight Word' buckets. There are also 'Working with Letters' and 'Working with Sounds.' Each topic has three different activities.

I used the results from my initial alphabet assessment in mid-September to identify students who knew fewer than 20 upper and lowercase letter names. Those students then worked with my classroom EA several times a week to practice tracing over and naming the alphabet letters. I created a simple alphabet book that displayed two letters per page, with each letter represented in upper and lowercase and a simple picture illustrating that letter. My EA pulled students for one-on-one time throughout the day to work with them on this booklet. Together they traced a finger over the letter as they said the name aloud and then named the picture. This series of steps helped to begin building the concept of letter-sound correlation.

By the end of October, we completed the alphabet study and began our second round of letter-a-day work, this time focusing on letter naming and letter-sound correspondence. I read a simple story loaded with words beginning with the target letter.

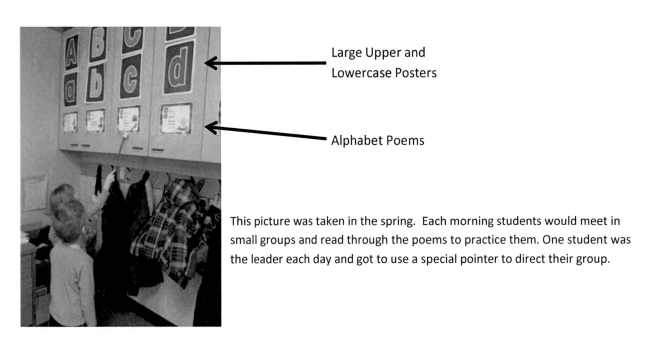

Large Upper and Lowercase Posters

Alphabet Poems

This picture was taken in the spring. Each morning students would meet in small groups and read through the poems to practice them. One student was the leader each day and got to use a special pointer to direct their group.

At the end of the story, we had a quick discussion about the target-letter words and the sound they made. I then taught the students a poem for that letter, having also created an accompanying poster for each poem. That poster was displayed along one side of our classroom under large upper and lowercase letter posters. We reviewed the letters and poems daily and encouraged the students to refer to the poems whenever they were stuck on a letter sound. The posters and poems became valuable tools to help students move toward independence in their reading and writing.

Linking Letters with Sight Words

After practicing the letter name and sound, everyone returned to their tables to participate in a guided drawing activity. Step by step, we drew a simple picture starting with the target letter. The students were given a page with six large boxes on it. When I began drawing on the Smart Board, students recreated it on their page and with the picture completed, we wrote a simple sentence at the bottom of the page about it. That activity offered great opportunities to teach, practice and point out sight words. We had learned a few key sight words by this point in the year and were able to talk about capital and lowercase letters, spacing, punctuation, word recognition and to begin practice sounding out words. I made a conscious effort to keep this process fun and exciting by using praise and encouragement whenever the students could identify words. They became so excited to put their hand up to tell me a word they knew. Soon they wanted to read the whole sentence to me!

The following morning, the students completed an alphabet flip-book independently.

Our Alphabet Flip Book

My objective with the alphabet flip-book was to provide each student with an easy yet engaging activity that introduced the previous day's target letter sound as the initial sound in simple words. The students all started with a full piece of paper. On the top half was the target letter in upper and lowercase (in large print) and the words "is for" and then a box with a word starting with that target letter and a picture to match it. At the bottom of the page were four boxes containing a simple word and a matching picture. The students cut apart the four boxes on the bottom on the page (fine motor practice), then layered all the cut pieces over the word box on the top half of the page and stapled all the pieces together. The students were asked to practice reading their flip book. For example, they would read "Pp is for

pot" then flip the picture over and read the sentence again using the next picture prompt "Pp is for pig" and so on. Once they had practiced the book themselves they could bring it over to me and read it with me. For students who needed the picture and the text clues we would look at both if they came to a word they were unsure of. With these students I'd always end with saying to them "What can Pp say?" For students who were stronger in their letter-sound correlation skills, I might cover up the picture and work with them to sound out the sounds and then

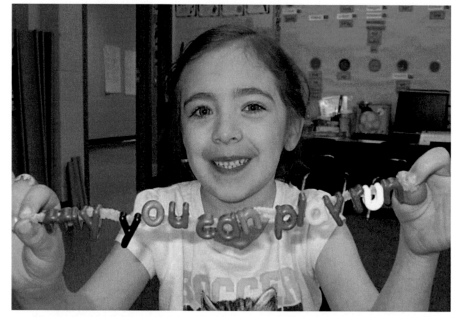

This student built her name using a letter construction kit. Students built sight words, practiced word families and built individual letters of the alphabet.

check to see if they were right by uncovering the picture. The students really enjoyed making the flip books and practicing reading all the different sentences within one book. They were also asked to take the book home and read it with at least one person who was older than they were.

Literacy Groups, initiated in January, were opportunities to platoon with the grade one class. The resource teacher, the grade one teacher, and I worked with small groups and if they were not working with a teacher, they worked at a literacy station.

During the morning group time, we sang the Alphabet song; later in the year we added two Dr. Jean songs, *Alphabet Forwards and Backwards* and *Letter Pops*. We then proceeded to the morning message, the daily agenda, and a story. As for journals, the children did their personal writing while the class EA and I circulated, working with individual or small groups. Center time was free-play time.

Literacy sessions were our alphabet or word-work time, and we usually began with a thematic or seasonal poem, staying with it for at least a week. Early in the year we did a guided drawing for each letter of the alphabet. At this time, we worked on word-family activities, sight words or reading strategies. If individuals or small groups were not ready for the concepts that I was covering, my EA worked with them on more appropriate skills and concepts to be reviewed at a different table.

The students are writing down sight words on hand shaped wipe off boards. I call out the words and ask them to print it on their 'hand' and put their hand in the air when they are done.

The knowledge, skills and concepts for social studies and science were covered with a literacy focus. I used these two subject areas to cover non-fiction literacy skills and concepts through the use of anchor charts, lists and vocabulary charts. Science or social studies vocabulary was then used to practice creating sentences and building simple writing skills. We learned about the features of non-fiction text and practiced labeling our drawings. We also learned how to read for information instead of just for the pleasure of a story.

The Trusting Joyful Environment

A key component to the students' success was the trusting, safe and encouraging environment that we worked so hard to build and sustain throughout the year. I believe that kindergarten is every child's first step into the formalized education system. The experience each child has there plays an important role in how they see themselves as a learner and how willing they become to take risks. My classroom EA and I worked hard to develop strong, understanding, supportive relationships with every student. With some children, my connection was stronger than the classroom EA's connection and vice versa. We tried from the first day of kindergarten to instil in the children their capability to learn, do, and acquire knowledge and skills. I purposely set up situations where the students could show me their knowledge or skills and followed this with acknowledgement and praise for their efforts.

Positive praise is so important in my classroom. The students love to make their teacher happy, and when they see genuine pride and happiness given in return, their confidence and smiles soar. Putting the effort into knowing and understanding each student helps me know how far I can challenge them and also, when it is appropriate to challenge them. I personally do not allow the phrase "I can't…" in my classroom. I begin from the first day of kindergarten helping the children to move from "I can't…" to "I will try…" statements and I continue working on this throughout the year. My intent is to help them see that they can do whatever it is they want, maybe with some assistance or a little change, so they can reach success. A student may say,

This student built his name using magnet letters. Uppercase and lowercase magnet letters are easy to use for a variety of student needs (identify letters, build words, etc.).

"But I can't read this book" and my response is, "You are a reader! Tell me what this word or letter is." My aim is to create a positive experience to show them that there are things they can do even if it requires a little help.

Results: Amazing! Unbelievable! Best Ever!

In my class this year I had a core group of 16 students who were with me the entire year: All 16 of them mastered their letter names and sounds. On our district kindergarten assessment in June, three of them were considered "at risk" for their phonological awareness skills, predominantly in the area of producing rhyming words. This is an area that I see needs more work such as new activities and resources. Twelve of the 16 students were assessed as reading [beyond grade-level expectations] in June. I have never had this many kindergarten students reading at the end of a year!

A core group of students seemed to take longer to acquire new skills, requiring more one-on-one assistance, and needing multiple opportunities to practice emerging skills. This group worked with our resource teacher four times a week for 20-minute sessions from October straight through until June. They generally received the same classroom instruction as all the other students, but when they were required to complete a task, my EA worked with them together for extra support. By modifying the requirements for a finished product, we helped them achieve success. The one-on-one and small group support they received eventually helped them to develop their confidence and begin trying tasks on their own. By the end of the year, one of these students was assessed as being at risk for P.A. (Phonological Awareness) skills, a second was at risk for both alphabetic knowledge and P.A. skills; the other two had mastered all the alphabet and P.A. skills required. A big accomplishment!

Janet's Comment

It is important as well to acknowledge frustrations and worries. It is so important that we seek the support of our administrators and other experts as early in the year as possible to help us deal with attendance and behavioral issues. We need vulnerable children to be present every day to make the kind of progress they need to close experiential gaps. Shauna describes her disappointment:

Janet

Not all children were as successful; however, there were competing issues that confronted me. One student who joined us in November did not know many letter names when he arrived. He had missed many days of school throughout the year; sometimes I saw him only once or twice a week. However, by the June assessment he was identified as being at risk for alphabet knowledge and phonological awareness skills. A second child with behavioral issues began the year with us but was withdrawn and enrolled in homeschooling in late September. He re-enrolled in April and attended a part-day program, starting with one hour a day in the afternoon and finishing the year attending school for two hours a day. He finished the year identified as being at risk for alphabet knowledge, phonological awareness skills, and social emotional needs on our June kindergarten assessment. [Special support will be needed next year, attendance being a key issue.]

The Future

I want to continue on this journey of discovering what really matters and what really works for early literacy learners. I intend to continue exploring what the experts are saying and implementing new ideas and strategies in my classroom. I want to continue looking into the area of writing instruction. My students this year are far better writers than previous classes, although I don't necessarily think it's because I did a better job of teaching them to write. I believe that the reading skills and strategies I helped them develop ultimately led them to greater understanding and awareness in their writing, as well as their ability to sound out words, and to use the class word wall.

I think that my classroom is more joyful now. The students and I are delighted to use their growing skills to unlock the joy of words. I can see the excitement in their eyes when they can ably use a new skill or identify a letter or word correctly. This is a journey that we are taking together: For every student the journey is unique, and they all reach a different place on the road to becoming readers and writers. However, we celebrate every achievement with a pat on the back for ourselves for a job well done. I feel privileged to be a part of every single student's journey!

This project has re-kindled my interest in working with teachers in a leadership or mentorship role towards improving literacy instruction. It is not that I think I have all the right answers or am a stellar teacher. Rather, I hope to spark encouragement in teachers that will lead them to think about their own instructional strategies. I have had a few opportunities already to engage in a leadership role, both within my district and at a regional Pro-D event. My hope is to continue finding opportunities to grow as a leader, not only for students but for teachers as well.

Students use a magnifying glass to find tiny sight words that are hidden in a picture. Once they find one they record it on a sheet.

A Special Story About Dominic

Dominic - A Success Story

Dominic enrolled in kindergarten with minimal literacy or social exposure. Despite the fact that his two older brothers attended our school, we had never actually seen Dominic in our building even though a *Strong Start Centre* had operated there since he was born.

Initially, Dominic was overwhelmed by the other students, the sheer number of new experiences he encountered and the classroom environment as a whole. He flitted from place to place in the classroom since so many things caught his attention. Keeping him focused on one thing at a time was very difficult.

We quickly learned that Dominic hadn't been exposed to the alphabet, nor could he recognize his name. He seemed surprised to learn of things called *letters*, then shocked to find out he must remember their names. We focused on learning the first three letters of his name since this was his nickname at home. With any activity, Dominic required a lot of adult support since he lacked the ability to hold a pencil and make a discernable shape; he wasn't capable of following more than one direction at a time or working quietly at a table. Despite the many challenges,

Dominic remained happy and was usually willing to try new activities with adult help.

We were surprised to discover that Dominic had never removed stickers from a sticker sheet. We realized that every experience we gave him would likely be new to him. This was going to be his year of firsts! In addition to EA support with all class activities, Dominic also received help from our LART four times a week for 20 minutes a session. Their work began slowly with learning alphabet names and as the year progressed, their work gradually included letter sounds and important phonological awareness skills.

Dominic thrived on praise. His chest would puff out and an enormous smile would spread across his face when we complimented him on his efforts and acknowledged his improvements.

In April, while working on a group word work project, Dominic offered to help another student who was struggling to figure out the *hu* sound belonging to *h*. Dominic leaned over saying, "That's the letter *h*." He said it in such a matter-of-fact way and was so sure of himself that the classroom EA and I were both shocked. Not only has this boy learned that there are 26 upper **and** lowercase letters, their

associated sounds, and that combining these sounds makes words, but he is confident enough in his new skills and knowledge to want to help out a friend! Slowly through the month we watched Dominic's confidence soar. When he announced one day, "I can read this book," we quickly sat down with him while he read the book, which he had memorized. He now saw himself as a reader and began offering answers during our daily morning message work. Earlier in the year, he had even had trouble sitting through the message, never mind being actively involved.

Describing the progress Dominic has made this year warms my heart. His positive, hard-working nature, the efforts of a variety of school staff, as well as the focus on early literacy instruction has given him a chance to be successful. He is going to enter grade one with more independence, skills, and knowledge than I would ever have thought possible in September. Dominic is one of our success stories: He is proof that it can be done!

Shauna Lothrop, Kindergarten Teacher

Case Study 2: School District 59 (Peace River South)

Please note: School District 59 Peace River South named its project the *SD 59 Primary Literacy Project.* For the purpose of the researcher's work (Janet Mort, PhD), all five projects she is involved in are called research pilot projects, hence the different name references. Janet will eventually report on the results of five different pilot projects for the purposes of research. From the perspective of School District 59 the project is considered to be an integrated three-year project, which will form a permanent curricular base for early learning. There is no discrepancy between these designations, rather viewed for different purposes (research vs. implementation). Each one informs the other.

Some of the 55 participants in the School District 59 Primary Project attending a Summit.

Background

Contact with the Director of Instruction

Through the Summit events, I had been actively seeking pilot sites that might be interested in exploring and implementing the latest research on early intervention, specifically, the skills identified in the NELP (National Early Literacy Panel) Report. I had been speaking publicly and candidly about the need for change in our primary programs – including explicit instruction of literacy skills in playful classrooms. Director Leslie Lambie of School District 59 approached me about the possibility of generating a project and providing leadership with her primary and district staff. My **real** interest was to establish pilot projects throughout the province that we could use to demonstrate what could happen for vulnerable children if we developed new literacy expectations at the primary level. Leslie's interest was to rejuvenate the school district's existing primary project in order to provide more successful opportunities for vulnerable children. It was clear to me that our interests and goals were symbiotic and compatible. We agreed to proceed with implementation.

Examining the Current State of Affairs

Prior to establishing the long-term vision, school district staff examined the existing state of affairs that would guide implementation decisions: The assessment included the following acknowledgements:

- Many inexperienced teachers are responsible for multi-age classes;
- Some teachers are very experienced;
- Ten schools are rural;
- Most schools have a literacy goal;
- All elementary teachers are required to have a literacy goal in instructional plans;
- There is strong general awareness of literacy but not necessarily strong practice;
- Literacy practices are stronger in primary compared to intermediate and there is much less emphasis on teaching reading after grade three;
- Some administrators are uncertain about literacy practices and therefore unable to supervise adequately;
- Many teachers want literacy in-service;
- There are coach/mentors in every school and helping teachers in every region but inconsistent use of them and some teachers do not "buy in" to the model;
- There are many good resources for literacy support – human and otherwise; and
- There is an excellent collection of long-term data on students' reading [decoding] already.

First Stage: Project Preparation

I prepared a description of expectations for the project for Director Lambie's consideration. (Since then, Director Lambie has become Superintendent of Schools.) Based on the prevailing research on change and literacy, my major expectations included the following:

- Participants would be volunteers in school teams and administrators would actively participate;
- Janet Mort would attend in the district at least four times a year to present research to in-service staff, provide coaching and monitor the progress;

- Participants would commit to honoring the research in their practice, teaching and tracking the identified essential skills, and submitting related data to the central office;

- The overall goal would be that 90% of all children entering kindergarten would be readers and writers at the appropriate literacy level by the end of grade three; the other 10% would be at the best of personal potential; and

- The district would be responsible for project supervision, support and coaching between my visits. The team was to be called The *Project Facilitators* and included key district staff.

In response, in June 2013, Director Lambie sent an invitation to primary teachers to attend an after-school district information session. Its purpose was to learn about the possibilities inherent in the project, the commitments required for participation and to respond to an invitation to commit to the project. She held an information session after school on June 27th, 2013 to discuss the possibilities for the project. At this session she distributed a "commitment" document, which teachers were to return before the end of the month. It was anticipated that perhaps a dozen teachers from up to six schools would commit to the project. Much to her surprise, almost 100 teachers attended the information session and (within the week) 65 teachers had returned the personal commitment letter to the central office. A total of 11 schools committed with all primary teachers involved; four schools had some individual teachers but not the full primary staff; two schools did not commit.

The following presentation was made to the School Board and other stakeholders.

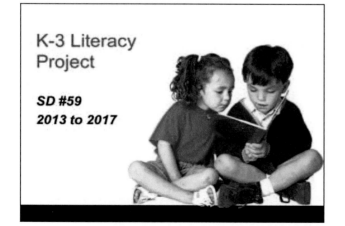

K-3 Literacy Project

SD #59
2013 to 2017

Our Goals

- 90% of students will be reading at grade level by the end of grade 3
- 100% of students will show growth in literacy and numeracy skills based on their personal learning profiles.

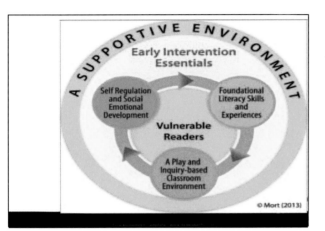

The Vision

- 120 minutes of daily, uninterrupted time for literacy.
- The 2 other focus areas that will be reported on are numeracy and social emotional learning.
- PE/Art/Music are integrated. These and any other prep blocks will be scheduled in the afternoon.
- Other curricular area themes are incorporated into the 3 focus areas but not reported on.
- An inquiry/activity based environment.

Who is Involved 2013/14

- K and 1 classes: pilot cohort
- Grade 2/3 classes: Participants but not required to collect supplementary data (2013/14)
- Teams : Teachers, Principals, LAT's, Coach/Mentors
- Recommended supplementary supports: SLP Dept., Counsellors, Helping Teachers, Reading Recovery Teachers, Pilot Facilitators, Strong Start, ECE and Support staff as appropriate to each site.

Teacher Commitment:

- Implement pilot classroom structure including Language centers which may be developed in collaboration with Speech/Language department
- Engage in monthly after school Professional Learning Community(PLC) sessions on a variety of early childhood teaching and learning topics
- Open classroom to peer and specialist visits
- Participate in 2 day working session in late August with Dr. Janet Mort who will share her research and expertise around foundational literacy and supporting practices

Teacher Commitment

- Share and reflect on data to inform planning and instruction
- Engage in structured data collection:
  - ongoing formative assessment data i.e. observation survey of early literacy achievement (running records ongoing grades 1-3)
  - summative assessment data twice a year i.e.,Fountas & Pinnell team scored writing assessment 2 times a year (Grade 1)
- Team scored writing assessment twice a year (Grade 1)

District Commitment

- The project will be ongoing and will be adjusted based on literacy data. The K cohort will be specifically tracked from 2013 to 2017 when these students will be exiting Grade 3.
- New participants will be welcomed at the **beginning** of any year and existing participants will continue to be supported.

District Commitment:

- Provide foundational resources (furniture, games & manipulatives) and access to limited funds for teachers to choose classroom enhancements
- Priority access to the Literacy Helping Teacher
- Investigate and implement, over time, the placement of a paraprofessional Early Childhood Educator (ECE) in each K/1 classroom

District Commitment:

- Provide targeted funding to support travel and Professional Development
- Facilitate the PLC's and provide meals for gatherings
- If there are sufficient number of participants in each community, PLC's will be held in those communities
- Provide facilitation for the development and endorse alternate report card
- Pilot facilitators commit to regular, on-site visits to classrooms

Pilot Project teachers and administrators were asked to commit to these tasks:

- Implementing a new assessment strategy based on the NELP (National Early Literacy Panel) report;

- Attending eight specified training days with Janet Mort over the course of the year;

- Focusing on literacy as the highest curriculum priority;

- Scheduling at least 120 minutes of uninterrupted literacy instruction per day;

- Collecting specified data with a goal of over 90% of present kindergarten readers/writers being able to read and write at grade level by the end of grade three in 2017;

- Implementing the Fountas and Pinnell assessment system (2009) and the *Circle Charts* for primary classes;

- Attending and participating in PLCs (Professional Learning Communities) between Janet's visits in evening sessions;

- Committing to working on the project on three additional Saturdays during the school year;

- Implementing a new pilot report card that reflects the focus on literacy and the above commitments; and

- Communicating regularly with parents regarding the project.

Communicating to Parents and the Public

The following is the SD 59 information letter that explained the project and its purpose:

Dear Parents:

The vision of the School District and (**NAME OF SCHOOL**) is that 90% of students entering kindergarten in the fall of 2013 will be reading, writing and using numbers confidently and competently, at grade level, when they enter grade 4 in 2017! Further, we have a vision that all students will be achieving to their fullest personal potential based on goals set forth in the individual instructional plans developed to address special needs.

To this end we are beginning an exciting primary project (Kindergarten – Grade 3) and your child's class will be participating. This project involves an intense focus on literacy, numeracy, inquiry-based learning and social emotional learning, which is based on current educational research. Other subject areas such as science and social studies will be integrated in the context of literacy and numeracy and not reported on separately. Teachers will be engaging in practices and ongoing professional development that supports this approach.

We are very fortunate to have Dr. Janet Mort, an adjunct professor and researcher from Vancouver Island University, working with us to ensure quality experiences for our students and in teachers' professional learning journeys. Also supporting the work of the classroom teachers will be the various District Helping Teachers for literacy, numeracy, speech and language development, and special needs. Partners in our school will be the (Principal/Vice-Principal, Learning Assistance Teacher, Coach/Mentor Teacher, Reading Recovery Teacher ...... (**INSERT WHAT APPLIES TO YOUR SCHOOL**)

The only big difference you will see at home is in the report card. The report will provide performance ratings and comments on language arts, math and social/ emotional development. Themes from the content areas will be covered through the literacy and numeracy programs. Physical education and fine arts will be integrated throughout.

We are very much looking forward to engaging in this work and to celebrating your child's achievements over the year and the years to come. In addition to reporting on your child's individual progress, we will regularly monitor our overall school progress and provide periodic updates at key points in the year (January and June).

Please feel free to talk to your child's teacher and me at any time you have questions or want ideas about how you can support our work at home.

Sincerely,

[Principal of School]

Creating a Long-term Vision

Prior to project commencement, the district established a long-term vision and commitment for the entire school district including:

- Ongoing literacy professional development for all administrators,
- Ongoing foundational teacher professional development,
- Revision of the Helping Teacher model and Learning Assistance Teacher model,
- A shift of resource allocations,
- A shift in assessment models to include Fountas and Pinnell (2009) including teacher training,
- Resource purchasing to align with new priorities,
- A summer institute revival (foundational understandings), and
- Transition plans with an up to grade eight focus on literacy.

Committing to an Intense Professional Development Plan

The Summits: The district committed to sending a team of randomly selected attendees to each of the *Vancouver Island University* sponsored *Summits on Vulnerable Children*. These representatives would be responsible for reporting back to the pilot participants to inform them about emerging developments.

Planning Pilot Participant In-service Dates

Four two-day dates were established for the year when Janet Mort would meet with all participants to conduct training sessions. Initial dates were set for August 2013, October 2013, January 2014 and May 2014. These sessions would provide participants with 40 hours of professional development. Additional training in Professional Learning communities and special guests would provide them with in excess of the 60 hours that Richard Allington recommends for annual training necessary for successful change processes.

Planning Professional Learning Community Dates

These sessions were intended to (a) support learning at the Janet Mort training sessions, (b) give the district Facilitator Team access to participants to monitor progress, (c) provide participants with time to share and problem solve, and (d) provide all participants with time for further planning for the next steps.

Providing Resources

Janet Mort provided a list of recommended resources for classrooms including games and activities, professional books and professional journal articles. Participants were invited to submit special requests. The District Resource Center ordered materials centrally; the new resources were displayed at the first training session in August. Kindergarten and grade one teachers would be given first priority followed by grades two and three. Materials would be bar-coded so that they could be traced and shared. Teachers were asked to return items when they were no longer using them. Once checked out, the resources were to be considered the property of the teacher for the school year.

Rich and varied resources make learning challenging.

The district invested an initial $30,000 to upgrade participating primary classes with essential items. To ensure ongoing maintenance and upgrading, the district requested that schools take responsibility for classroom furniture purchase through internal adjustments and make a long-term purchasing plan to accommodate future needs.

Second Stage: Project Implementation

The three main features of the yearlong project implementation were:

1. Training Sessions with Dr. Janet Mort
2. Classroom Implementation; Teacher Action; District Support
3. Ongoing Professional Learning Communities

Teacher Training Sessions with Dr. Janet Mort

A total of four two-day training sessions were held between August 2014 and June 2014, the first just before school started in August 2014. The planned curriculum for teachers was based on the items named in the NELP Report as having the greatest impact on future reading ability and success as well as related research and books and articles. At each session Janet asked for feedback from staff related to (a) issues they were facing where they would like more information, (b) a better understanding of the research, or (c) more detailed training. Janet began every session with an overview of the latest research (post-2005). She also provided each staff member with a binder organized into sections that focused on each facet of the NELP Report as a personal reference.

The two-day presentation format comprised a combination of research overviews, discussion activities, content presentations, article analysis, problem-solving strategies, report-outs on implementation successes and roadblocks, data analysis, storytelling and teambuilding. (Janet also conducted a special one-day session for district staff and administrators in late September. School and district-level administrators were expected to participate in all workshops and Professional Learning Communities. The purpose was to develop an understanding of how district and leadership positions could help to support teachers during the project.)

Topics addressed in the four teacher training sessions (as well as personal coaching, interviews and site monitoring):

August 2013

- Early Learning Research in British Columbia (Hertzman, 2009),
- The NELP Report highlights,
- The essential literacy skills,
- Janet's graphic of the balanced classroom,
- Introduction of the reference binders,
- A new tool for tracking skills – *The Circle Charts*;
- The role of learning centers in a balanced classroom; and
- The relative roles of shared reading and guided reading.

October 2013

- Review of the NELP Report;
- Alphabetic principles and phonological awareness;
- Sight words and spelling;
- Shared reading;
- Change and transitions;
- Print awareness;
- Emergent writing;
- The connection between oral language and other skills;
- Revisiting learning centers;
- Essential literacy skills review; and
- Role of oral language.

January 2014

- The role of administrators in supporting change,
- Human resource support options for classroom teachers,
- Review of strengths, issues and opportunities,
- Emerging district data-analysis,
- Success stories and challenges,
- Roadblocks to 90% success rate, and
- Curriculum expectations: Clarification.

May 2014

- Story and experience sharing,
- Data collection and *Circle Chart* sharing,
- Summer reading loss: How to intervene,
- Transition from this year to next year,
- Family meetings, and
- School groups planning for next year.

An additional visit was arranged for data collection, document reviews and small group meeting and interviews as part of documenting the project and student results.

What is the Essence of a Professional Learning Community?

The implementation of professional learning communities, in essence, is an effort to move the focus of leadership from central office control to a focus on supporting school-level improvements. In the process, systems, processes and access to resources become the responsibility of those at the school level, supported by central systems. There is a strong emphasis on gradual and continued improvement.

While central staff realizes that the results that matter are found at the school level, the essential role of district level staff changes to a focus on helping school staff to implement their improvement plans. Long-standing practices and procedures that interfere with school improvement need to be modified. School administrators have the responsibility to ensure professional learning communities thrive at the school level. District administrators have the responsibility to ensure professional learning communities thrive at the district level while focusing on system-wide initiatives such as the Early Learning pilot projects.

School District 59 Primary Literacy Project: The Professional Learning Community

Peace River South pilot participants and district staff collaborated to host regular PLCs between Janet Mort's four professional development sessions. These were held on a monthly basis. They took place after school hours in two of three communities served by the district (Dawson Creek and Tumbler Ridge) with dinner provided. Momentum was maintained through an agenda that was action-oriented and generated by participants, not in-service or generated by district staff. Highlights included door prizes (Starbucks cards, stickers, children's books, stickers). Celebrations with balloons and table treats were the order of the day. Checking-in and checking-out activities kept staff involved and engaged. Sticky notes, games, emotional tributes and sharing and fun announcements kept the pace upbeat. When one teacher had a story about a child to share, it was often accompanied by appreciative applause and standing ovations.

The participants reported that "Table Talk" was invigorating. It involved selected sharing, videos, rapid-fire brainstorms, book draws, perusal of resource displays, generation of inquiry questions to be organized for next sessions, problem solving and colleague-solution presentations.

Examples:

- The group of 65 teachers assembled in small groups to prepare a report card model that would be consistent with the pilot project approach to literacy.

- Data was being collected on skill mastery for individual children and presented on a composite chart; it was a complex process. The PLC assisted by generating a list of questions that could be used to explore and analyze the data at the classroom and school level.

- Areas of concern were always (and normally) bubbling under the surface. The PLC made certain that processes were consistently in place to raise even the most minor issues in safe ways, then follow up by making them part of future agendas.

- In the early stages of implementation, the following topics were of universal interest: learning centers, use of resources, daily schedules, differentiation for children, building relationships and how to incorporate each issue into the classroom. At one popular PLC meeting, the 65 participants were divided into seven small groups – each given a specific question and challenge. The refreshing recommendations and suggestions at the end of the PLC session heartened participants.

The fact that **all** participants attended **all** sessions after a hard day of classroom work is testimony to the importance and effectiveness of the SD 59 *Primary Literacy Project's* Professional Learning Community in Peace River South.

Ten Months Later: Pilot Results

Quantitative Data

District Analysis

The project began in August 2013. Screening for alphabetic principles and phonological awareness were completed by the end of October and the intervention plan began. In January 2014, we were eager to know how we were doing district-wide so that we could target resources as necessary, troubleshoot together and provide support in creative ways. This required considerable trust, as teachers were asked to submit the results of their assessments, documented on the *Circle Charts*, to the central office.

There was some individual anxiety but district staff promised that the results would be used respectfully and individuals would not be identified. Results were aggregated district-wide; school results were provided to school teams. Individual classroom results were not identified (although it was possible to guess class results by considering numbers of students and other clues). The following chart was projected on a screen followed by a group discussion and analysis.

Sorting Alphabet Soup letters and finding words.

Primary Pilot Project Data

Date	Grade	# of Students	Alphabet Knowledge K/1 (M NM)	Phono Skills Rhyming/Discrim K (M NM)	Rhyming Production K (M NM)	Isolation K (M NM)	Blending Syllables K (M NM)	Segmentation K (M NM)	Deletion K (M NM)	Isolation Medial 1 (M NM)	Isolation Final 1 (M NM)	Blending 1 (M NM)	Segmentation 1 (M NM)	Segmentation Phonemes 1 (M NM)	Meeting in All Areas
Jan 23, 2014	K	21	0 21	14 7	11 10	13 8	19 2	17 4	18 3						
Jan 23, 2014	K	20	4 16	16 4	12 8	16 4	17 3	10 10	13 7						
Jan 23, 2014	K	7		6 1	6 1	5 2	5 2	4 3	4 3						
Jan 23, 2014	K	22	0 22	12 10	12 10	8 14	13 9	8 14	8 14						
Jan 23, 2014	K	17	2 15	5 12	2 15	14 3	9 8	7 10	12 5						
Jan 23, 2014	K	17	2 15	5 12	2 15	14 3	9 8	7 10	12 5						
Jan 23, 2014	K	4	3 1	4 0	2 2	1 3	3 1	3 1	4 0						
Jan 23, 2014	K	4	0 4	0 4	2 2	3 1	2 2	1 3	3 1						
Jan 23, 2014	K	5	2 3	5 0	2 3	5 0	5 0	2 3	5 0						
Jan 23, 2014	K	1	0 1	0 1	0 1	0 1	0 1	0 1	0 1						
Jan 23, 2014	K	22	8 14	14 8	7 15	12 10	15 7	8 14	10 12						
Jan 23, 2014	K	12	1 11	8 4	8 4	12 0	10 2	10 2	10 2						
Jan 23, 2014	K	18	2 16	2 16	3 15	3 15	0 18	12 6	0 18						
Jan 23, 2014	K	21	15 6	4 17	6 15	15 6	15 6	15 6	4 17						
Jan 23, 2014	K	7	1 6	2 5	2 5	2 5	2 5	2 5	2 5						
Jan 23, 2014	K	9	1 8	6 3	4 5	6 3	6 3	8 1	6 3						
Jan 23, 2014	K	15	1 14	12 3	10 5	12 3	10 5	3 12	10 5	12 3	10 5	8 7	9 6	9 6	
Subtotal	**K**	**222**	**42 173**	**115 107**	**91 131**	**141 81**	**140 82**	**117 105**	**121 101**	**12 3**	**10 5**	**8 7**	**9 6**	**9 6**	
Jan 23, 2014	1	3	0 3	2 1	0 3	2 1	2 1	0 3	2 1	0 3	0 3	1 2	0 3	1 2	
Jan 23, 2014	1	21	16 5	18 3	19 2	21 0	20 1	21 0	20 1	5 16	15 6	14 7	17 4	11 10	
Jan 23, 2014	1	8								5 3	8 0	5 3	8 0	6 2	
Jan 23, 2014	1	14	11 3							10 4	11 3	11 3	11 3	11 3	
Jan 23, 2014	1	22	11 11							20 2	22 0	21 1	22 0	19 3	
Jan 23, 2014	1	10	4 6							4 6	6 4	4 6	5 5	3 7	
Jan 23, 2014	1	10	5 5	7 3	8 2	9 1	9 1	8 2	8 2	2 8	9 1	7 3	2 8	2 8	
Jan 23, 2014	1	11	4 7							6 5	9 2	8 3	8 3	6 5	
Jan 23, 2014	1	7	5 2							5 2	5 2	3 4	3 4	0 7	
Jan 23, 2014	1	4	1 3	4 0	3 1	4 0	4 0	4 0	4 0	1 3	4 0	4 0	4 0	3 1	
Jan 23, 2014	1	24	18 6	20 4	14 10	22 2	21 3	20 4	17 7	14 10	16 8	9 15	19 5	6 18	
Jan 23, 2014	1	9	3 6	8 1	5 4	9 0			2 7	7 2	8 1	6 3	7 2	2 7	
Jan 23, 2014	1	13	6 7	13 0	12 1	13 0	13 0	12 1	13 0	4 9	11 2	13 0	12 1	13 0	
Jan 23, 2014	1	14	3 11							6 8	12 2	9 5	9 5	3 11	
Jan 23, 2014	1	16	10 6							13 3	13 3	13 3	11 5	10 6	
Jan 23, 2014	1	10	6 4							5 5	5 5	5 5	5 5	5 5	
Jan 23, 2014	1	7	1 6							3 4	5 2	6 1	7 0	2 5	
Jan 23, 2014	1	3	2 1							3 0	3 0	3 0	3 0	3 0	
Jan 23, 2014	1	4	3 1							4 0	4 0	3 1	3 1	0 4	
Jan 23, 2014	1	5	0 5							0 5	0 5	0 5	2 3	0 5	
Subtotal	**1**	**215**	**109 98**	**72 12**	**61 23**	**80 4**	**69 6**	**65 10**	**66 18**	**117 98**	**166 49**	**145 70**	**158 57**	**106 109**	
Grand Total		**437**	**151 271**	**187 119**	**152 154**	**221 85**	**209 88**	**182 115**	**187 119**	**129 101**	**176 54**	**153 77**	**167 63**	**115 115**	

We identified discrepancies on the chart. We asked questions. We speculated using
sentence stems like "Why is it that…? Could it be that…? Compare this column with
that column…" We identified what appeared to be concerns: "No children have
mastered that letter of the alphabet yet, shouldn't some have mastered it by now?"
We kept the conversation speculative although, from time to time, a teacher would
call out, "No, that was my class – I just haven't taught it yet!"

We then put participants into school groups with administrators who already had the school results. Their assigned task was to examine their individual class and student results to determine:

1. How were the children faring related to each skill?

2. Why was there such little mastery of some skills?

3. Did the class seem on track or were there worrisome areas?

4. Is there a particular student who seems to require assistance beyond the classroom?

5. Were there areas that needed to be "blitzed" (targeted with an intensive effort to improve results)?

6. Did school resources need to be realigned to improve results and if so, how?

7. How were the individual teachers feeling: Did they need collegial support? How could the others provide it?

Within a month of this meeting there were significant changes in the aggregate results with marvelous stories of school and district teams providing support.

Summary of Data to July 2014

In the fall of 2014 final data sets will be completed. They will include the district analysis of aggregate achievements for each of the alphabetic principles and phonological awareness skills; Fountas and Pinnell (2009) reading levels; completed *Circle Charts* and other benchmarks. In June 2014 we were able to examine partial data sets for the *Peabody Picture and Vocabulary Test,* and pre- and post-kindergarten screening results conducted by speech pathologists. We were able to reach the following conclusions with confidence:

- Significant numbers of vulnerable children are reading and writing at the end of kindergarten compared to previous years;

- Many vulnerable children are exceeding one year of anticipated progress in less than 10 months;

- The *Circle Chart* tracking device is popular and working well to inform daily instruction;

- Vulnerable children are thriving and learning to read and write in joyful, challenging environments;

- All pilot sites outperformed non-pilot sites in the first 10 months as measured on a standardized test;

- Teachers are excited, enthusiastic and proud; they are learning new skills and applying them with results they can measure; and

- Quantitative data is confirming the qualitative data.

Qualitative Data

I returned to Peace River to conduct interviews with staff and to collect stories. In spite of the job action, many teachers were eager to share their stories and attended meetings off school sites and after school hours – this was a reflection of their commitment to the project. Eleven teachers, eight district staff, and four administrators were interviewed; comments were recorded with permission. The resulting transcription was a total of 28 pages. Their comments have been collated in categories. All comments were included unless they were repetitive. All negative comments are included (there were very few).

Peace River Interviews:
Teachers and Administrators

- We have a high rate of ESL (English Second Language) students in our school yet the results from this year's k and grade 1 classes are the best we have ever had. Our K and grade one results on the district K screener indicate almost 100% skill success rate—the greatest success ever in our records. I think the teachers understand the process, the instructional requirements of the reading program, and the process of engaging children through small group work.

- The implementation of the project has made a definitive, constructive change in the classroom. We now always know each child's skill level. We understand each child's learning needs and we coach the child accordingly. A most exciting moment for me was promoting and witnessing how children can teach each other and the power that is engendered. Previously, when I worked with a small group here, I gave the others something that perhaps wasn't quite so meaningful. I am ashamed to admit it, but as I worked with a group with guided reading or writing, I gave the others something like worksheets that would keep them quiet. Now they are practicing in learning centers and every minute of their time is useful.

Reading and learning together.

- I think the children are a lot more joyful. They appear to be more engaged, more confident and proud of themselves.

Building patterns together with pattern blocks.

- The project gave me a great sense of each student's progress. This year's class had many challenges—a class with over 50% vulnerable, the majority of the students coming from a classroom comprising just play-based activities; some of the children had been in that classroom for two years and had very few literacy skills. Now, at this year's end, there is only one extremely vulnerable child and three on the edge of grade level literacy. What a transformation from over 50% vulnerability to only three students needing extra support! I will be keeping these children next year and targeting them to ensure they master all their skills.

Program

- Our school composition is 63% aboriginal children. The kindergarten teacher has struggled with a play-based program, not knowing exactly how to implement it effectively. She really enjoyed this year, especially because she was moving into the learning centers and away from the more unstructured play-based program. We found in the last four years that the vulnerable children entering kindergarten after a play-based program were still vulnerable at the end of their year.

- I changed my schedule so that the whole morning was language arts, reading, writing and playing. In the afternoon we had more quiet reading time, shared reading and buddy reading. The children never tired of reading—even during playtime some of them wanted to read and write. One of the little girls came to me with black around her mouth; I looked down to see that she had words all over her arm. I looked at two of her friends; they had words all over their arms. That was playtime, and they had chosen to write instead of play (albeit in an unusual way). They infused more reading and writing into their play than I ever imagined possible.

- You might be asking, "Why didn't I do this before?" My answer is that I didn't know **how** to do it before. I think in some respects I put more of the onus of learning on the students this year. I was asking more often, "What should we do next?" I posed more questions and listened to their responses to guide my planning. Previously, I would plan activities without even asking them what they would like to do. Now they have become partners in the planning and have helped me set up some of their favorite learning centers.

- I know the project made a huge difference in what I am currently doing with my students who are like the rest of the school, aboriginal children in poverty. They have many challenges. One of my delights is observing their happiness about working hard. It gives me goose bumps! How often do you see children who want to get the centers out and are excited about them? They leave me notes saying, "I love you Mrs. D. Thank you for this center." They have their favorites, and I give them the choice of their favorite center because I want them to be independent as well as accountable. In their center book they write the date, their name and the center they worked on. Then, as I look through the book, I can see they are not just sticking to the ones they prefer.

The cook in "My Little Restaurant."

- The children vote on centers they want or don't want to create. My Little Restaurant transformed from playtime into mainstream learning center time because they loved it; they were writing in it. However, I decide which skills will be practiced.

Classroom Support

- We created a program for high school students interested in education. They received a credit for working with our vulnerable students. These secondary students came to our school every morning from recess to 11:30 a.m. to manage a center; they felt really important while also earning community action credits.

- The speech pathologist offered a training day for support staff so they could apply specific strategies in the primary program.

- We switched our delivery of learning assistance to devote a two-week period to vulnerable students. For one-half hour a day I worked one-on-one with them to teach phonemic awareness. Our learning assistant practiced other skills with the remaining children. I hope we can maintain this structure.

- In January we went to the high school to ask for volunteer students to help during a block of 10:30 to 11:30 every day; we found enough volunteers for each class to have one helper for that hour. We showed them what to do; my 16 boys loved having a male literacy coach. They were upset when occasionally he couldn't be there, but I explained to them that his own schooling had to come first. Games were the order of the day.

Collaboration

- Learning and understanding more about the vulnerable children's needs enabled us to bring the entire school on board. The excitement tumbled into the whole school when everyone became involved in the project. It was very satisfying to open those doors and learn with my colleagues because, together, we all began to understand the connection between early learning and future success.

- The PLCs (Professional Learning Communities) were invaluable keys to success for everybody and especially for our school.

- I partnered with a first-year kindergarten teacher, meeting every week, checking our data, and creating weekly plans. For example, we would conclude that we needed to blitz rhyming but how were we going to do that? We decided to put some poems on the board and experience them as a group. Next, we modeled it together; then we each taught the lesson, and finished with the students working independently. We followed that by creating learning centers that focused on rhyming. The "blitzing" was a good focus for me as well as my partner teacher—collaboration was the key. It was useful to see what other teachers were doing and how they were adapting the idea. Identifying the vulnerable students was the

"We can do it!"

foundation of our program. We talked about a lot about how many "doses" we had to provide for those children.

- I was quite pleased to have 22 students this year, with only two not fully meeting the alphabet knowledge mastery guide. I don't usually do formal guided reading until after spring break; however, I started it in January and February. As a result. my k children were just reading up a storm.

- When I asked my administrator for some training sessions with a Reading Recovery (RR) teacher, she volunteered to help with some centers so that the RR teacher could coach me. In just a few mini-sessions, I was able to take children who were struggling with alphabetical knowledge and accompany them to the RR session. I sat one-on-one with both of them, observing her mini demonstration lessons with the strugglers. That became a great resource for me, helping me understand how I could support vulnerable children. Sometimes I paired up with the other classes or combined another teacher's children with my own lower students; in that case, my more able students would go with the other teacher.

Stories About Individual Children

A student I am concerned about is actually one of my success stories even though he is still vulnerable and on an IEP (Individual Educational Plan). He had been diagnosed as low-average intelligence with multiple related issues. He was held back in kindergarten and came to our school last year as a new student, entering my class for grade one. I spent the first three months just building a relationship with him. It seemed he hated me, the principal, the school and everyone in the school. Consequently, he spent most of his days in the kindergarten class in the *quiet* desk.

Now, however, if we look at his *Circle Chart*, we see he has come a long way. In spite of entering at a preschool skill level, in ten months he finished at the kindergarten skill level. The most significant change was his happiness, his joy. I went from being called *teacher* and the students from being *him* or *her* to being called by our proper names. He began to attend every day, on time, despite a lengthy history of unexcused absences. His mother appreciated the fact that it was no longer a fight to get him to school. Although his skill level did not match the rest of the class, by the end of the year he was able to cope and could rotate to every station where he had his own assigned activities. I always try to include an expert student at every center so that children such as this boy have help when I am busy. This strategy was a big success and center time came to be his favorite part of the day.

We still have a long way to go skill-wise, but he hugs me and has friends. He has stopped hitting, fighting and biting and he behaves almost like a regular student

He needed to feel safe and know that people cared, that they didn't consider him stupid. His biggest achievement was to be at the practice centers cooperating and learning along with the other children. I am a little emotional just telling this story.

Another struggling child, very vulnerable, diagnosed with ADHD, and on the margin of being mentally handicapped was at a pre-primer level; we didn't expect her to advance much farther. At the beginning of the year she couldn't even point at anything in a book. Now she can actually sit down and read, find her mistakes and apply strategies that we taught her. I am going to cry if I talk any more about her. She is really so special

Assessment and Tracking

- The constant assessment allows teaching to stay at the leading edge and negates assumptions about what the children know or don't know. We so often make mistakes, either over- or underestimating a child's skill level, but by using the *Circle Charts*, the teacher can maintain an accurate reading of those levels.

- I think our Superintendent is right when she says that this project or approach should never stop. Next year, I will be excited to see where students will achieve in their intermediate grades. Our principal said, "You know, I questioned putting all of this money, time and energy into primary at the expense of other students, but now I get it."

- Considering the reading data alone, this was the first time that all the grade 1s, including ESL (English Second Language) students entering kindergarten were reading at a level eight or higher by year's end. Our school has never had those kinds of results. Also, all my kindergarten children have mastered phonological awareness skills as well as some grade 2 skills. One little girl with disability issues is showing significant progress. Half the kindergarten students have mastered the alphabet and the ones that haven't are missing only two sounds.

- Our *Circle Charts* are demonstrating such growth. I love the *Circle Charts* because they are simple and concise to fill out and clearly illustrate each child's learning requirements. I think it is not only the children's joy, but also my own sense of confidence and competence that has grown so much this year. It has been my best school year ever.

Recording words with a "spooky" O sound and covering them with fruit loops which have spooky Os, too!

Comments from Teachers:
How Has This Project Affected Me?

- I am much more intentional than ever before. I have a clear concept of what we need to comprehend and how to achieve success. For me, that is the most significant change: I am purposeful as to what I teach and how I set up my schedule and resources. Becoming more intentional, anticipating the skills for the week ahead and focusing on them has changed the way I teach.

- Additionally, recognizing that none of my students need to be left behind has really helped me. They can all succeed!

- As a teacher, I used to regard struggling students and think, "They are struggling and that's just the way it's going to be," not realizing how my perception affected the children. This whole project has given me a new perspective. The students might not be reaching the benchmarks for a specific grade level but they are succeeding continue to master skills. They will eventually get there because we have the resources, research and knowledge, and we are helping them along the way.

Creative practice makes perfection.

- The project has given me a new understanding of what success means for each student. Achievement rates may differ, but all can be successful. Are we, as teachers, going to make sure they reach mastery or are we going to give up on them? My perception of struggling students has changed to the point where I now recognize and acknowledge the need to reach out to students even though they may be giving me a run for my money.

- Whether you are new to teaching or not, you probably feel as I often did— sometimes spinning your wheels, not getting anywhere or at least not as successful as you felt you should be. This project has paved the way for me. Now all the children in my class are going to be so much richer than what I could have provided them before. I would not have stayed in teaching since I suspected I wasn't giving the children what they needed. Now I know what I am doing, I can be effective and I can say that I feel proud of myself. That is a long way from where I used to be.

- I urge you to not give up on your students. See them through and get the resources you need for support along the way. In the end, when we see these children in grades one, two and three, we are going to see students in a world of people who are literate and successful because that's what this project is about – reaching all students and making sure that no child is left behind. Our project is so much more because it addresses implementation, the teaching concepts, assessment strategies and tracking techniques.

- There is no reason why the majority of struggling children can't attain success. It depends on us, as teachers, and what we do for them!

They feel successful—and happy—and proud.

- My toolbox is brimming now. We are always looking to grow and do what is best, using the research as a major part of that. My eyes are opened to best practice rather than the automatic adoption of the latest trend. I understand that, as a professional, I must focus on the research and what our experts say about literacy. I am certain that next year my success will be ten-fold because I will have greater awareness of the students, skill-wise, and as a result I will be able to complete more circles for those children until they reach mastery.

The School District that Persuaded Me!

Case Study 3:School District 23 (Central Okanagan)

89% Literacy Success by the end of Grade Three

(Kelowna, 2009)

Executive Summary: Program Review

Vulnerable Children Becoming Thriving Primary Readers

Early in my work at University of British Columbia the late Dr. Clyde Hertzman asked me to explore school districts that seemed to be doing better than others in the primary grades. Having no primary measuring tool that would indicate degrees of success, I sent an inquiry to districts asking them to self-identify if they believed reading levels were improving in the primary grades, due to any specific intervention they were applying. I had 13 school districts (out of 60) that volunteered to be part of the study. A team of two of us visited each district for several days interviewing staff, documenting quantitative data and recording interviews.

I remember flying out of the city of Kelowna (School District 23 Central Okanagan) with a box of data and my head spinning: I commented to my research partner, Neil, "Someone should be doing a detailed study of what's going on in that district." It was clear to both of us that in the short time we had, we could not do justice to understanding the depth of what we witnessed, but we certainly were aware that something very important was underway in the culture of the school district. Staff were beginning to be able to provide evidence of that in an almost overwhelming data collection system. We needed to know more, but it was beyond the parameters of the commissioned study.

Little did I know that several years later I would be invited to be the researcher who would independently document the district's literacy experience over the course of ten months. What an incredible experience that turned out to be! Clyde Hertzman had been telling me for years that, from a clinical medical perspective, 93% of all children were capable of learning to read in spite of their life circumstances prior to school attendance. I wanted to believe him and SD 23 seemed to confirm his belief. In the year of our study, the Kelowna School District had, indeed, achieved an 89% success rate by the end of grade three!

When I decided to write this book I knew it would be important to tell the School District 23 story. I want to introduce you to Clara Sulz, one of the driving forces in Kelowna who made it happen out of pure determination, tenacity and love for vulnerable children, most of all. She became the inspiration that drove me forward and continues to do so as my very dear friend.

Celebrating The Early Learning Evaluation Results
(Donna Kozak, Janet Mort, Clara Sulz, Pat Smith)

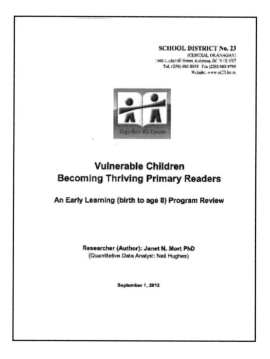

The following document is the Executive Summary of the 96-page full report that tells the essence of the Kelowna story.

Janet

SCHOOL DISTRICT No. 23
(CENTRAL OKANAGAN)
1940 Underhill Street, Kelowna, B.C. V1X 5X7
Tel. (250) 860-8888   Fax (250) 860-9799
Website: www.sd23.bc.ca

"Together We Learn"

July 5, 2012

Dear Colleagues and School District Staff:

This timely review of the Early Learning programs/initiatives in School District No. 23 is a testament to all who have participated. The interconnected initiatives that have been implemented since 1999 have continuously evolved to meet the needs of vulnerable learners and to support the dedicated educators who have made this possible.

The improving trend-line of student performance exhibited in this document is unprecedented in the history of our school district. The data collected, while sometimes arduous, has been the driving force to inform teachers, administrators and school district staff for future strategies and structures to personalize the learning of all individuals. Our STUDENTS have always remained at the heart of what we do and their successes have guided our commitment to continue to cultivate an early learning community that permeates beyond the mandate of our school district into our community at large.

The conversations resulting from the *Early Learning Profile* have led staff to connect with our early learning partners, with parents to initiate the Early Learning for Family evenings (ELFF), and to support educators (both Early Childhood Educators and district staff) with ongoing, connected professional development. Our joint efforts have continued to build a vision shared by all who work with young children in our school district as well as with our community partners.

The results of our initiatives (most notably our long term data collection on all of our primary students since 2005) speak to the combined efforts of those who work in support of our students, and how powerful it can be when everyone collaborates and is committed to the same goal. We are confident that our results continue to flourish because our work is grounded in both the science of best practices, as well as the art of understanding what is needed for young children to grow and develop as they should.

As we take pride in celebrating the successes of the past and as we learn from the recommendations, we continue in next steps of assuring that our students exit our system acquiring the *Attributes of a School District No. 23 Learner for Success in the 21st Century: Learner, Thinker, Innovator, Collaborator and Contributor.*

For colleagues outside our school district, we are always pleased to share our experiences as you share yours with us. We welcome conversations and inquiries and would be pleased to share our expertise with you.

In summation, I am honored to be the Superintendent of a district with such dedicated staff who are committed to stay on the cutting edge of practices, partnerships, research and collaboration to ensure our students are on the receiving end of the best we can offer.

Sincerely,

Hugh Gloster
Superintendent

Executive Summary

Vulnerable Children Becoming Thriving Primary Readers
in
SD No. 23 Central Okanagan

Janet N. Mort PhD
Researcher

The Purpose of the Study

The purpose of this study was to examine the effectiveness of the school district's decade-long effort to enhance literacy success in preschools and primary grades. The following queries guided the study:

1. In June 2011, on average, only 12% of the student population in grade 3 remained at risk in critical literacy skills – a significant improvement over a documented five-year period of time. How was that achieved with the other 88% of the population?

2. Would qualitative and quantitative data verify this statistic?

3. Were applied practices consistent with recent prevailing research?

4. What are the ramifications for future planning in SD 23 and other jurisdictions?

The Researcher's Context

I am a former primary teacher with 35 years of experience in administration as teacher, principal and school superintendent. Since obtaining my PhD in 2007 in Language and Literacy (with a specialty in Early Learning), I have conducted nine provincial research projects on innovative practices in Early Learning (birth to age 8) in 26 School Districts throughout British Columbia, all of which were striving to increase literacy success for young children.

As a researcher, my greatest interest has been to find and document promising practices that could be published and shared with others so that the 30.9% of vulnerable young children who struggle when they enter Kindergarten (HELP, 2011) could achieve earlier and greater success in all domains of learning.

Therefore, when I was approached by SD 23 to conduct this case study I agreed to do so with great professional interest, on the understanding that I was free to conduct the review and publish the report with consultation but without censorship or interference, whatever the results may be. This report is, therefore, presented without bias and with my full integrity and professional wisdom.

The Research Methodology

The study began in early February 2012, concluded in July and was presented to SD 23 in August 2012. It examined all Early Learning (birth to age eight) implementation activities sponsored by the school district from January 1999 to February 2012.

Data were gathered through the following processes:

- A three-week visit to the school district in February 2012,

- The collection and examination of approximately 46 district and professional documents,

- Examination of related data from HELP and the Ministry of Education,

- Interviews with principals, ECEs and district staff members (focus groups during the visit with kindergarten teachers had to be postponed so as not to interfere with provincial job action),

- Surveys distributed to and returned from principals, ECE staff, primary teaching staff and parents attending ECE events, and

- Telephone interviews conducted weekly from April to June to clarify data as the report was being written.

Data were cross-referenced, categorized and analyzed. Facts were checked throughout the process and again before publication in August 2012.

The district examined multiple layers of prominent research to determine its direction. Some of the most important references included topics such as:

- The needs of at-risk students,

- The importance of early intervention,

- The importance of phonological and phonemic awareness, and

- The critical role of staff development.

Please refer to the reference list for detail.

The core belief of SD 23 Early Learning program reflects the most recent research that reveals:

- That children who struggle to read comprise approximately 15% to 20% of the school population;

Reading and enjoying the story together.

- That between 90% to 95% of all children should be reading at grade level by the end of Grade 3. This is best achieved in a personalized Early Learning program that meets their individual skill needs, and offered in a playful and inclusionary classroom environment; and

- That the other 5% to 10% may have genetic or health-related issues that require specialized services outside of the classroom environment (HELP, 2012; Allington, 2009).

The science of reading research is clear about the skills children must have in order to be literate by the end of their primary years. Each skill that they do not master will magnify their spelling mistakes, decrease their fluency rates, reduce their reading comprehension capacity, and minimize their self-confidence and therefore their school success and dreams for the future.

SD 23 has mandated the implementation of the latest research on literacy skill development; the intervention that must be applied when mastery is not achieved; and professional development on how to achieve that intervention invisibly, collaboratively, and inclusively in a play-based classroom environment.

The magic of a fridge box.

Summary and Conclusions

Six key organizers emerged as a result of the analysis of the district vision and the research base for Early Learning Initiatives.

1. Initiative One: Achieving a Necessary Future (1999)

This pilot initiative (ANF) was SD 23's first major effort to change trajectories for young children based on the premise that small class sizes, carefully structured and managed might play a pivotal role. Even though, during the first five years of implementation some data suggested a trend towards improvement, the data were never consistent enough to conclude that the ANF project was, in itself, worthy of continuation and replication.

The ANF project, in retrospect, became an important catalyst for reflection, discussion and collaborative planning to enhance opportunities for children. What is most significant is that the dialogue that began with the ANF vision has resulted in the following five other integrated and dynamic initiatives that have resulted in increasing success for at-risk children.

2. Initiative Two: The *Early Learning Profile* (2001)

SD 23 developed the *Early Learning Profile* (ELP) screening tool that established benchmarks for kindergarten to grade 3, carefully constructed using the latest research findings on early literacy success. It was developed by a committee of teachers and specialists in speech pathology, learning assistance and learning disabilities, and coordinated by district staff.

The purpose of the (now district-mandated) ELP is to track each child's skill development, plan for sequential skill development on a personalized basis and intervene as necessary with at-risk children who are still struggling. The process benefits all children but particularly the 15% to 20% of children who typically do not read at grade level by the end of grade 3.

Every child is screened for these skills at the beginning of kindergarten so that at-risk children can be immediately identified. The teacher designs a cycle of screening, teaching and tracking skill development as well as a targeted cycle of play-oriented intervention in small group instruction, before any time is lost. The children with needs are tracked daily, weekly and monthly.

SD 23 tracks every primary child centrally and summarizes the children who remain at-risk at each grade level for September school opening, so that schools can organize and plan resources to continue necessary interventions without losing any time.

The ELP is revised annually to maintain its relevance and to be responsive to teacher input and new research. Teachers, therefore, are provided with annual in-service for updates and new teachers are trained in its use. The ongoing professional development program provides innovative strategies for responsive teaching and other promising practices.

As a result of this initiative the district is able to proudly announce that 88% of its children are reading at grade level by the end of grade three in 2011. As an example of the progress made over time, the following quantitative figure illustrates a data summary of the at-risk trends for three cohort groups moving from kindergarten through to grade 3. The stories and quotes in Chapters One through Five provide clarification and interpretations of how SD 23 has achieved such significant results.

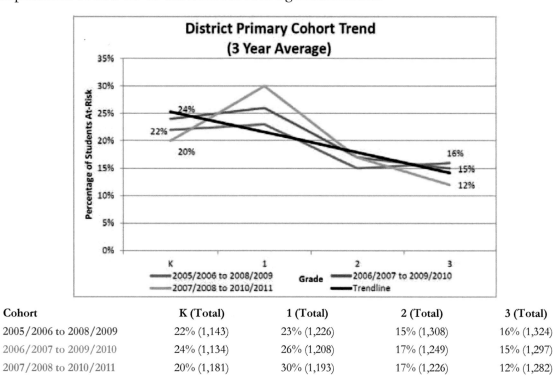

Cohort	K (Total)	1 (Total)	2 (Total)	3 (Total)
2005/2006 to 2008/2009	22% (1,143)	23% (1,226)	15% (1,308)	16% (1,324)
2006/2007 to 2009/2010	24% (1,134)	26% (1,208)	17% (1,249)	15% (1,297)
2007/2008 to 2010/2011	20% (1,181)	30% (1,193)	17% (1,226)	12% (1,282)

Please refer to Chapter Five for more details and individual school trends.

3. Initiative Three: Universal Preschool (2002)

In 2002, after a review of prevailing research SD 23 decided to establish a system-wide preschool program in schools that had space and where vulnerable children might benefit from preschool experiences. The main objective was to support a successful and high-quality universal preschool system and to provide affordable access for low-income families.

Shared reading, talking and writing.

Program operators were asked to commit to participating in innovative district professional development offerings, parent support programs, and be active participants in school activities – all to build a strong transition between the preschools and kindergarten entry expectations. In turn, the district provided subsidized offerings.

Presently, out of a total of 30 schools, 13 preschools are hosted in SD 23 schools. All preschool operators are active participants in family participation programs and have recently begun to participate in Early Learning professional development activities with k teachers. District staff members visit preschool programs for related coaching and demonstration purposes.

Initiative Three brings preschools, StrongStart BC programs and community-based childcare and early learning programs into schools as part of SD 23's Early Learning Partnership. Interventions with parents begin well before the children arrive at school.

Schools are reporting a steady decrease in the numbers of at-risk children arriving in kindergarten as measured by the EDI (Language and Cognitive Domain) and the ELP (*Early Learning Profile*). One principal reported the following ELP results at the beginning of the K year:

> 2008 – 76% at-risk; 2009 – 49% at-risk; and 2010 – 23% at risk

She attributes the results to intensive preschool interventions offered at her school. Without this type of intervention at-risk children will enter kindergarten and grade 1 already a year behind according to Allington (2009).

In addition, further evidence that Early Learning programs have made a difference to preschoolers is that the EDI (Early Development Instrument) scores dropped from 14% of children vulnerable in Wave 2 (2004/2007) to 5% vulnerable in Wave 4 (2009 to 2011) in the Language and Cognitive Development domain (the average provincial vulnerability is 10%).

4.   Initiative Four: Professional Development Offerings

SD 23 has a done an exceptional job of establishing research-based principles for professional development strategies and offering high-quality professional development (Pro D) opportunities for teaching staff, administrators, ECEs and district staff – as identified in the comments included in Chapter Four. Participant comments indicated gratitude and appreciation for district staff efforts, and enthusiasm for their own growth and learning, and the impact it has had on children.

5.   Initiative Five: The New Initiative – The Collaborative Model of Support (2011)

The C-MOS project, which was piloted in select schools in the 2010/2011 school year, is leaving the pilot stage and entering the district implementation stage. Refer to Chapter Five for teacher comments and conclusions related to the project.

A Collaborative Model of Support (C-MOS) **district** team has been launched to include five resource teachers (department heads) including early resource transition (entry to K), resource low-incidence, foetal alcohol spectrum disorder, autism and behaviour resource teachers. The district team will work collaboratively to support school-based teams, co-teach and provide in-service to staff to further develop a resource team model for learning structures and strategies.

The ultimate goal of this team is to create classrooms and schools where all students belong and learn according to their individual needs.

6.   Initiative Six: Data Collection – Assessment for Instruction (2005)

Any major program change should be accompanied by both qualitative and quantitative data as a part of making change in programs. (Goodwin & Goodwin, 1996)

"At the same time…the dynamics of the developmental change process and an in-depth understanding of its nature might well be better assessed via qualitatively oriented observations or interviews. Together, the two sets of measures [quantitative and qualitative] – one addressing how well and the other how and why – would paint a much fuller picture of the development occurring… That is, the quantitative aspect of the study could be planned and finalized while qualitative data was taking place and, very likely, also was providing guidance for aspects of the quantitative effort to follow. Each approach can inform and assist the other approach."

SD 23 has developed a unique and impressive quantitative approach that accompanies teacher assessments and observations that guide decisions related to each child's literacy skill development.

The data analysis, documents, stories and specific quotes described in this report logically support a number of conclusions:

Conclusion 1:   That involving preschool programs and activities in the school system has provided a powerful connection for young learners and their families and provides a helpful transition from home to kindergarten. Pre-school intervention programs have strongly influenced outcomes for at-risk groups where they have been applied in a coordinated way.

Conclusion 2:   EDI vulnerability rates have been reduced in a number of areas, particularly in Language and Cognitive domains and especially in areas where strong ECE programs are offered.

Conclusion 3:   That the *Early Learning Profile* (ELP) data has demonstrated a consistent downward trend in at-risk percentages of students from kindergarten to grade 3 (except for grade 1). It seems reasonable to conclude that the trend spikes upward in grade 1 as literacy expectations in the grade one tool increase.

Conclusion 4:   That the application of screening and tracking individual progress over time at both the school and district levels has provided a confident measure for better decision making for children and programs; and

Conclusion 5:   That teachers and administrators in SD 23 have succeeded in making a significant and innovative effort to change at-risk trajectories for vulnerable children who are already becoming thriving primary readers.

The message on the report cover is a graphic interpretation of School District No. 23's belief system. It demonstrates that without a solid foundation in basic literacy skills, children will not be able to engage in the rich experiments, inquiries, innovations, reflections and research promised in the cover's highway graphic. The graphic depicts the opportunities and choices that lie ahead in their educational journey and life. The journey starts with the ABCs in a playful early learning environment.

It has been an honor to spend six months working with such a determined, passionate and proactive group of educators. As a researcher, I have been enriched by the time I have spent working with them.

Sincerely,

Janet N. Mort, PhD
Researcher
Language and Literacy (Early Learning)

Recommendations for Next Steps

The following recommendations are made in the spirit of encouraging the district as it plans its next steps on an already highly successful journey that supports vulnerable young children as they become thriving primary readers.

1. That the full report be reviewed with district primary staff (who were unavailable due to the provincial labour dispute) so that they can be informed and provide their input for each Initiative, and that an addendum be attached to the report that summarized their responses.

   Rationale: Findings were based on input from principals, ECE staff, parents and district staff; it will be important to include the voice of teachers who are most important in applying the processes and programs.

2. That in subsequent professional development sessions the following topics be addressed or re-visited:

- The concept that the complete Profile should not need to be administered more than once at the beginning of the school year. Subsequently, with careful tracking, only individual skills for individual children should need to be re-assessed as mastery is achieved.

- The importance of isolating skills for the purpose of knowing what the children know, what they need to know, and what the teacher needs to teach.

- Strategies for tracking individual students on a daily basis to facilitate small group instruction until skill mastery is achieved.

- Use of ongoing classroom data to be used for planning daily and weekly instruction.

- A review of specific items in the Profile to ensure they are age appropriate as identified in the research and to reinforce the fact that individual children are developmentally ready for some skills at different ages; it is important that program offerings include all ages and stages without being imposed on those who are not ready.

- How resources can be purchased, adapted, planned and targeted more efficiently.

- Others topics that teachers may request.

Rationale: These were the issues that were raised in the principal survey and seemed to be misunderstood or of importance and/or concern.

3. That student portfolios be implemented for all primary classes; portfolios would include results of ongoing ELP assessments (not just the year-end summary) as well as samples of other significant student work for the purpose of reporting to parents and passing the portfolio to the next teacher for school start-up in September. Teachers should participate in creating a proposed Table of Contents for the Portfolio so the approach is consistent throughout the system.

Rationale: Most teachers have done an exceptional job of administering the ELP and preparing end-of-year data reports on individual students. With minimum effort, a profile system would enhance transitions between classes and teachers as well as provide concrete examples for reporting to parents.

4. That district staff review with principals and share strategies about:

- The ways they provide support to release teachers for the initial screening of the ELP at the beginning of the school year; and

- The ways they review the individual student results of the ELP (from the previous year) at the start of the new school year for the purpose of planning instruction for at-risk children.

Rationale: It appears from the survey results that principals are using different ways to release teachers and to plan for resource applications once results are received. While it is important that schools have autonomy, it is also important that there be equitable release and planning time for teachers.

5. That district staff ensure that the C-MOS (Collaborative Model of Support) project focuses on the use of the ELP results for planning student programs, purchasing resources, releasing teachers for ELP assessments and preparing year-end reports.

Rationale: The ELP process, while highly valued by most, has been challenging and there is inconsistent application between schools. The collaborative model will allow creative and helpful new ways to maximize the use of the ELP process.

6. That the numeracy part of the ELP be removed at least temporarily.

   Rationale: The ELP is a complex process that has gradually increased in sophistication. The numeracy program, while considered important, is not yet fully evolved and poses an additional challenge for staff who are uncertain about the new approach and intended outcomes. Once the numeracy program is fully implemented and professional development is underway, this recommendation should be revisited.

7. That the ELP tool be simplified. Build in descriptions and explanations about why each component is important and how it should be implemented, and package it in separate grade levels.

   Rationale: Many staff commented on the complexity and overwhelming size of the document. Other districts have discussed the possibility of applying components in their own districts; however, it is not a stand-alone document. Re-packaging and simplifying it will allow the district to provide it as a resource for others to enhance student literacy success.

8. That creative strategies be developed to make contact with more vulnerable families to encourage them to participate in the preschool programs.

   Rationale: A number of principals commented that the most needy families were not attending the programs. When StrongStart BC was first implemented, many creative strategies were developed to encourage attendance. Examples include linking with health and recreation programs to track and personally invite participants; a taxi and bus pass system for those who lacked transportation; posters in neighbourhood facilities; invitations in local newspapers and a booth at markets and public gatherings.

9. That the number of preschool and/or StrongStart BC offerings be increased when it is financially feasible and if the school population can sustain the program.

10. That the district approach local service groups, foundations, or corporations to seek financial partnerships to expand preschool offerings.

11. That SD 23 work with other Ministries and intersectoral groups to pursue the possibility of combining staff and resources to enhance services to vulnerable families. Such offerings could be delivered through the Neighbourhood Hub concept presently being piloted in the province.

    Rationale: For over ten years, SD 23 has been investing considerable financial resources and staff time in preschool programs. The data analysis in Chapter 6 identifies a trend of improvement in student success in primary grades where significant investments have been applied. Additionally, given the enthusiasm among most principals and ECE professionals about the benefits to children, there appears to be a strong base for future expansion in preschool programs. The district does not receive external funding for this investment (other than StrongStart BC) yet this is a community issue. SD 23 has proven that its 2001 vision is worthy of financial support from other agencies concerned with child development.

12. Please review Recommendations #2, 3, 4 and 5 in other chapters because these recommendations will most likely be addressed in further professional development activities.

13. Keep up the great work as you proceed into the C-MOS and other projects!

Rationale: The district has created a winning pattern for professional development that pleases participants; the district team has paid particular attention to integrating the needs of attendees with the needs of the children and district, and the research findings.

14. That the district carefully document changes in data that appear to occur as a result of C-MOS and add it as an addendum to this report at the end of the year.

Rationale: Research indicates that collaborative efforts make a significant contribution to student success. The C-MOS initiative requires a substantial investment in human resources and expertise; it will be important to demonstrate that its value is worthy of the expenditure by enhancing student success.

15. That the school district consider a pilot project to explore the possibility of developing an application that could be used with iPads in primary classrooms to support teachers in their efforts to track skill development.

Rationale: The district is taking important steps to improve the use of technology to track student records. Current, or newly developing technology may provide teachers with new ways to improve or simplify daily record keeping techniques.

16. That efforts increase to track and study cohort groups throughout primary, in an effort to determine the various factors at play in schools where significant changes in at-risk trends are noted.

Rationale: It appears that some schools are having more success than others at achieving the downward at-risk momentum. It is probable that in those schools there are specific factors that could be studied and replicated especially as the C-MOS project further develops.

17. That the district office continue to provide summative spreadsheets at the start of the school year regarding ELP results.

Rationale: This was raised as a question by district staff. In principal responses it was clear that almost all valued the information, as a way to enhance decisions about student needs, student assignments and application of resources.

Janet N. Mort PhD
Researcher
Language and Literacy
(Early Learning)

Kindergarten classes with most kindergarten students identified as at-risk in one or more areas of the ELP at the beginning of the year. By year-end (depending on the cohort), the number of vulnerable students has decreased.

Kelowna's Assessment, Teaching and Tracking System

The district developed an Early Learning Profile (ELP) to support and guide teachers from kindergarten through to grade 3. Each year new teachers received at least one day of in-service on how use the tools within the document. The School Board mandated that all primary teachers would be required to teach the series of skills identified within the document and track the degree of progress each child made throughout the year. At the end of the year student results were placed in portfolios to be transferred to next year's teacher. Class results were sent to the district office where they were collated and analyzed. In September, results were examined at the school to inform resource allocations and instructional services for planning for children's services for the new year.

Each booklet contains:

- Background and introduction,
- Components of a detailed literacy program,
- Research that supports the program,
- An explanation about the intervention approach,
- Suggested timelines for skill instruction,
- Definitions of key terms,
- Lists of defined skills,
- Sample pages on how teach the skills,
- Summary pages to track individual and class development,
- A Writing Rubric, and
- Guidelines for using *PM Benchmarks*.

Excerpts from Kelowna's K-3 Early Learning Profile (ELP)

Foreword

The principles of evidence-based practice support the revisions contained in the 2009 S.D. No. 23's Early Learning Screener and Profile and the revised 2012 S.D. No 23 *Early Learning Profile*, if used as intended, can be a highly effective tool in reaching those children who are exhibiting early signs of vulnerability to get the attention they need to eventually become literate, but also to identify skills and abilities of all students.

Evidence-based practice in teaching is a continuous, cyclical process involving three elements:

Information of the highest quality from the available scientific evidence,

Assessment of a student's needs, and

A teacher's own expertise.

Grade One ELP Language and Literacy Profile

Sample pages from the Early Learning Profile (ELP) for Grade One.

ELP Suggested Timeline for Grade One					

☐ Find the student's K ELP Portfolio

Grade 1 Term 1		Grade 1 Term 2		Grade 1 Term 3	
Phonological Awareness		**For At-Risk students re-check using the Oral Language Checklist**		**Re-check At-Risk students from previous terms**	
Re-teach and re-screen any students who were at risk (1) at the end of kindergarten	☐	• Receptive	☐	**Word Recognition** Grade 1 List 3	☐
Screen all students for:		• Expressive	☐		
• Isolation of final phoneme	☐	• Social	☐	**Reading Level/ Fluency – PM Benchmark**	☐
• Blending – phonemes	☐	**Letter Recognition** (Rescreen students who were at-risk at the end of term 1			
• Segmentation – syllables and phonemes	☐			**Writing Sample With Rubric**	☐
• Deletion - phonemes	☐	• upper case, lower case, phoneme word	☐		
Letter Recognition				**Developmental Spelling Test**	☐
Re-screen students who were at risk at the end of kindergarten	☐	**Word Recognition** List 1 & 2	☐		
Check K Word Recognition Levels 1, 2, & 3	☐	**Reading Level/Fluency –** PM Benchmark	☐	*Prepare the ELP portfolios for the next receiving teacher*	
Check Concepts of Print and Rescreen if necessary	☐				

© ELP Suggested Timeline for Grade One (page 14)

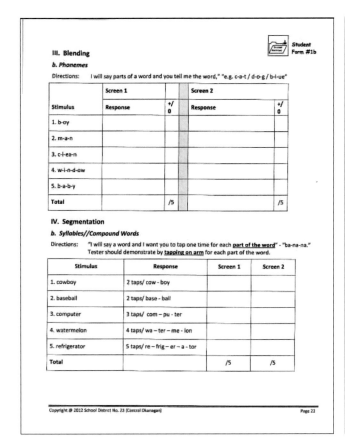

III. Blending

b. Phonemes

Directions: I will say parts of a word and you tell me the word," "e.g. c-a-t / d-o-g / b-l-ue"

Student Form #1b

Stimulus	Screen 1 Response	+/0	Screen 2 Response	+/0
1. b-oy				
2. m-a-n				
3. c-l-ea-n				
4. w-i-n-d-ow				
5. b-a-b-y				
Total		/5		/5

IV. Segmentation

b. Syllables//Compound Words

Directions: "I will say a word and I want you to tap one time for each **part of the word**" - "ba-na-na."
Tester should demonstrate by **tapping on arm** for each part of the word.

Stimulus	Response	Screen 1	Screen 2
1. cowboy	2 taps/ cow - boy		
2. baseball	2 taps/ base - ball		
3. computer	3 taps/ com – pu - ter		
4. watermelon	4 taps/ wa – ter – me - lon		
5. refrigerator	5 taps/ re – frig – er – a - tor		
Total		/5	/5

Copyright @ 2012 School District No. 23 (Central Okanagan)   Page 22

ELP: Phonological Awareness Summary (Grade 1)

Student Form #2

Student name ____ Teacher ____ School ____

	Kindergarten		Grade 1			
	Term 1	Term 2	Term 1	Term 2		
I Rhyming						
a. Discrimination	/5	/5	/5	/5		
b. Production	/5	/5	/5	/5		
II Isolation						
a. Initial	/5	/5	/5	/5		
b. Final			/5	/5		
c. Medial						
III Blending:						
a. Syllables	/5	/5	/5	/5		
b. Phonemes			/5	/5		
IV Segmentation:						
a. Sentences	/5	/5	/5	/5		
c. Syllables			/5	/5		
d. Phonemes			/5	/5		
V. Deletion:						
a. Compounds	/5	/5	/5	/5		
b. Phonemes			/5	/5		

Grade 1 Total:	/55	/55
Grade 1 Key:		
1 =not yet meeting	≤34 = 1	≤39 = 1
2 = minimally meeting	35-40 = 2	40-44 = 2
3 = meeting	41-44 = 3	45-47 = 3
4 = exceeding	>44 = 4	>47 = 4

Copyright @ 2012 School District No. 23 (Central Okanagan)   Page 24

Student Screening and Tracking Form (page 22)   Student Phonological Awareness Summary (page 24)

Most children can, and do, learn to read and write. But too many children read and write poorly. When schools fail to teach any child to read and write, they fail all of us. We must ensure that all children receive the excellent instruction and support they need to learn to read and write. – *Making a Difference Means Making It Different – Honoring Children's Right to Excellent Reading Instruction (2000)* Position Statement by the International Reading Association.

Note: The package of the Report and four grade level K, 1, 2, 3, *Early Learning Profiles (ELP's)* can be purchased as a set from the school district offices for approximately $275.00 (CDN). Contact http://www.sd23.bc.ca for further information. These documents contain all the information a school or district would need to start a primary assessment, teaching and tracking system. I highly recommend this resource so you can start this journey whether at a classroom, school or school district level.

Janet's Summary

The Real Heroes in This Book

Bold First Initiators

BOOT CAMP? In my travels in the province while I was conducting the research for my PhD I kept hearing about the district who was conducting 'boot camp' in the summer for five-year olds—skilling-and-drilling them in August before they came back to school. I, too, would have been horrified if I thought it was true: But I knew that some of our best professionals worked in School District 23 Kelowna, so I was delighted when the late Dr. Clyde Hertzman assigned me the task of researching why the district was improving vulnerability scores against all odds.

It was a memorable research project: The **true** story was about passionate, committed educators who were far ahead of their time: They had conducted their own research on the Internet, had found the studies reflected in the 2009 NELP Report and designed their own summer intervention plan for vulnerable readers. It included an invitation to the families of the most vulnerable to attend a summer camp complete with games, balloons, enticing food, books and take-away literacy fun—all designed to mitigate the "*Summer Loss*" solutions that Richard Allington champions in his co-authored book. Shame on those educators who spread the boot-camp stories about Kelowna professionals as if they were true! This district has a success rate of 89% at the grade three level—well ahead of any other school district in the province!

Brave Risk-takers

I believed, after 40 years in the system as a teacher, principal and superintendent; and after seven years of being immersed in university studies while I earned a doctorate; I had finally determined what we needed to do to achieve over 90% success in literacy for all children by the end of grade two. I was excited and eager to implement the theories but had no school of my own. I put out the word that I was looking for risk takers.

What a delight it was to receive calls from School District 28 (Quesnel), School District 59 (Peace River South), School District 84 (Vancouver Island West), all wanting to establish pilot projects to implement the most recent literacy theories and research. We did so. We have had so much fun and learned so much from each other. The Peace River South District started six months before the other two districts so we were only able to report on their aggregate results in this publication, but we look forward to continuing our professional development and data-driven evidence that our strategies are working. Special thanks to teacher Shauna Lothrop from Quesnel for her case study; she initiated and documented it herself.

Researchers like me have nothing to offer without professionals like these!

Janet

References

Allington, R. L. (2006). *What really matters for struggling readers* (2nd ed.). Boston, MA: Allyn & Bacon.

Allington, R. L. (2009). *What really matters for RTI (Response to Intervention)*. Boston, MA: Allyn & Bacon.

Allington, R. L. (2012). *What really matters for struggling readers: Designing research-based programs*. Boston, MA: Pearson.

Allington, R. L. (2014, May). *Early Intervention*. Paper presented at the meeting of Summit 5, Victoria, BC.

Allington, R. L., & Cunningham, P. (1996). *Schools that work: Where all children read and write*. Scarborough, ON: Harper-Collins.

Allington, R. L., & Cunningham, P. (2007). *Classrooms that work: They can all read and write* (4th ed.). Scarborough, ON: Harper-Collins.

Allington, R. L., & McGill-Franzen, A. (2013). *Summer Reading: Closing the rich/poor reading achievement gap*. New York, NY: Teacher's College Press.

Bear, D., Invernizzi, M., Templeton, S., & Johnston, F. (2012). *Words their way: Word study for phonics, vocabulary, and spelling instruction* (5th ed.). Boston, MA: Pearson.

Beatty, J. J., & Pratt, L. (2012). *Early literacy in preschool and kindergarten: A multicultural perspective* (3rd ed.). Boston, MA: Pearson.

Burkey, L. C., Lenhart, L. A., & McKeon, C. A. (2008). *Developing early literacy: Report of the national early literacy panel*. Washington, DC: National Institute for Literacy. Retrieved from http://lincs.ed.gov/publications/pdf/NELPReport09.pdf

Canadian Council of Learning. (2006). *Let the children play*. Retrieved from http://www.ccl-cca.ca/pdfs/LessonsInLearning/Nov-08-06-Let-the-Children-Play.pdf

Cunningham, A., & Zibulsky, J. (2014). *Book smart*. New York, NY: Oxford University Press.

Curtis, D., & Carter, M. (2003). *Designs for learning and living*. St. Paul, MN: Redleaf Press.

Diller, D. (2003). *Literacy work stations: Making centers work*. Portland, ME: Stenhouse.

Diller, D. (2005). *Practice with purpose*. Portland, ME: Stenhouse.

Diller, D. (2008). *Spaces and places: Designing classrooms for literacy*. Portland, ME: Stenhouse.

Edwards, C., Gandini, L., & Foreman, G. (Eds.). (1998). *The hundred languages of children* (2nd ed.). London, ON: Ablex.

Flemington, K., Hewins, L., & Villiers, U. (2011). *Journey to literacy: No worksheets required*. Markham, ON: Pembroke.

Fountas, I. C., & Pinnell, G. S. (2011). *Literacy beginnings: A prekindergarten handbook*. Portsmouth, NH: Heinemann.

Johnson, J., & Keier, K. (2010). *Catching readers before they fall: Supporting readers who struggle, K-4*. Portland, MA: Stenhouse.

Lyons, C. A. (2012). *Teaching struggling readers: How to use brain-based research to maximize learning*. Portsmouth, NH: Heinemann.

McGee, L., & Morrow, L. M. (2005). *Teaching literacy in kindergarten*. New York, NY: The Guildford Press.

McGill-Franzen, A. (2006). *Kindergarten literacy: Matching assessment and instruction in kindergarten*. New York, NY: Scholastic.

Middendorf, C. (2009). *Building oral language skills*. New York, NY: Scholastic.

Morrow, L. M. (2012). *Literary development in the early years: Helping children read and write* (7th ed.). Boston, MA: Pearson.

Mort, J. (1983). *Teaching with the winning touch*. Carthage, IL: Good Apple.

National Association for the Education of Young Children. (2003). *Chopsticks and counting chips: Do play and foundational skills need to compete for the teacher's attention in an early childhood classroom?* Retrieved from https://www.ccl-cca.ca/pdfs/LessonsInLearning/Nov-08-06-Let-the-children-play.pdf

National Early Learning Panel. (2009). *Developing early literacy: Report of the early learning panel*. National Center for Family Literacy. Retrieved from http://lincs.ed.gov/publications/pdf/NELPReport09.pdf

National Strategy for Early Literacy. (2009). *The Canadian Language and Literacy Research Network*. Retrieved from http://research4children.com/data/documents/NationalStrategyforEarlyLiteracyReportsandRecommendationspdf.pdf

Payne, C. D., & Schulman, M. B. (1998). *Getting the most out of morning message and other shared writing lessons.* New York, NY: Scholastic.

Pinnell, G. S., & Fountas, I. C. (2009). *When readers struggle: Teaching that works.* Portsmouth, NH: Heinemann.

Rog, L. J. (2001). *Read, write, play, learn: Literacy instruction in today's kindergarten.*   Newark, DE: International Reading Association.

Routman, R. (2003). *Reading essentials.* Portsmouth, NH: Heinemann.

Routman, R. (2005). *Writing essentials.* Portsmouth, NH: Heinemann.

Routman, R. (2014). *Read, write, lead.* Alexandria, VA: ASCD

Schultze, B. (2008). *Basic tools for beginning writers.* Markham, ON: Pembroke.

Sousa, D. A., & Tomlinson, C. A. (2011). *How neuroscience supports the learner-friendly classroom: Differentiation and the brain.* Bloomington, IN: Solution Tree Press.

Trehearne, M. (2011). *Learning to write and loving it.* Thousand Oaks, CA: Corwin.

Vacca, J., Vacca, R. T., & Gove, M. K. (2012). *Reading and learning to read* (8th ed.). Boston, MA: Pearson.

Weisman, C., Gandini, L., & Gandini, T. (1999). *Beautiful stuff: Learning with found materials.* Worcester, MA: Davis.

Wikipedia. Dolch Word List. Retrieved from en.wikipedia.org/wiki/Dolch_word_list

Appendix

Site License for Assessment and Tracking *Circle Charts*: Primary Grades

(Copyright Janet N. Mort PhD)

Why are the 'Circle Charts' so Innovative and Important?

Recent research (2009) has affirmed that without specific foundational skills in kindergarten and grade one, most vulnerable children will struggle throughout their school experience due to a lack of specific skills, confidence and diminished self concept. Research not only has identified skills essential in kindergarten and grade one but also maintains that 90% of all children should be able to be successful if these skills are mastered in kindergarten, grade one and grade two. In many jurisdictions fewer than 70% of children enter school ready for literacy expectations, yet the most recent research suggests most 4-year- olds are developmentally ready. The problem is that many young children have not had rich literacy experiences between birth and age five.

These *Circle Charts* provide teachers with a simple tool that will guide the initial assessment at kindergarten entry and track each child's progress on a daily basis. This ongoing assessment will guide daily small-group instruction for vulnerable children in a play-based environment enabling many to reach grade two or three achieving at the same level as their more fortunate peers. The charts were developed professionally. The skills identified on them are based on the NELP (National Early Learning Panel, 2009) report and the work of major literacy experts who present at the Summits and are well informed about the most recent research.

The most important implementation issue for vulnerable children is that these skills MUST be introduced and embedded invisibly in a PLAY-BASED environment. This integration of play, literacy and additional explicit instruction for vulnerable children is challenging for teachers—especially those new to the profession.

The Literacy Circle Charts: Site License
These charts are available in a site license. In the set of 43 circle charts (8.5 x 14.5) you will be provided with pdf files with skills listed horizontally and student spaces listed vertically for the skills.

Essential Research-based Literacy Skills

Alphabet, Phonological Awareness, Sight Words, Print Concepts, Word Work, Reading and Writing

The following pages are included in each full set of *Circle Charts*:

- 1 page - Alphabet Letters lower case chart,
- 1 page - Alphabet Letters capitals chart,
- 1 page - Vowel chart,
- 2 pages - Phonological Awareness skill charts (k/1),
- 12 pages – 210 Dolch Sight Words in 'Circle Chart' format,
- 1 page - Oral Language and Comprehension: Expressive (speaking) and Receptive (listening),
- 1 page - Print Concepts,
- 1 page – Reading and Writing skills,
- 1 page - 1 blank circle chart (not in pdf) that can be replicated and used for other skills (math etc.),
- 1 page - A summary of the skills children should have at the end of grades 2 and 3, and
- 21 pages: 210 Dolch Sight Words—formatted and print-ready for recipe card sized labels.

Sight words, which comprise over 60% of all grade 3 level books are the connector words and are one of the fastest ways to encourage reading in young children. All 210 Dolch words are printed on single sheets—ten per page for a specific size of commercial labels—so that teachers can run off labels and paste them onto recipe cards for games, or in sets for individual children. Sight word cards can then be assigned to children, as they are ready, collected on key rings or placed in boxes of personal word collections. This saves hours of work printing, cutting and pasting them and makes it possible to give children their own individual sets.

Blank circles indicate the skills that have not yet been mastered by the child; half circles identify skills that require review and re-assessment; filled-in circles indicate skill mastery, and the colors indicate in which term the child mastered the skill. Skills are taught in a joyful play-based environment in large groups or small groups informed by skill needs or individually as necessary. The goal is skill mastery for tier one and tier two children before the end of grade 2. Tier three children will likely require external support and pullout services. *Circle Charts* should be passed on from kindergarten to grade 1 to avoid unnecessary re-assessments.

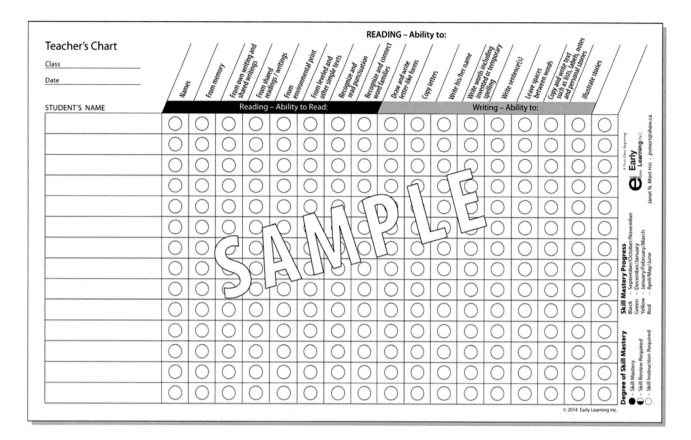

Sample Circle Chart

Site-License Pricing (63 Circle Chart Pages in Total)	
Type of Site	Site License Fee
Single Classroom	$ 75.00
Small School (1 - 10 classrooms)	$ 300.00
Large School (10 + classrooms)	$ 600.00
Small School District (1 - 10 schools)	$1500.00
Large School District (10 + schools)	$3000.00

This license is a permanent license. *Circle Charts* can be ordered by emailing vulnerablereaders@shaw.ca

Please contact me for further discussion. I am flexible with all of the above—except to reiterate that this skill-development process should only be implemented in a play-based environment.

Sincerely,

Janet N. Mort PhD

Made in the USA
San Bernardino, CA
12 June 2015